1199

THE
HISTORY
ATLAS OF
EUROPE

THE
HISTORY
ATLAS OF
EUROPE

Ian Barnes
and
Robert Hudson

MACMILLAN • USA

MACMILLAN

A Simon & Schuster Macmillan Company
1633 Broadway
New York, N.Y. 10019-6785

Library of Congress Cataloging-in-Publication Data

Barnes, Ian.
   The Macmillan history atlas of Europe / Ian Barnes and Robert Hudson.
      p. cm.
   Includes bibliographical references and index.
   ISBN 0-02-862584-6
   1. Europe—Historical geography—Maps.   I. Hudson, Robert.
   II. Title. III. Title: History atlas of Europe. IV. Title: Atlas of Europe.
   G1797.21.S1 B3   1998   <G&M>
   911'.4—DC21

                          98-12582
                           CIP
                         MAPS

Printed in the United States of America
10 9 8 7 6 5 4 2 1

FOREWORD

Europe has been forged through conquest, occupation, and hegemony, while its peoples have shared and disputed a variety of philosophical, religious, economic, and cultural beliefs, values, and practices.

The History Atlas of Europe explores the extraordinary sweep of Europe's development, commencing with the origins of the earliest peoples and the classical past, through Christendom, to the balance of power politics of the seventeenth and eighteenth centuries, before concentrating on issues and developments in the nineteenth and twentieth centuries. The Atlas discusses aspects of art, culture, trade, thought, and religion to provide a more rounded treatment than more conventional historical atlases. The spread of Celtic peoples through Europe is juxtaposed with the end of Greek Mediterranean hegemony through the Peloponnesian War and the rise of Rome on the Italian peninsula, with its growth of empire and path of conquest. The gradual decline that set in after Diocletian's reforms at the end of the third century is followed by collapse from internal weakness in the face of Germanic invasions.

Since the time of Diocletian the empire had divided into two parts, and this cleavage would persist with the rise of the Byzantine empire in the East and the Frankish kingdoms in the West. East-West differences would deepen with the schism between Orthodox and Catholic variations of confession in 1054 and impact upon Europe yet again in the Early Modern period. The onset of new directions in faith, trade, politics, and society would widen the rift even further. The effect of the Enlightenment, the ideas and ideals of the French Revolution, and industrialization would widen and exacerbate this difference, in a process that has continued well into our own century.

One thing becomes clear throughout the progression of this work: that the constantly changing boundaries of Europe have expanded or contracted due to influences from beyond, with Europe as little more than a peninsula on the edge of Asia, spreading at its greatest extent from the Atlantic to the Urals and from the North Cape to the Mediterranean. This book therefore traces the thread of a common European identity based on common historical experiences in a celebration of diversity.

The origins of feudalism are illustrated by the map on Charlemagne and analyzed throughout the remainder of the section on "Christian Eruope." Conflicts over religious differences are examined against the backdrop of the rise of the state and the growth of absolutism as a political formation and the balance of power through the wars of Louis XIV and the collapse of the Swedish empire.

One area which we considered most significant was revolution and the rise of nationalism. Here we found that changes in the nature of kingship in England, new political forms in the Dutch Republic, the impact and legacy of the French Revolution, and state-building in Germany and Italy all had their specific roles to play. The Bolshevik Revolution—a critique in action of previous liberal and capitalist developments—seemed to provide a logical conclusion to this section.

The last two sections of the book locate Europe within the wider world and consider the rise and fall of European colonial empires and the impact of two major wars upon the European continent. As Europe enters the twenty-first century, two key issues, "deepening" and "widening," confront the European communities. To what extent will Europe progress down the road toward becoming a federal, supranational state; and how does Europe respond to the enormous changes that have taken place in eastern Europe since the fall of the Berlin Wall, the end of the Cold War, and the break-up of the Soviet Union? Might the return to nationalism, irredentism, and debates over sovereignty and self-determination result in further European discord?

In putting this book together, we both realize that some areas of European history have received less attention. This is both a reflection of our personal interests and editorial constraints.

Ian Barnes and Robert Hudson

CONTENTS

FOREWORD   5

Part I   **Earliest Peoples and Settlements**   8

Human Colonization   14
First Farmers, 6500 BC   16
Minoan Crete   18
Mycenaean Greece   20
Early Greece   22
Etruscan Expansion   24
The Hallstatt Culture–The Celts I   26

Part II   **The Mediterranean World**   28

Greek and Phoenician Colonization   32
Peloponnesian War   34
The Rise of Macedonia   36
La Tène Culture–The Celts II   38
Roots of Rome, 753 BC   40
Punic Wars   42
Rome–From Republic to Empire   44

Part III   **Legacy of Rome**   46

Imperial Rome   48
Diocletian–The Empire Reorganized   52
Enemies at the Gates   56
Germanic Kingdoms   58
The Empire in the East   60

PART IV   **Christian Europe**   62

The Empire of Charlemagne   66
Fire and Sword   68
Empire and Papacy   70
The Crusades   72
Russia and the Tatar Invasions   74
The Fall of Constantinople   76
Reconquest and Unification of Spain   78
The Ties of Trade   80

Part V	New Directions	82
	Ottoman Threat	86
	Protestant Reformation	88
	Habsburg Rule	90
	Thirty Years' War, 1618–1648	92
	Expansion of Russia	94
	French Designs	96
	The Baltic Balance	98
Part VI	The Idea of State	100
	English Civil War	104
	Republics of Trade	106
	Revolution in France	108
	The Napoleonic Empire	110
	The Congress of Vienna	112
	State Unification	114
	The Russian Revolution	116
	The New Russia	118
Part VII	Imperial Echoes	120
	Global Empires	124
	The Road to Self-destruction	128
	World War I	130
	Versailles, 1919	132
	The Great Depression	134
Part VIII	Modern Times	136
	The Fascist States	140
	World War II, 1939–1942	142
	World War II, 1942–1945	144
	Ruin, Bankruptcy, and Recovery	146
	European Union	148
	New Hope, Old Divisions	150
CHRONOLOGY		152
SELECT BIBLIOGRAPHY		154
INDEX		156
ACKNOWLEDGMENTS		160

PART I: EARLIEST PEOPLES AND SETTLEMENTS

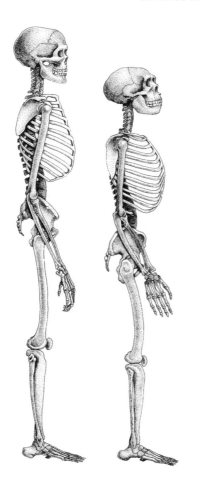

Myth, legend, and debate shroud the origins and history of Europe's early peoples and settlement. The first hominids traveled from Africa some million years ago, probably being related to *Homo erectus* and survived by hunting and gathering, working in harmony with the seasons. Early hominid archaeological finds are scattered throughout Europe, with the earliest sites situated around the Mediterranean. Northerly areas were only occupied during warmer periods in the Ice Ages. More evidence of hominid activity derives from discoveries like pebble tools, butchered animal bones, and stone hand axes. These sites tend to follow river valleys as a means of penetrating new territories and to be by lakes, reliable supplies of water being essential for survival. Dwelling in cave communities or in huts at Bilzingsleben, these early man-ape peoples tamed fire and were capable of cooperation in big-game hunting, evidenced by elephant remains at Terralba-Ambrona in Spain. Large animals, including rhinoceros, were driven over cliffs, as seen at La Cotte de St. Brelade in the Channel Islands, although late Neanderthal man might have been responsible for this massacre.

The discovery of Neanderthal man in Germany in 1856 eventually sparked a controversy over the origins of early man. In 1921, a Neanderthal skull, differing slightly from the first, was found in Zambia and was classed as a new subspecies, Rhodesian man. In reality, Neanderthals varied as to climate, but the apparent minor differences led to theories of parallel development claiming that modern man evolved simultaneously, with Europeans from Neanderthals and Africans from Rhodesian man. Archaeology now suggests a widely held "Out of Africa" theory that Rhodesian man changed into *Homo sapiens* and broke out of sub-Saharan Africa to eventually populate Asia and Australia, and then entered Europe, gradually extinguishing the Neanderthal population. The Neanderthals are often sterotyped as primitive and brutish cavemen, but evidence suggests few differences between them and modern man; certainly their brains were equal in size. Living in social groups and using tools, particularly the Mousterian stone type, Neanderthals were dispersed from the Mediterranean to the glacial areas of northern Europe, and from Portugal to

Comparative skeletons of Neanderthal (right), and Cro-Magnon (left). The Neanderthal shows a shorter, more powerful build, while Cro-Magnon, with a taller and lighter build—apart from the heavier brow ridge—could almost be a modern human.

central Asia, with heavy concentration of finds in the caves of southwestern France. That at La Ferrassie displayed a Neanderthal cemetery of two adults and three children. Elsewhere, in Iraq at Shanidar, a body was accompanied by flowers. Evidence, therefore, suggests that Neanderthals were strong, socially organized, and adaptable to different environments, and showed compassion in

Stonehenge is perhaps one of the most famous prehistoric sites in the world. Its building began around 3100 BC and was then rearranged over a period of some 1,200 years. Its final form, seen today, dates from 1550 BC. From the beginning the main axis of the structure has been aligned with the midsummer sunrise, and it is possible that the stones also align with other astronomical objects. The site allowed its builders to mark the changing seasons, as well as providing a focus for religious ceremony.

burial rites. The spread of hunter-gatherers into Europe generally followed river valleys, often along deer migration trails, movements often being dependent on fish supplies, especially salmon, an important dietary component. Technology developed apace, seeing the introduction of new stone flaking techniques, spear throwers, spears, harpoons, bows, fish hooks, and nets. Social organization and communal hunting methods grew throughout Europe, but cultural evolution became more specialized. Although the distribution of Venus figurines is widespread, suggesting some common cultural elements and contact, regional variations about stone tools might lead to speculation about regional identities and cultural differences.

The existence of Paleolithic Venus figurines points to an interest in art and maybe religion. Highly significant are the variety of cave paintings. The basrelief painted Venus of Laussel in the French Dordogne is arguably an earth-mother goddess, and pinnacle of a matriarchal society. Cave art was often carried out in inaccessible places, implemented by ladders and artificial light. The pictures at Altimira are particularly interesting, with an eighteen-meter-long painted ceiling of bison coexisting with many other animal representations, some now extinct. The Stone Age societies were superseded by Neolithic civilizations reaching the Atlantic coast by about 4000 BC (via the Danube and partly through the Mediterranean), bringing agriculture, stock-breeding, and pottery. Accompanied by megalithic building, predominantly in the British Isles, France, and Denmark, this civilization suddenly disappeared, possibly at the hands of invading battle-axe peoples entering from southern Russia and the Balkans; these groups introduced the Bronze Age, with its skilled metallurgy, spreading slowly from what are now the Czech and Slovak Republics to the Atlantic.

The first three recorded European civilizations thrived in the Bronze Age and were nurtured by Mediterranean trade. Minoan Crete was virtually an Aegean

hegemonic power between 2200 and 1450 BC, succeeded by Mycenae on mainland Greece between 1450 and 1200 BC. In Italy, the Etruscans created western Europe's first civilization between 800 and 300. Each civilization made major contributions to trade, technology, art, and religion. Crete also supplied the legend of the Minotaur, while Homer's *Iliad* and *Odyssey* brought the world classic verse and riddles for archaeologists yet to solve. Furthermore, historians have been introduced to "functional" history in Roman accounts of Etruscan life. Portrayed as vice-ridden and evil, Rome constantly sought to overshadow a civilization that had contributed so much to its own.

Aegean culture originally generated a Cycladic civilization, as seen in excavations made on Thera, Delos, and surrounding islands. Pottery, jewelry, and marble idols of human size have been unearthed, the latter being associated with the central fact of Cycladic life–the sea. Theran frescoes showed similarities with Minoan examples, but the island was destroyed by a volcanic eruption (c. 1625 BC). The islands exported obsidian, supported a fishing community, and developed an important shipbuilding technology.

The Lion gate at at Mycenae, built around 1300 BC. So impressed were the ancient Greeks when they viewed the ruins, they believed that the huge stones had been moved into position by a race of one-eyed giants, the "Cyclops."

Having ready access to quality timber, the Aegean peoples were constructing sail-driven boats, with keels, ribs, and cutwaters. Evidence from a vase fragment found on the island of Syra, together with pictures on Cretan gems and seals, show ship development. After the fall of Knossos, some Minoans fled to Egypt, taking their skills with them, and a ship model from the tomb at Medinet Haba near Luxor is reminiscent of Aegean craft.

In terms of trade, Crete and Mycenae were locked into an ever-increasing web of communications based upon mastery of the sea. The search for minerals was extremely important, since the civilizations were based on copper and tin, the former from Cyprus and the latter from Spain, and maybe Cornwall in southwestern Britain. Pottery vessels containing perfumed oil were sent to Cyprus, Egypt, the Sudan, the Hittite empire in Anatolia, Sicily, Sardinia,

Malta, and Etruria. In return, gold, ebony, and ivory came from Egypt and Nubia, lapis lazuli from Afghanistan, and amber from the Baltic. Knowledge of trade comes from both shipwrecks and grave finds. The existence of ritual burial with grave goods suggests a belief in an afterlife and religion. Lack of knowledge concerning Bronze Age religion prevents an accurate depiction of Cretan and Mycenaean cults. In the Cyclades, an open-air sanctuary with marble figurines was found on the island of Karos. The early period of Minoan culture likewise developed hilltop and mountain sanctuaries. The use of shrines seems prevalent, but little is known about the deities except that pictures of a goddess holding snakes are not uncommon. This snake deity's worship involved symbols of fertility and lunar and solar cycles. The major figure of reverence was a goddess or goddesses. Some clay figures were discovered at Ayia Irini in Ceos and at Mycenae. Many Mycenaean sites have terra-cotta figures with a woman's form. They possess beaklike noses and prominent breasts and might represent a fertility goddess. They wear flat head-dresses and long skirts and appear to hold up their arms in an attitude of worship. Unlike Homer's Hades, Minoan Crete appeared to offer the dead the Isles of the Blessed.

The Minoan and Mycenaean architectural experiences are entirely different. The Minoan palaces were multifunctional, possessing spaces for worship, storage areas, workshops, and living quarters. These were organized around a central courtyard and were totally unfortified. At Mycenae, Tiryns, and Pylos, palaces tended to have a dominant central hall entered from a courtyard and were fortified with massive, irregular masonry blocks. Where painting but not sculpture are concerned, the Minoans outclassed Mycenae. Cretan murals depicted nature, animals, and the notion of movement, and their techniques and styles were exported to the Greek mainland. On Thera a recent excavation has uncovered one fresco representing the Aegean world with highly decorated ships sailing from port to port. Minoan sculpture includes bronze figurines in attitudes of worship and somersaulting bull-jumpers and statuettes incorporating and decorated with several different materials. The Cycladic civilization produced not just the life-sized painted women but many seated male figures playing harps or holding drinking cups. Mycenae produced geometric and figural commemorative plaques, some reliefs on the Lion Gate, ivory containers, and statuettes. Both Minoan and Mycenaean pottery created pottery jars, mainly decorated with aspects of marine life such as octopuses, cuttlefish, and seaweed. Minoan pottery pictures tended to be free-flowing, while a more disciplined Mycenaean style introduced animal and human figures. Little Minoan metalwork survives, but Mycenaean craftsmanship is very impressive. Their shaft-graves produced Agamemnon's golden death mask, as well as gold and silver vases, and ornamental bronze weapons inlayed with precious metals and sheathed in gold and ivory. Such beautiful items were prized all over the Aegean, and a most memorable piece was the holed pomegranate pendant made by a Mycenaean jeweler around 1300 BC and found in Cyprus, a refuge for many

"In the ruins of Mycenae are the underground chambers of Atreus and his sons where they kept the treasure-houses of their wealth."
Pausanias,
The Guide to Greece

This detail from a fresco in the Palace of Knossos dates from about 1600 BC and shows part of a procession of gift-bearers.

Greeks when the Mycenaean civilization eventually crumbled.

In contrast to the eastern Mediterranean, the western Etruscans have been overlooked by many historians. Whether sailing from Asia Minor or migrating from eastern Europe over the Alps, the Etruscans established (c. 800–400 BC) a confederation of twelve city-states in central Italy (modern Tuscany), gradually extending their control to the Po Valley and to the Adriatic at Spina and Adria and also to the bay of Naples, where they won control over Greek colonies, including Capua and Pompeii. They even turned the modest settlement of Rome into an Etruscan city ruled by the Tarquin kings. Eventually, the Gauls invaded the Po Valley, Campania fell to local Italic peoples, while Rome steadily acquired the rest of Etruria, crushing its culture and turning it into a Roman province. Originally, each city was ruled by a king lording it over serfs and slaves. Wealth was based on iron ore extraction, Elban copper, cinnabar, tin, silver, lead, and alum, used to fix pigments in cloth. Minerals were traded with Greeks and Phoenicians, and economic forces appear to be at the root of Etruscan internecine wars, alliances, and conflicts with Greeks and Romans. The author and poet D. H. Lawrence, in his poems "Cypresses," portrays the "long-nosed, sensitive-footed, subtly-smiling Etruscans" with their "fanciful long shoes" as being ephemeral, artistic, and evasive, these views taken from Etruscan murals. Bright colors were used to depict vivacious games, dancing, music, and banqueting. Women were shown sharing couches with men at mealtimes, riding in covered wagons to inspect estates, and playing musical instruments at funerals, suggesting that aristocratic women were treated with more respect than their Roman and Greek counterparts, and that they achieved high social status and economic influence. In art, men are always engaged in activity; games, boar-hunting, processions, dances, banquets, and diving. Toward the end of Etruscan civilization, murals became gloomy, portraying war scenes and demons after death, maybe instinctively depicting the inevitability of defeat at the hands of the dour Romans.

Etruscan tombs are witness to the power, wealth, and sophistication of their owners. Grave gifts provide microcosms of life through mirrors, bowls, and other artifacts left with the dead. Frescoes such as that in a tomb at Chiusi picture hunting scenes, exotic birds, and flowers, together with the journey to the afterlife. Religion took note of natural forces deified as gods of the sea, earth, and rising sun. Greek gods and goddesses were renamed: Zeus, Hera, and Athena became Tinia, Uni, and Minerva; Vulcan, Bacchus, and Mercury had counterparts. Catha was the sun god; Tiv, god of the moon; Thesan, god of the dawn; Turan was Venus, and Applu, Apollo. Oriental and Greek symbols coexist; Egyptian sphinxes watch Etruscan winged demons charge dangerous Greek furies. Many elements of Etruscan religion were appropriated by the Romans. Other Etruscan influences on the Romans were considerable, giving them the toga, town planning, the villa, and an alphabet only slightly modified. Etruria never died; it survived culturally.

An Etruscan bronze statuette of a warrior (originally he would also have been equipped with a shield and spear). Cast in bronze, it was found near Arezzo, Italy, and dates from around 550 BC.

Human Colonization

Many scientists assume that early hominids developed in southern Africa, but remains have been found in Tanzania, Kenya, and southern Ethiopia. This *Australopithecus africanus* is associated with pebble tool industries; these crude tools were adequate enough for pounding plants and shredding meat. Some forms of these hominids are classified as *Homo habilis*, showing advanced tool skills; they may have hunted animals but more probably were vegetarians, supplementing their diet by scavenging carcasses. *Homo erectus* probably developed from this earlier hominid, as it is recognizably a human creature and capable of flaking stone to produce choppers. Evidence suggests that he was both a cave and river or lake bank dweller. Remains of *Homo erectus* at Vértessölös near the Danube revealed stone implements and stone chips and what appears to be a hearth pointing to control of fire.

Homo erectus survived for some one and a half million years, probably thriving in the warm periods during the Ice Ages. By 250,000 years ago, new peoples were evolving and adapting to living in cold periods, and about 150,000 years later, Neanderthal man emerged. He can be regarded as a separate species and lived during the last Ice Age in Eurasia. Remains from a number of sites have been found, noticeably in the Neander Valley, La Chapelle-aux-Saints, Le Moustier, La Ferrassie, La Quina, Gibraltar, Monte Circeo, Saccopastore, Ehringsdorf, and Krapina, showing a geographic distribution in Germany, France, Spain, Italy, and the Balkans. Were they a species adapted to the cold, a specialized offshoot from the human tree becoming extinct as the climate improved? Some Neanderthals are thought to have avoided cold-adaptation and developed into *Homo sapiens*. Another view places Neanderthals within human evolution and attributes their extinction to absorption into modern man, scattering a few genes in the process. Fossil finds show that Neanderthal tool kits, especially of the Mousterian culture, demonstrate spearmaking, a use of stone flakes, and bone. They hunted large animals (elk), gathered nuts, roots, and tubers, had domesticated fire, and could make huts constructed of animal skins on a frame of branches or mammoth bones.

When modern man emerged through natural selection, a process with huge gaps in the historical story, a variety of human types such as Cro-Magnon, Grimaldi, and Brünn were capable of making flint-tipped spears and arrows, hunting in coordinated groups, developing bone tools (awls), flint drills, scrapers, and cutters. Early man lived in caves, rock shelters, and huts, developing an appreciation of decoration, sculpture, and art. Engraved bone tools depicting a bison followed by a man were found at Laugierie Basse, France, while carved horses' heads on bone from Le Mas d'Azil show clear artistic appreciation. Venus figurines found all over Europe (Brno, Willendorf) show faceless, large-breasted, wide-hipped pregnant women and are assumed to be a fertility symbol. Painting using mineral colors was fairly widespread, communicating views about wildlife, hunting, and perhaps even tradition, and ritual. The techniques used were often sophisticated, using cave wall surfaces to achieve a three-dimensional effect.

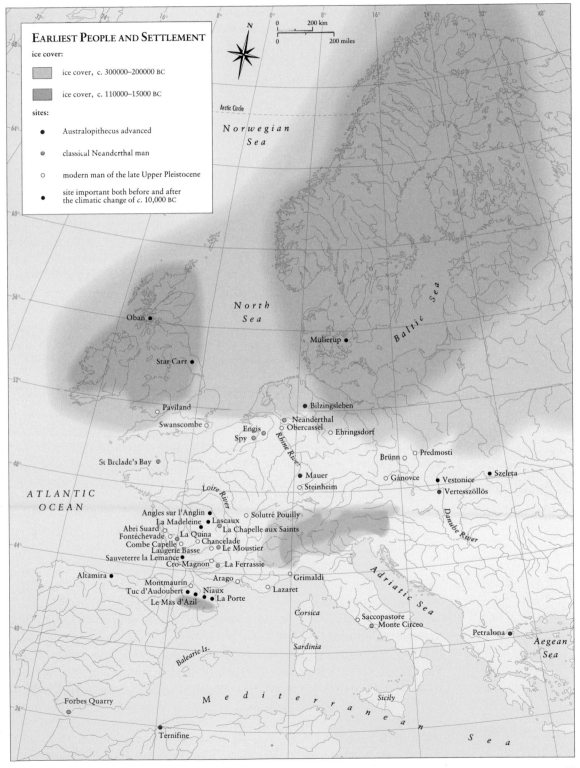

EARLIEST PEOPLE AND SETTLEMENT

ice cover:

◻ ice cover, c. 300000–200000 BC

◻ ice cover, c. 110000–15000 BC

sites:

● Australopithecus advanced

◉ classical Neanderthal man

○ modern man of the late Upper Pleistocene

● site important both before and after
the climatic change of c. 10,000 BC

0   200 km

0   200 miles

N

Arctic Circle

Norwegian Sea

Baltic Sea

North Sea

Oban ●

Mulierup ○

Star Carr ●

Paviland ○

Swanscombe ○

Bilzingsleben ●

Neanderthal ◉
Engis ○   Obercassel ○
Spy ◉   Ehringsdorf ○

St Brelade's Bay ◉

Rhine River

Brünn ○   Prédmosti ○

Mauer ●   Gánovce ○   Vestonice ●   Szeleta ●
Steinheim ○   Vertesszöllös ●

ATLANTIC OCEAN

Loire River

Angles sur l'Anglin ●   Solutré Pouilly ○
La Madeleine ●   Lascaux ●
Abri Suard ○   La Chapelle aux Saints ●
Fontéchevade ○   La Quina ●
Combe Capelle ○   Chancelade ○
Laugerie Basse ○   Le Moustier ○
Sauveterre la Lemance ●
Cro-Magnon ○   La Ferrassie ○

Altamira ●   Arago ○
Montmaurin ○   Grimaldi ●
Tuc d'Audoubert ●   Niaux ●   Lazaret ○
Le Mas d'Azil ●   La Porte ●

Danube River

Adriatic Sea

Corsica

Saccopastore ○
Monte Circeo ◉

Balearic Is.

Sardinia

Petralona ●

Aegean Sea

M e d i t e r r a n e a n

Sicily

Forbes Quarry ◉

S e a

Ternifine ●

15

FIRST FARMERS, 6500 BC

A shepherd tends his flock in the Provence region of southern France. In many areas across Europe the keeping of livestock has changed little, and traditional methods still exist, handed down from earliest times.

Agriculture and cattle farming reached the Aegean about 6500 BC but took another 2,000 to 3,000 years to spread throughout the temperate regions of Europe. Neolithic farming villages allowed the population to rapidly increase and to push settlements farther north and west. Settlements spread up the Vardar River to the north Balkans and into the lower Danubian Basin, complete with their common Starcevo-Körös style of painted and impressed-ware pottery. Villages made of mud-brick buildings were sometimes continuously occupied for hundreds of years, steadily accumulating debris until the village ended on a mound. This *tell* style of settlement is best exemplified by Karanovo in Bulgaria. The next phase of expansion saw movement through middle Europe into the Rhineland, the Low Countries, and northern France in the west; into north Germany and Silesia in the north; and east into the Ukraine. The settlements comprised groups of rectangular wooden farmhouses surrounded by walls and ditches, but the population was still mobile. Slash-and-burn agricultural techniques meant a move every few seasons after soil exhaustion set in. Rested land would be reoccupied later. Gradually, Neolithic culture split into separate but overlapping cultures defined by their pottery styles. The Boian settlements developed in Romania and in the Tripolye around the Bug and Dnieper, while the funnel-necked beaker culture and the battle-ax culture lasted into the second millennium.

The movement from loess soil settlements along river valleys and plains to heavier, less productive ones made ploughing essential. The felling of forest land necessitated large supplies of flints, and flint factories were established. Neoloithic mobility was aided by travel on rivers in dugout canoes and skin-covered boats and on land by sleds in snow, on oxen or reindeer-drawn wagons, later pulled by horses, and by building trackways of logs and branches in wetlands. Trade was extensive in grinding stones, knapped flints, and amber and followed a variety of routes, along the Rhine, Elbe, Rhone, and Danube. Neolithic ingenuity is further evidenced by the construction of standing stones (menhirs) and various stone alignments (megaliths), the most famous being at Carnac in Brittany and Stonehenge in England. Dependence on stone tools gradually diminished as copper was mined by the different groups in central, northern, and eastern Europe. These people produced knives, daggers, and pins. Eventually, the mixture of tin and copper produced bronze, a harder metal. A variety of important Bronze Age cultures emerged; the Unetice culture of the Early Bronze Age was established in central Germany, Bohemia, and Lower Austria, linking with Bell-beaker groups in Bavaria. The area was an important transit region for trade between the north and the Mediterranean. The Urnfield culture spread after 1300 BC, practicing cremation of the dead and the burial of ashes in urns. Sites have been found from Spain to eastern Europe, in Italy, southern Scandinavia, and Britain. The degree of specialization involved in mining and smelting bronze would suggest that society was becoming differentiated, with tradesmen coexisting with farmers. Grave finds containing bronze swords would suggest the growth of a warrior caste.

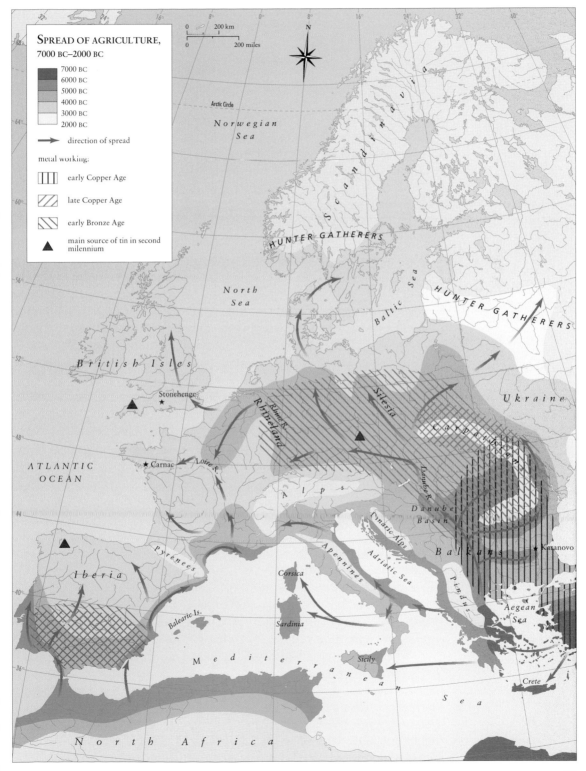

SPREAD OF AGRICULTURE,
7000 BC–2000 BC

7000 BC
6000 BC
5000 BC
4000 BC
3000 BC
2000 BC

→ direction of spread

metal working:

early Copper Age

late Copper Age

early Bronze Age

▲ main source of tin in second milennium

*Norwegian
Sea*

Arctic Circle

Scandinavia

*North
Sea*

Baltic Sea

HUNTER GATHERERS

HUNTER GATHERERS

British Isles

★ Stonehenge

Ukraine

Rhine R.

Rhineland

Silesia

Carpathians

*ATLANTIC
OCEAN*

★ Carnac

Loire R.

Alps

Danube R.

*Danube
Basin*

Iberia

Pyrenees

Dinaric Alps

Balkans

★ Karanovo

Apennines

Adriatic Sea

Corsica

Pindus

*Aegean
Sea*

Balearic Is.

Sardinia

Sicily

*Mediterranean
Sea*

Crete

North Africa

MINOAN CRETE

A pouring vessel (rhyton) carved from serpentine in the form of a bull's head, from the Palace of Knossos.

Minoan culture was one of the three main cultures of Aegean civilization, the other two being the Cycladic and Mycenaean. This Bronze Age civilization has been associated in myth with Theseus and the Minotaur, but archaeological discoveries by Sir Arthur Evans in 1900 unearthed an example of a flourishing palace culture at Knossos, other buildings being found at Phaestos, Mallia, and Zakros. The kings of Knossos achieved their greatest power between 2200 and 1450 BC, when they influenced the whole Aegean, trading widely with Egypt, Sicily, Cyprus, and Syria while building colonies at Kastri on Cythera, on Rhodes, and Miletus in Anatolia. Cretans also lived in towns such as Phylakopi on Melos and Agia Irini on Ceos. Copies of Cretan frescoes and motifs have been discovered in Tell-el-Daba in Egypt. Moreover, the bull-jumping scenes associated with Minoan bull sports were painted with Cretan, not Egyptian, colors.

The Cretan thalassocracy survived several rebuildings of its palaces following natural disasters and developed a brilliant culture that might have been crossfertilized by mainland refugees from the Near East. So successful were the Minoans that letters found in Mari on the Euphrates attest to the quality of Cretan craftsmanship. Exports included woven wool textiles, pottery, metal vases, daggers, stone lamps and vases, and timber products; imports included copper, scarab seals, iron, precious stones, and ostrich eggs.

The most significant monument of Minoan history must be the Knossos palace. Rooms, on up to four levels, surrounded a central courtyard, demonstrating architectural sophistication best observed in the distinctive, downward-tapering Minoan columns and walls made of doors, allowing privacy and ventilation. The palace walls were often richly decorated with frescoes depicting landscapes and seascapes vitalized by animals, birds, and foliage. Minoan artists excelled in carving marble figures, creating bronze figurines of bull-jumpers, replicating scenes on Knossos murals.

Cretan religion is portrayed by the sanctuaries within the palace at Knossos, associated with worship of a mother-goddess, possibly Rhea, and linked to pictures of a double ax appearing on the palace walls. A snake goddess also appears to be a figure of veneration, and the sympathetic portrayal of nature in the arts suggests a form of nature worship.

The collapse of Minoan culture coincided with the growth of the Mycenaean civilization in Greece, suggesting that this culture eclipsed and destroyed the Minoan cultural age.

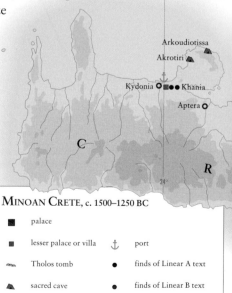

Arkoudiotissa
Akrotiri
Kýdonia ◾●● Khania
Aptera ◯

C

R

24°

MINOAN CRETE, c. 1500–1250 BC

◼	palace		
◾	lesser palace or villa	⚓ port	
⌒	Tholos tomb	●	finds of Linear A text
▲	sacred cave	●	finds of Linear B text
▲	peak sanctuary	◯	places mentioned in linear B text

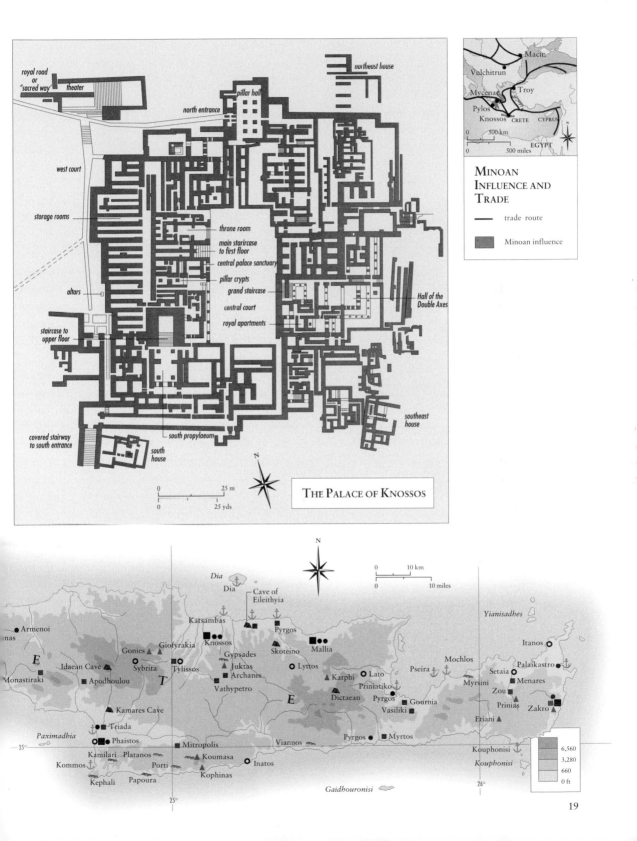

THE PALACE OF KNOSSOS

royal road or "sacred way"

theater

pillar hall

northeast house

north entrance

west court

storage rooms

throne room

main staircase to first floor

central palace sanctuary

pillar crypts

grand staircase

Hall of the Double Axes

altars

central court

staircase to upper floor

royal apartments

covered stairway to south entrance

south propylaeum

south house

southeast house

0   25 m
0   25 yds

MINOAN INFLUENCE AND TRADE

—— trade route

⬛ Minoan influence

Macin
Vulchitrun
Mycenae
Troy
Pylos
Knossos CRETE CYPRUS
EGYPT

0 500 km
0 500 miles

Dia
Dia
Cave of Eileithyia
Katsambas
Pyrgos
Armenoi
nas
Gonies Giofyrakia
Knossos
Gypsades
Skoteino
Mallia
Yianisadhes
Itanos
E
Idaean Cave
Sybrita
Tylissos
Juktas
Archanes
Lyttos
Karphi Lato
Priniatiko
Mochlos
Pseira
Palaikastro
Setaia
Menares
Monastiraki
Apodhoulou
T
Vathypetro
E
Dictaean
Pyrgos
Gournia
Myrsini
Zou
Prinias
Kamares Cave
Vasiliki
Etiani
Zakro
Triada
Phaistos
Viannos
Pyrgos Myrtos
Kouphonisi
Paximadhia
35°
Kamilari Platanos
Mitropolis
Kommos
Porti
Koumasa
Inatos
Kouphonisi
Kephali Papoura
Kophinas
Gaidhouronisi
26°

0 10 km
0 10 miles

6,560
3,280
660
0 ft

MYCENAEAN GREECE

Mycenae, on the plain of Argolis, gave its name to a culture developed on mainland Greece during the late phase of the Bronze Age. Other major centers of Mycenaean culture included Tiryns, Pylos, Thebes, and Argos. Mycenae, reputably the city of Agamemnon in the Homeric epics, was one of a series of heavily fortified strongholds built in a palatial style, following the example of Knossos. These edifices served as the military headquarters and administrative centers for the surrounding countryside.

Mycenae was the most powerful of the mainland Greek states between 1450 and 1200 BC. Shaft-grave finds including Linear B early Greek inscriptions have been found at numerous sites together with pottery, considerable quantities of weapons and armor, and funeral masks in beaten gold.

The German archaeologist Heinrich Schliemann uncovered Mycenae, with its massive cyclopean walls (1876–1878), its famous Lion Gate, and the beehive tombs known as the Treasury of Atreus and the Tomb of Clytemnestra. His discoveries confirmed Homer's description of Mycenae as being "rich in gold." Grave finds include amber, ivory, ostrich egg beakers, gold and silver vases, amethysts, and other objects demonstrating the extensive trade routes used and how Mycenaean culture was a fitting heir to Minoan Crete. Indeed, the palaces were similar to those in Crete, particularly in the utilization of frescoes, bathrooms, and storage rooms. However, the more sophisticated Cretan style gave way to massive stone constructions demonstrated in the Lion Gate, but serving a similar function as storage and status centers.

A golden burial mask from a tomb at Mycenae, excavated by Heinrich Schliemann, so excited by this find he wrote:"I have looked upon the face of Agamemnon."

The power and influence of Mycenae was considerable if not dominant in the Aegean, where its sea power colonized the Cyclades, Crete, Cyprus, the Dodecanese, northern Greece, Macedonia, and western Anatolia. Trade spread to Sardinia and southern Italy, as well as former Cretan markets. Mycenaean pottery has been found as far afield as Sudan and western Asia.

The art and architecture of Mycenae is reminiscent of Minoan Crete. Minoan artists carried their crafts to the mainland, as evidenced in the change of Mycenaean royal graves from shaft-graves to the Minoan tholos tomb, sometimes vaulted with thick stone roofs before being covered with earth tumuli.

The facade of one, named the Treasury of Atreus, is decorated with contrasting green and red marbles in the form of columns. Art flourished in the adornment of pottery, closely following Minoan themes, such as an octopus-painted jar found in a cemetery at a Mycenaean colony on Rhodes and a cuttlefish-decorated cup.

In 1900, a British archaeologist, Sir Arthur Evans, found baked clay tablets

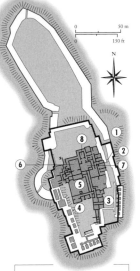

at Knossos, dating from the middle of the second millennium BC, with two types of writing on them. These are called Linear A and Linear B; the former, the written language of Minoan Crete, has yet to be deciphered, but the latter is an early form of Greek. The discovery of Linear B on Crete supports one historical explanation that Mycenaeans gained ascendancy over the Minoans.

Mycenae was destroyed about 1100 BC by fire. Historians cannot yet agree why this should have occurred, nor can they satisfactorily explain the collapse of Mycenaean civilization. Invasions by Dorians from the north might have caused this destruction, but equally famine or sea raiders might explain its demise.

TIRYNS CITADEL

———	old citadel 1400 BC
1	main gateway
2	inner gateway to palace
3	greater propælum
4	lesser propælum
5	court to chief Megaron
6	chief Megaron
7	court to lesser Megaron
8	lesser Megaron

MYCENAEAN GREECE

- ■ Mycenaean capital
- ● major city
- · Mycenaean site

EARLY GREECE

At the end of the Bronze Age, waves of invaders (c. 1200–1000 BC) sifted down into ancient Greece, subjugating the indigenous peoples. These invaders, perhaps set in motion by Illyrian pressure, were militarily superior, using mounted warriors with iron weapons against the more primitively armed bronze weapons of the attacked. Some northwestern Greeks settled in Epirus, Aetolia, and Acarnania, but the Dorians reached into the Peloponnesus by land and to Crete, the Dodecanese, and southwest Anatolia by sea. Attica, Euboea, and the Cyclades, inhabited by Ionians, either remained untouched by the Dorians or repelled them, and eventually settled Chios and the western coast of Anatolia. The Aeolians, from Thessaly, occupied Lesbos and areas farther north in Anatolia. Historians have debated the nature and timing of the Dorian invasions, but whatever theories are proffered, there is no denying that large-scale population movements occurred, and many Bronze Age sites were destroyed by fire (Mycenae, Tiryns, Pylus), setting in motion two centuries of chaos, after which the distribution of peoples is reflected by the disposition of the most important dialects. At the end of the Dark Ages, the Greeks spread throughout the Mediterranean, trade being a prime motive. The Greeks were therefore in a position to transmit aspects of advanced cultures from the Near East to western Europe. Many of the colonies became extremely rich. Legend has it that the people of Sybaris in southern

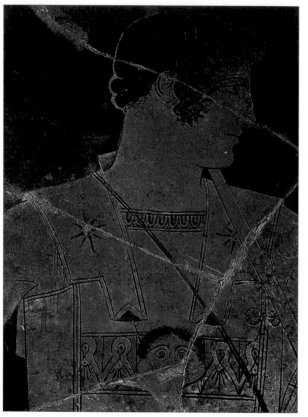

Achilles, the heroic ideal, admired by the Greeks, portrayed here on a vase of the 5th century BC.

Italy slept on beds of rose petals, and roosters were banned from the town, lest the inhabitants would be woken up too early by raucous crowing. Eastern trade with Egypt and Syria became very important for Corinth, Rhodes, and Ephesus.

The geography of Greece informs its political development. Living on islands, on promontories, in valleys separated by mountains on the mainland, people in small areas inaccessible from other parts developed a series of independent communities competing for the best land and creating a miscellaneous collection of city-states. Each state possessed a strong identity, and citizens were extremely loyal to that home state and its patron deity. Despite their individuality, the city-states did sometimes league together against common enemies.

The city-states gradually produced a new property-owning noble class, developing aristocratic rule. Other forms of politics included oligarchies and despotic tyranny, but some states eventually created early forms of democracy.

Athens provided an assembly where ordinary citizens, rich or poor, could speak and vote, making important decisions such as declaring war. In religion, the Greeks made use of shrines and temples, with a pantheon of deities each possessing their own spheres of influence: Apollo was associated with healing and medicine, while Athena was the goddess of wisdom and warfare and presided over literature, the arts, and philosophy. This latter "love of wisdom" involved science, mathematics, and political ideas. Heraclitus created an atomic theory, while Pythagoras developed theorems. Associated with philosophy are political thinkers who gradually reformed society. Leading figures are Solon, who outlawed debt slavery, and Cleisthones, who developed equality of political rights, strongly influencing many modern democratic systems.

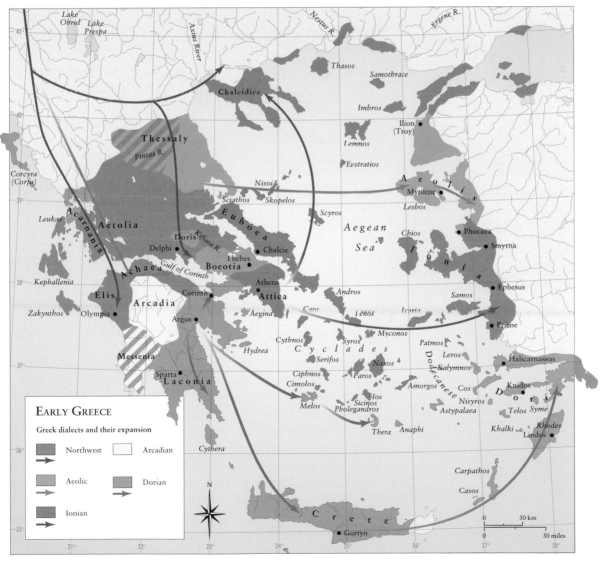

EARLY GREECE

Greek dialects and their expansion

- Northwest
- Arcadian
- Aeolic
- Dorian
- Ionian

ETRUSCAN EXPANSION

A detail from "Tomb of the Leopards" showing musicians at an Etruscan funerary banquet, 6th century BC.

The Etruscans, a people allegedly from southwestern Asia Minor, Lydia according to Herodotus, built the first civilization of western Europe from the eighth to third centuries BC in central Italy, in a region known as Etruria, modern-day Tuscany. Subjugating the mineral-wealthy region between the Arno and Tiber, an Etruscan nobility founded a loosely knit League of Twelve Cities, probably dominating the local population. Some major cities were at Veii, Tarquinii, Vulci, Volaterrae, and Visentium. Their power expanded by colonization to the north into the Po Valley and to the south beyond Rome into the Latium and Campania. Etruscan power was impressive, but the city-states, although mutually aligning themselves for economic and political gain, never united to fully coordinate their policies. The threatening power of Etruria eventually drove Romans, whose city was allegedly once ruled by the Etruscan Tarqin dynasty, and Greeks together against it. Trade rivalry resulted in a Greek-Etruscan battle of Alalia (535 BC), leaving Corsica in the Etruscan sphere of influence, but in 474 BC, an allied Etruscan fleet was defeated off Cumae by a Syracusan fleet. A later effort to control the seaways saw the Etruscan League allying with Athens against Syracuse in a disastrous assault in 413 BC. The gradual weakening of Etruria saw a series of piecemeal conflicts between individual Etruscan cities and the growing power of Rome initiated by the fall of Veii (396 BC) after a ten-year siege. By 283 BC, Rome had conquered Etruria, and by the reign of Caesar Augustus the region was becoming increasingly romanized.

Etrurian wealth was originally based on iron, which attracted Phoenician and Greek traders. The Etruscan city of Spina on the Adriatic traded with Istria and the Greek Dalmatian colonies. Contacts were made with La Tène Celts in Gaul, and the mercantile network included trade with Tartessos, and Ampurias near Barcelona in Spain. This thriving commercial and agricultural civilization was mirrored by artistic and architectural achievements, eventually incorporated into the Roman tradition. House styles were later copied in Rome, with colonnades around a courtyard with gabled or flat roofs decorated with terracotta statuary, as at the Etruscan site of Pogo Civitate near Siena. Their design has been found on ceramic votive models. Etruscan tombs repeat the design of houses, some being built aboveground and covered with earth tumuli, while others were dug into volcanic rock. The excavation of these tombs revealed many valuable artifacts, which allow archaeologists to reconstruct Etruscan life. Pottery developed a distinctive black bucchero ware with incised designs or with decorations in relief. Bronze work was particularly fine, including temple tripods, bowls, and candelabra for divination in religious ceremonies. The Etruscans also made gold, silver, and ivory jewelry, particularly gold earrings and wreaths of gold ivy leaves. Despite being defeated by Rome, many Etruscan practices continued in the forms of frescoes and reliefs, architecture, and a peculiar sombrero-style hat that is still worn in the Sienese countryside.

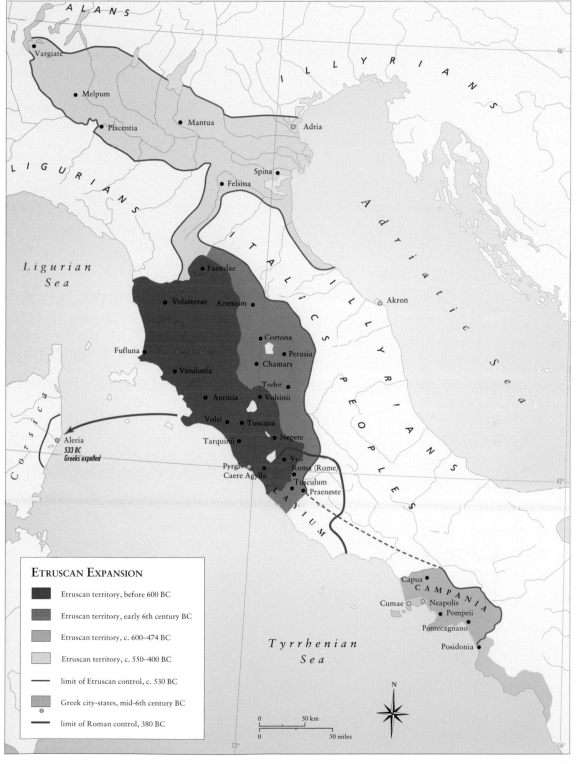

ETRUSCAN EXPANSION

Etruscan territory, before 600 BC

Etruscan territory, early 6th century BC

Etruscan territory, c. 600–474 BC

Etruscan territory, c. 550–400 BC

limit of Etruscan control, c. 530 BC

Greek city-states, mid-6th century BC

limit of Roman control, 380 BC

THE HALLSTATT CULTURE–THE CELTS I

The Hallstatt Celtic culture (750–450 BC), named after a burial ground in the Salzkammergut in Austria, spread its Iron Age technology and civilization throughout the Balkans, central Europe, France, and Spain. Archaeological evidence suggests that these Celts probably began to settle in Britain. Artifacts recovered at the Hallstatt necropolis demonstrate elaborate funeral rites, whether by cremation or interment. Some graves contain four-wheeled carts and bronze harness mounts and bits, suggesting economic and cultural links with the Russian steppes, whether by origin or by the absorption of peoples moving westward from a steppe homeland. Finely decorated burial sites in Bohemia, complete with Greek wine amphora and pottery, in southern Germany and in northeastern France would appear to be those of chieftains.

The increasing utilization of iron and technological skills in its work mark the Hallstatt Age. However, this culture continued to use Bronze Age materials and techniques of the earlier Urnfield culture. The widespread use of iron allowed the Celts to fell forests and clear land for agriculture as well as engaging in raids and warfare among themselves or with other peoples such as the Iberians, who settled in the Iberian peninsula. An indication of increasing warfare can be found in the construction of strongly fortified settlements and the later hill forts. The first fortified "castle" of the late Hallstatt period was found at Heuneburg on the Danube, where rich grave finds were uncovered.

This design of horse and rider is part of an elaborately decorated sword scabbard excavated at the Salzkammergut graves, Hallstatt. It shows a well-equipped cavalryman, armed with a lance, off to do battle.

The wealth of Celtic chieftains is well demonstrated by the interred works of art. Greek bronze, northern amber, gold, and wine vessels point to an increase in trade. Greeks certainly acted as merchants at Massilia (Marseille). The grave furniture of an aristocratic young woman at Vix, near Châtillon-sur-Seine in the Côte d'Or, contained a five-foot-high bronze wine container (krater), emphasizing the importance of trade between the Hallstatt Celts and Greece. Other sites provide evidence of links with the Etruscan civilization in Italy. During and after the heyday of Hallstatt culture, there is evidence for an increase in salt extraction, both for domestic use and as a trade product, as is demonstrated by the Hallstatt mines with shafts that reach a depth of 1,300 feet.

Despite a prevalence of intertribal rivalry, the Hallstatt Celts made a great contribution to European art, inheriting their techniques from the Urnfield culture and thus laying the foundations for the flowering of art during the La Tène Celtic period. Hallstatt artifacts were generally decorated with repeated, rigidly designed, symmetrical geometric patterns, as can be seen on the pottery vessel in the Württermbergisches Landesmuseum in Stuttgart. Their stylization of chevrons and curves derives from the Scythians and other steppe peoples, but this did not preclude the Hallstatt Celts from occasionally creating artwork with images of animals and people. A thirty-five-cm-long vehicle was found at Strettweg in Austria, this comprising a group of bronze figures on a wheeled platform. In the center stand a goddess surrounded by mounted warriors and sacred animals, including a horned god.

As far as Hallstatt Celtic society is concerned, it seems that was made up of tribes and subdivided into families, with loyalty being accorded to the chieftain. Society comprised chiefs, warriors, Druids, craftsmen, farmers, servants, and slaves. The burial at Vix appears to show that aristocratic women were given parity with men, this being sustained by the existence of Boudicca, Queen of the Iceni in a later period in Britain.

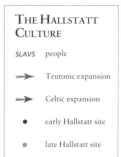

THE HALLSTATT
CULTURE

SLAVS   people

→   Teutonic expansion

→   Celtic expansion

●   early Hallstatt site

●   late Hallstatt site

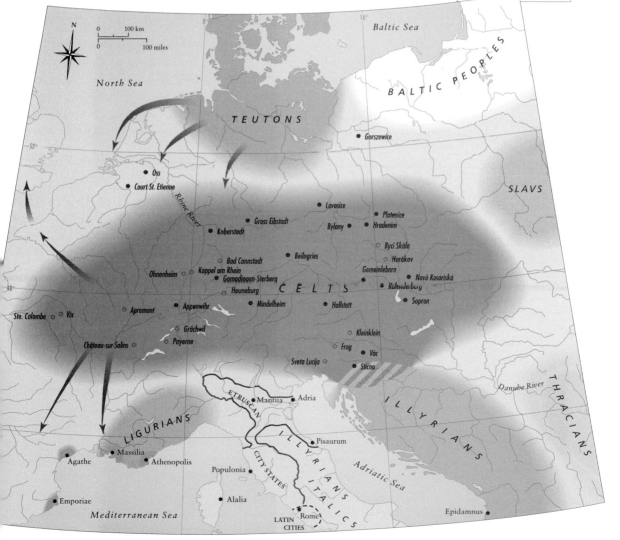

PART II: THE MEDITERRANEAN WORLD

The rise of the city-state *(polis)* in the eighth century BC became a key feature in the spread of Greek civilization. It has been said that the city-state, a small, politically independent community of citizens who were protected by a fortified citadel, was a natural product of Greek physical geography, for the Greek peninsula was a mountainous land with small coastal plains and valleys separated by mountains. Between the eighth and the seventh centuries, the economy, technology, and culture flourished, with notable contributions in the field of Greek epic literature and lyrical poetry, provided by Homer and Hesiod.

The feeling that the city-states were united by a common Greek identity, based upon culture, language, and religion, was best demonstrated by the foundation of the Olympic Games, in 776 BC, yet despite this, the city-states engaged themselves in a state of almost perpetual conflict, most notably between Athens, Sparta, Thebes, and Corinth.

Far right: This terracotta tablet shows a woman preparing a trousseau for a forthcoming marriage ceremony, and dates from the 5th century BC.

During the same period, economic and social developments, boosted by colonial expansion, took place, enhancing the importance of the Greek nobility. Yet by about 600 BC a transfer of power from the nobility to the citizens took place, which was particularly demonstrated in the military sphere of society, with the creation of heavily armored infantry units, the Hoplites, among the wealthier citizens.

Although the Greeks had been hemmed in from the north by the Celts, colonial expansion gradually took place in Eretria, Chalcis, Corinth, and Megara in central Greece; in Miletus in Asia Minor and the island of Rhodes, it was stimulated by Greek military superiority, land hunger, and a desire for increasing trade and profit. Around the shores of the Mediterranean, Greek settlements were also established in Marseille (Massilia), Naples (Neapolis), Byzantium, and Syracuse, which would become lasting centers of trade. The Greeks would learn much from their contacts with other cultures around the eastern shores of the Mediterranean, which would in turn influence their technical and philosophical development.

The Greek religion was centered upon the twelve Olympian gods, whose home, according to Greek mythology, was on Mount Olympus, the highest mountain in Greece. Here Zeus, "the father of all gods and men," held sway over the other deities and mortals in what can be described as a patriarchal system of hierarchy. The main deities were introduced by the Dorians who had invaded from the north. Each of the gods governed a variety of activities and human experience, as well as lying at the heart of Greek mythology, about whom a raft of stories of relations between the gods and ordinary mortals were recounted, forming the basis of classical Greek literature. The Olympian gods would in turn influence Roman religious beliefs, thinking, and practice.

Another aspect of the Greek religion was the oracle, of which the most important was the Delphic Oracle, presided over by the god Apollo, who gave oracular utterance through the intermediary of a young priestess, the Pythia, who conducted her duties in a state of ecstasy. These oracles were

then translated by priests in charge and conveyed to the suppliant. Oracles formed an important feature of Greek cultural, social, and even political life, and were used for advice on a variety of matters. The Delphic Oracle was usually consulted on the planning and conduct of military campaigns, and had even discouraged resistance to Persia, no doubt reflecting the attitudes of several influential Greek political advisors who wished to see Greece absorbed into the powerful Persian empire in 480 BC. Similarly, the oracle had given support to the Spartan cause against Athens, and during the period of Greek colonial expansion, the advice of the Delphic Oracle was also sought on where to site the new cities.

A limited form of democracy developed in the fifth century BC, although women, foreigners, and slaves were denied political rights, against a backdrop of continuing conflict between the militarized state of Sparta and the democratic state of Athens, where every male citizen had the right to speak and vote in the assembly.

By the beginning of the fifth century, a new danger began to threaten the Greek city-states, which were obliged to unite to confront incursions from the Persian empire in 490 and 480. In the heat of battle, well-trained Greek Hoplites proved to be more than a match for Persian cavalry, who at the time were considered to be the best soldiers in the world. In the battle of Marathon in 490 BC, the phalanx of Athenian Hoplites, fighting at close quarters in a rigid formation of serried ranks, put the Persian troops to flight. Later, in 480 BC, three hundred Spartan Hoplites, led by Leonidas, King of Sparta, were able to hold a Persian army for a period of three days, before being defeated in action. It should be noted that the Persians were a hundred times superior to the Spartans in terms of manpower strength and had been led by their King, Xerxes.

In the meantime, Athens grew in power as the leader of a free alliance of Greek maritime states, yet, despite the period of unity brought about by the threat of Persian conquest, unity among the city-states was short-lived, and a bloody war, known as the Peloponnesian War, soon broke out between Sparta and Athens, lasting twenty-seven years, between 431 and 404 BC.

The fifth century witnessed a further flowering of Hellenic culture, which has made a deep impact upon European civilization. This classical "Golden Age" was represented by historians, such as Heodotus and Thucydides; dramatists, such as Aristophanes, Aeschylus, Euripides, and Sophocles; and the great philosopher Socrates, who would be followed in the fourth century by Plato and Aristotle, who worked together, as teacher and pupil, for a period of twenty years. Although scientific questioning had begun in the sixth century BC, influenced by contact with other cultures bordering the Mediterranean world, the greatest period of the kind of speculative thinking, argument, and counter-argument that lie at the heart of the classical European philosophical tradition took place in the period between 550 and 400 BC. This period witnessed a growth in the number of sophists and professional teachers, who were a prod-

> "The sense of wonder is the mark of the the philosopher. Philosophy indeed has no other origin."
> *Socrates*

uct of the wealthy and leisured class that could be found in developing societies such as Athens.

Yet despite their thoughts upon the nature of Greek identity, Greece remained politically divided. Then, in the mid fourth century, unity would be imposed upon the city-states by the rising power of Macedonia under Philip and later its great and able leader, Alexander, who compelled the Greek city-states to form an alliance with him prior to his attack on the Persian empire.

The military conquests of Alexander the Great had a huge impact upon the Hellenistic world, spreading Greek civilization from the Mediterranean shores deep into the heart of Asia. In 334, his combined Macedonian and Greek army of 35,000 men crossed the Hellespont into Asia Minor, winning the battle of the River Granicus and conquering all before them in Anatolia. They continued their advance upon Syria, defeating the main Persian army under Darius in 333 BC. With the conquest of Egypt, Alexander had gained control of the whole of the eastern Mediterranean and strategic control of the sea. Alexander's army then pushed east and southeast into Babylon and the Tigris and Euphrates Rivers, defeating Darius once and for all at the battle of Guagamel in 331 BC. The Greco-Macedonian forces then turned upon Persia, penetrating into the Hindu Kush, Bukhara, and Tashkent. At its greatest extent, Alexander's empire spread as far as present-day Afghanistan and Baluchistan and northward into Bactria and Sogadiana.

A Roman stone funerary stele, made around AD 70, showing a cavalry soldier, spear held high, riding to attack.

Although Alexander had achieved such noteworthy military victories, he had totally failed to organize his empire politically. He had made no provision for his succession, so that on his death, in 323 BC, Alexander's huge empire broke up and was divided among his generals, who would fight among themselves for a period of fifty years. The ensuing rivalry and internecine strife throughout the third century BC eventually led to the development of a federal system among the city-states, of which the Aetolian and Achean leagues were the most prominent.

By the second century BC, great advances had been made in the expansion of trade by the Greeks with eastern Africa, Arabia, India, central Asia, and even China. In the meantime, to the north, Rome, having conquered the whole of the Italian Peninsula south of the Rubicon River, including Etruria, began to threaten the borders of Greece. When Philip V of Macedon allied with the Carthaginian leader Hannibal in 215 BC, the Romans struck south, intervening in the Greek Peninsula for the first time.

By the end of the third century, the Roman republic had become the dominant military and political power in the Mediterranean, so that by mid second century it had effectively consolidated itself as an empire, although true imperial status would not be achieved until after the battle of Actium in 31 BC, when Octavian defeated the armies of Anthony and Cleopatra, and was granted the title of Augustus by both the Senate and the people of Rome.

GREEK AND PHOENICIAN COLONIZATION

The Phoenicians were a Semitic people inhabiting a group of city-kingdoms on the eastern Mediterranean coast, the most important being Tyre and Sidon. After 1100 BC, the Phoenicians became prominent traders and sailors. Their fleets sailed throughout the Mediterranean and even into the Atlantic, founding many colonies, notably Utica and Carthage in North Africa, and on the islands of Cyprus, Sardinia, and Sicily. Other Phoenician centers included the Balearics, Sexi in southern Spain, and Tortessus (Gades) on the Spanish Atlantic coast to exploit silver, copper, and tin deposits. Phoenician exports included cedar and pine, linen, material dyed with Tyrian purple, Sidonian embroidery, wine, metalwork, and glass. Imports and transit goods included papyrus, ivory, Anatolian wool, and Arabian resins, and Cypriot copper, while Tyre formed an entrepôt for goods delivered down the Amber Road and by caravan routes to Memphis, Nineveh, and Babylon, and hence to the Indus. Phoenicia eventually succumbed to a variety of imperial powers: Assyria, the Chaldean empire of Nebuchadnezzar II, Persia, and Macedonia. The most significant contribution to civilization was the Phoenician alphabet, the probable ancestor of the Greek and thus all western alphabets.

Greek colonization paralleled the Phoenician, predicated upon demographic increase, the expansion of maritime

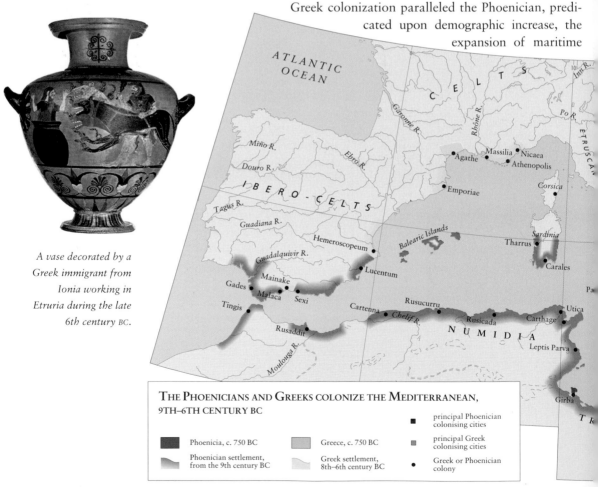

A vase decorated by a Greek immigrant from Ionia working in Etruria during the late 6th century BC.

THE PHOENICIANS AND GREEKS COLONIZE THE MEDITERRANEAN, 9TH–6TH CENTURY BC

- Phoenicia, c. 750 BC
- Phoenician settlement, from the 9th century BC
- Greece, c. 750 BC
- Greek settlement, 8th–6th century BC
- principal Phoenician colonising cities
- principal Greek colonising cities
- Greek or Phoenician colony

trade, and social conflict. Colonies were founded by a mother-city but owned political autonomy, while keeping contact through common customs and religious cults. Expansion to the east was prevented by the growth of Middle Eastern empires, so colonization was focused on the western Mediterranean. After earlier colonization of the Black Sea, centers were established in Egypt, Cyrene, Sicily, Campania, southern Anatolia, and southern France. These colonies eventually controlled the Black Sea grain trade and the tin route through Etruria. This Greek trade and cultural imperialism changed the whole complexion of the Mediterranean world. The Greeks imbibed ideas from Egypt, Mesopotamia, and India, and developed their own synthesis, resulting in an unequaled flowering of culture, especially in Athens. New political structures were tested, from democracies to tyrannies, the latter exemplified by Dionysus I of Syracuse; the Ionians adopted a money economy, probably following Lydian examples, aiding the growth of a merchant class. In addition, art developed–by devising new forms of pottery; through drama writing by Sophocles and Euripedes; via comedies by Aristophanes; through the histories of Herodotus and Thucydides; and by schools of philosophy, forerunners of Socrates, Plato, and Aristotle.

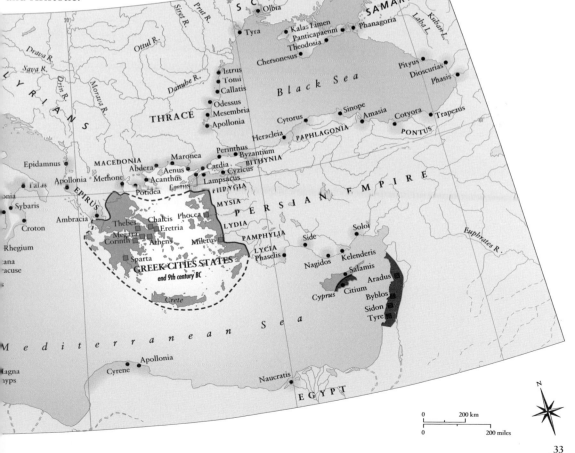

PELOPONNESIAN WAR

In 478 BC, the Delian League, a voluntary alliance, was established to drive the Persians from Greek city-states and the coastal islands of Asia Minor. Under the Athenian General Kimon, the Greek fleets defeated the Persians at Eurymedon in Pamphylia. Athens gradually dominated the league, and its members soon became subjects rather than allies, paying tribute instead of supplying ships to the league. Athens' tributaries became discontented under Athenian rule, and rebellions occurred such as those at Naxos and Thasos, whose fortifications were destroyed in reprisal.

Under Pericles, Athenian imperialism became harsher, and Athens entered a Golden Age as a major artistic, architectural, and cultural center. However, Sparta led an alliance of independent states and had a stronger army than Athens, which possessed a superior fleet. Competition and conflict broke out but was ended by a Thirty Years' treaty (445 BC). In 433 BC, Athens allied herself with Corcyra, a Corinthian colony. When Sparta and its allies accused Athens of breaking the treaty, Athens stood her ground. The Peloponnesian War began when, in 431 BC, a Spartan ally, Thebes, attacked Plataea, an Athenian ally. The war can be divided into two distinct periods broken by a brief truce. The initial stage of the war saw annual Spartan incursions into Attica, which persuaded Pericles to withdraw his soldiers into Athens rather than facing superior military might. Instead, his fleets waged a campaign against coasts and ships. Crowded Athens suffered the plague, killing large numbers of soldiers and civilians, temporarily weakening Athenian morale. Elsewhere, Spartan attacks in western Greece were halted, and an attempt to aid an anti-Athenian revolt on Lesbos was thwarted; the capture of Plataea (427 BC) was the sole success. Athens then took the initiative, moving into western Greece and the Peloponnese and interfering in Sicily, where Sparta and Athens

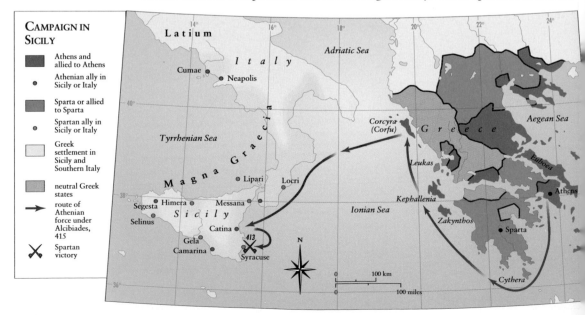

CAMPAIGN IN SICILY

- Athens and allied to Athens
- Athenian ally in Sicily or Italy
- Sparta or allied to Sparta
- Spartan ally in Sicily or Italy
- Greek settlement in Sicily and Southern Italy
- neutral Greek states
- route of Athenian force under Alcibiades, 415
- Spartan victory

supported different cities in an intraisland dispute. However, Sparta made important gains in Chalkidike, and defeated Athens at the battle of Amphipolis (422 BC). Exhausted, the enemies agreed on the Peace of Nikias (421 BC).

The war soon renewed, the Athenians suffering a major catastrophe in Sicily, where their entire force was destroyed (413 BC). A naval campaign was fought, with Athens gaining victories at Abydos (411 BC) and Cyzicus (410 BC), thereby securing the sea route to the Black Sea and its grain supplies. Events turned around when Athens suffered serious losses at Arginusae and the destruction of her fleet at Aegospotami (405 BC) by the Spartans. A further blow to Athenian prestige was the capture of Byzantium and Chalkedon, giving Sparta control of the Bosporus. A general revolt by Athenian allies broke out, and Athens was rapidly placed under siege by both land and sea. Starvation forced Athens to capitulate, her Long Walls and those of Piraeus were destroyed, and she submitted to rule by a Spartan-sponsored oligarchy known as the Thirty Tyrants (404 BC). Similar rule was established throughout the cities and islands of Asia Minor; Spartan rule was found more oppressive than Athenian. In 403 BC, an Athenian exile, Thrasybulus, liberated Athens, expelled the Spartan garrison, and restored Athenian democracy and independence.

PELOPONNESIAN WAR, 431–404 BC

- ■ Athens and members of the Delian League, c. 431 BC
- ■ Athens's allies
- → Athenian campaign
- ✗ Athenian victory
- ■ Sparta and Spartan allies, c. 431 BC
- → Spartan campaign
- ✗ Spartan victory
- ✳ revolt against Athens
- ■ Persian empire
- ■ neutral states

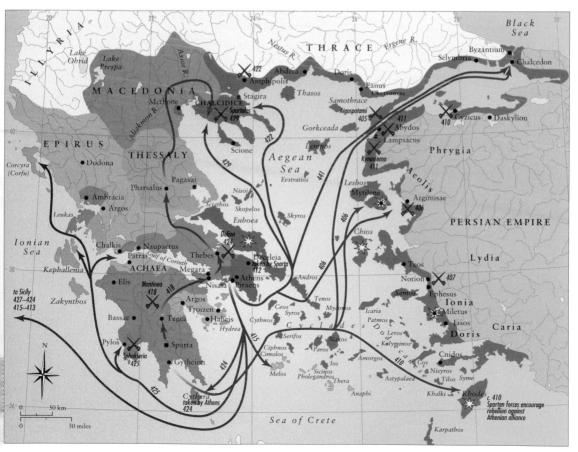

THE RISE OF MACEDONIA

Macedonia (359–336 BC) achieved major historical importance during the reign of Philip II. On returning to Macedonia after being a hostage in Thebes, he reorganized his army into a mixture of cavalry regiments, a phalanx of infantry armed with pikes (*sarissa*), javelin throwers, and archers. These were coordinated in battle in mutually supporting positions. Philip quickly reduced internal opposition (358 BC) after he usurped the throne, and then sought to expand his kingdom's borders to secure improved access to the sea. In 357 BC, he captured the Athenian colony of Amphipolis in Thrace, acquiring the gold mines of Mount Pangaeus, which helped finance subsequent military adventures. Rapid military campaigns and conquests followed: Potidea in Chalcidice and Pydna on the Thermaic Gulf; Thracian Cremides; and Methone, with an advance into Thessaly. By 348 BC, Philip had conquered Thrace and Chalcidice.

A beautifully decorated golden quiver from the royal tomb of King Philip II of Macedonia, showing soldiers in action, made around 340 BC.

In 346 BC, Macedon and Athens (which had been defending its ally Chalcidian Olynthus against Philip) made the Peace of Philocrates. Philip then intervened in a war between Thebes and Phocis; his victory and replacement of Phocis in the Amphictyonic League gave Macedonia the right to participate in Greek political issues, while making Philip commander of the league forces.

The spread of Macedonian power spurred Demosthenes to attack it in his oratorical *Philippics*, warning of Macedonia's control of the grain route into the Black Sea. The subsequent alliance between Athens and Thebes was crushed by Philip at Chaeronea (338 BC) making him the master and arbiter of Greece. Philip organized the League Council of Corinth of all Greek cities, except Sparta, and, while preparing to invade Persia, he was murdered.

Philip undoubtedly laid the foundations for his son, Alexander the Great, to consolidate the control of Greece and then to construct a vast empire in the east. On his accession, Alexander immediately executed those accused of his father's murder, together with all possible rivals and opposing factions. His ruthless methods, unexpected in a former pupil of Aristotle, continued with an advance to the Danube to kill and burn out the Getae, the crushing of an Illyrian invasion, and then a move south to put down a Theban and Athenian revolt. Thebes was razed to the ground; thousands were killed and the rest sold into slavery. Other dissenting states submitted and accepted Macedonian garrisons. In 334 BC, Alexander crossed the Hellespont into Asia Minor, defeated the Persian armies, captured Syria and Egypt, campaigned into Afghanistan and Uzbekistan, and invaded the Punjab into the Mauryan empire. In 325 BC, his troops demanded a return, but Alexander died (323 BC) aged thirty-three years, leaving his commanders to carve up his empire into Macedonia, the kingdom of Antigonus in Asia Minor, Ptolemaic Egypt, and the Seleucid empire.

Alexander was important in spreading Greek culture and language as far as India and establishing multiethnic cities based on equal rights for Persians and Greeks. New foci of culture and learning were established at Antioch,

Pergamon, and Alexandria, and trade between the Mediterranean, the Near East, and India was vitalized. Alternatively, Alexander might be seen as a megalomaniac, dying while dreaming of expanding into the western Mediterranean and the Carthaginian sphere of influence.

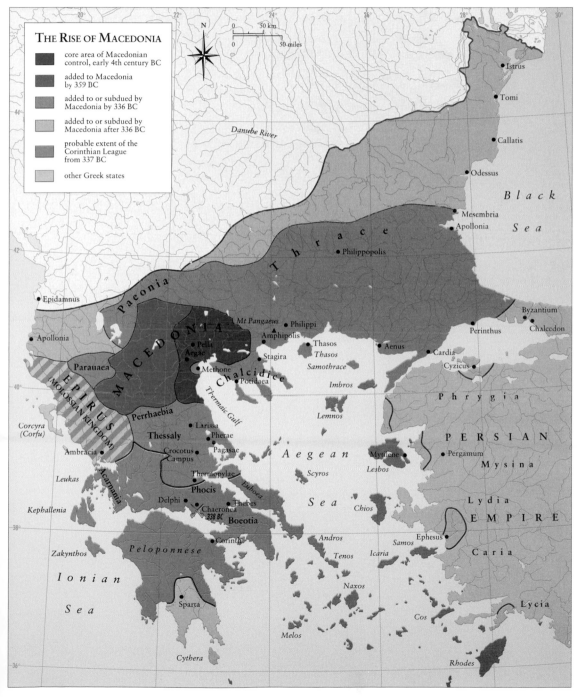

THE RISE OF MACEDONIA

- core area of Macedonian control, early 4th century BC
- added to Macedonia by 359 BC
- added to or subdued by Macedonia by 336 BC
- added to or subdued by Macedonia after 336 BC
- probable extent of the Corinthian League from 337 BC
- other Greek states

LA TÈNE CULTURE–THE CELTS II

Bronze brooch from Iberia showing a horseman carrying a severed head.

The La Tène culture, named after a Celtic archaeological site on Lake Neuchâtel in Switzerland, existed from about 450 BC to the conquest of Gaul by Julius Caesar in 58 BC. During this period, many Celts left their homeland to cross the Alps and settle in the fertile river valleys of northern Italy, fighting and destroying many Etruscan cities on their way. In 38 BC, the Celts sacked Rome and raided down to Sicily; the Romans eventually recovered under Marcus Furius Camillus and drove the invaders back to the Alpine foothills. The Celts next enlarged their control in Europe, with incursions into central Europe, the Carpathians, and the Balkans. The Roman historian Livy, as well as recounting the sack of Rome, describes how branches of the Celts settled in southern and central Germany. Under their leader, Brennus, they stormed into Bulgaria, Thrace, and Macedonia. In 279 BC, Brennus fought the Greeks and looted the temple of the god Apollo at Delphi. Eventually, the Celts were driven out. After this defeat, surviving Celts built a fort on the eventual site of Belgrade, and one band crossed the Dardanelles into Anatolia, where they settled, giving their name to Galatia. Some even reached the Sea of Azov in Russia. Eventually, the Celts were squeezed between the military might of Rome and the pressure of expanding German tribes, which forced many Celts to the south and west, where later they would be conquered by the Romans; the absence of political unity contributed to the Celts' ultimate downfall. The La Tène culture in Britain was brought under Roman control in the first century AD. In time, the remnants of Celtic tradition and languages survived in Brittany, Cornwall, Wales, the Isle of Man, Ireland, and the Highlands of Scotland–recently described as the Celtic fringe.

The La Tène culture developed the Hallstatt art forms and incorporated Greek and Etruscan styles but eventually Celticized these into its own legendary animals, plant motifs, and human masks. The designs appeared on military accoutrements, bowls and vessels, and mirrors. Examples of Celtic art are neck rings (torcs), brooches, and particularly the silver Gundestrup cauldron (in the Danish National Museum in Copenhagen), on which the figures were hammered out from behind using the repoussé method. Other well-known finds are in the British Museum, including a bronze lozenge-shaped shield with medallions and enamel work, and a bronze mirror with enamel decorations. In Britain and Ireland, La Tène art acquired a different style, especially in metalwork such as the Tara brooch and Ardagh chalice.

The legacy of the Celts is considerable. They were christianized during the fourth century and were under immense pressure during the fifth-century invasions of Britain by pagan Angles and Saxons (after the Romans had left). This forced the Celtic

Christians into Ireland, Wales, and Cornwall, with St. Patrick founding the center of Christianity in Ireland. Irish monks preserved knowledge by keeping learning and the Christian religion alive. The manuscripts they created are beautifully illuminated, such as the *Book of Kells,* while the Celtic crosses surviving in Ireland and the Isle of Man have a beauty of their own, most notably the Manx examples at Maughold, on an ancient monastic site.

A second inheritance is the survival of Celtic literature and stories. Although the Celts did not write, they passed on law, history, and stories through the oral tradition, and parts of these are preserved in the Welsh *Mabinogion,* the Irish legends of Cuchulainn, and the story of Bricriu's Feast.

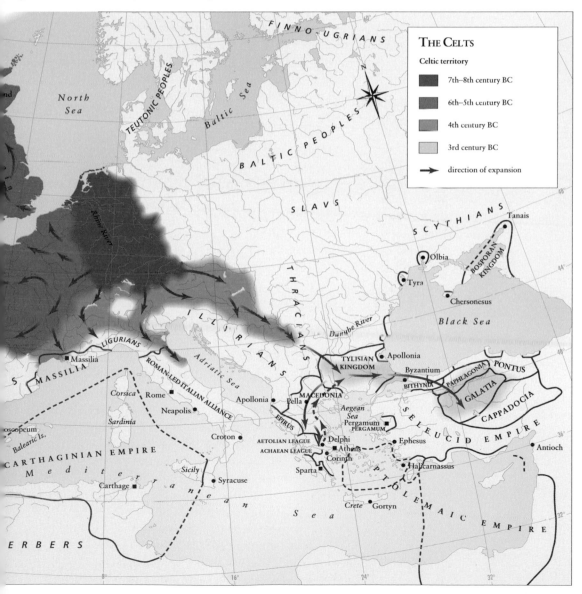

ROOTS OF ROME, 753 BC

Since its foundation in 735 BC and for a period of nearly two and a half centuries, Rome would remain within the Etruscan sphere of influence, growing from a cluster of villages in the region known as Latium, into a city-state. This was the period before recorded history, bathed in myths about a Roman descendency from the fall of Troy; myths that were played to the accompaniment of the saga of Dido and Aeneas, and the story of Romulus and Remus, who were suckled by a she-wolf, against the background of the rape of the Sabine women and the rape of Lucretia.

Bone tablets from Palestrina in Italy, carved during the 4th century BC, give a clear idea of the arms and personal equipment of Roman soldiers of the period.

Dominated initially by the Etruscans in the north, with Greek settlements in the south of the Italian peninsula, Rome commanded a strategic crossing point of the Tiber River, the fullest-flowing river in central Italy. For a period of two centuries, the Romans extended their power over one tribe after another–Sabines, Aequi, and Volsci–ultimately gaining ascendancy over the Etruscans.

The last Etruscan king, Tarquinius Superbus (the "Proud"), was overthrown in 510 BC, and Rome became a republic, governed by two consuls who were

elected on an annual basis. Nevertheless, Rome's position remained insecure, and Tarquin, with the help of the Etruscan leader, Lars Porsena, returned in a bid to retake Rome, only to be beaten off, according to Livy, by Horatius' heroic stand on the Tiber bridge. Rome would be joined by the other Latin cities, which, by the major victory of Aricia in 506 BC, were eventually able to win their political independence from the Etruscans.

Now an important city, Rome was, during the fourth century, able to expand its power southward and throughout the Italian peninsula, absorbed by warfare and diplomacy. Eventually the Romans defeated their onetime allies the Samnites, in the Second and Third Samnite Wars of 327–304 and 298–290 BC.

By 266 BC, the Romans controlled the whole of the Italian peninsula south of the Rubicon River, spreading Roman citizenship throughout the region. By the middle of the third century BC Rome, having behaved as an expansionist power, united all of Italy, by defeating Pyrrhus, King of Epirus, in northwestern Greece, between 282 and 272 BC. The Romans consolidated their hold on the Italian peninsula. In the second century BC, the Roman army crossed the straits of Messina onto Sicily and in so doing faced a new enemy, Carthage.

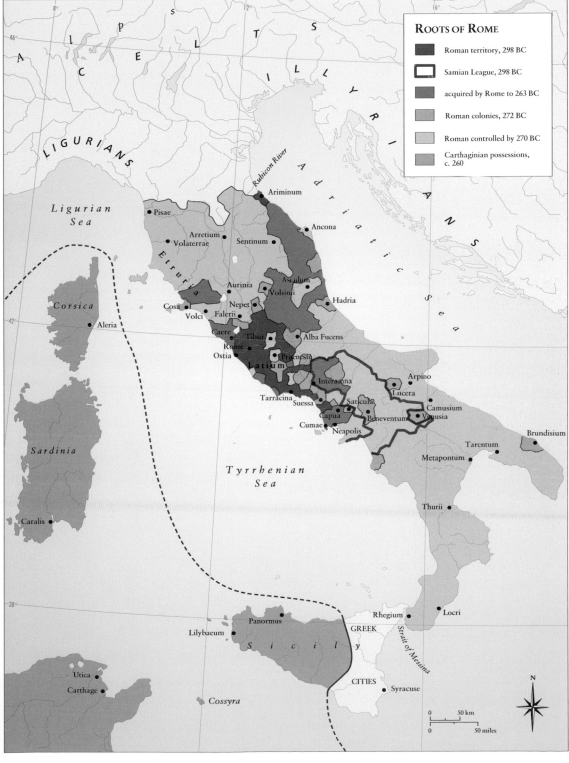

ROOTS OF ROME

Roman territory, 298 BC

Samian League, 298 BC

acquired by Rome to 263 BC

Roman colonies, 272 BC

Roman controlled by 270 BC

Carthaginian possessions, c. 260

PUNIC WARS

Once the Romans had conquered the whole of the Italian peninsula south of the Rubicon, they became involved in a series of three wars against the Carthaginians (*Poeni* in Latin). The first Punic War (264–241 BC) was largely waged at sea, which at first disadvantaged Rome, since Carthage was a maritime power, whose skilled sailors had extended its commercial interests in the western Mediterranean, establishing settlements in North Africa, Sicily, and Sardinia. Although successful when fighting on land in Sicily, Rome would take a further eight years to secure victory over the Carthaginians in a sea battle off the Aegates Islands in 241 BC. By now, Rome had built a large fleet of warships and had mastered naval skills, enabling them to drive the Carthaginians first from Sicily, then from Corsica and Sardinia (238 BC).

During the second Punic War (218–201 BC), because the Romans had gained undisputed control of the Mediterranean sea routes, the famous Carthaginian general Hannibal marched across the Alps from the Carthaginian base in Spain. With a large army of 20,000 infantry and 6,000 cavalry, supported by sixty elephants and reinforced by Gallic tribesmen, he forced his way south into Italy, defeating a number of large Roman armies over a period of sixteen years' fighting, although he failed to capture Rome. When elephants were used against unprepared troops, they easily created panic; however, at the battle of Zama in 202 BC, the Roman commander Scipio, using experienced soldiers, was able to stand firm against Hannibal's elephants, which in turn bolted and ran amok among the Carthaginian forces, adding to their crushing defeat. Eventually, the Romans conquered Spain, which they divided administratively into two Roman provinces, and the Carthaginians were obliged to pay war indemnities and surrender their navy to Rome.

This detail from a 3rd century pottery dish from Campania shows an elephant, probably Indian, carrying soldiers and a "driver" equipped for war.

Fearful that Carthage was beginning to develop once more as a commercial power, the Senate and Roman public opinion, influenced by Senator Cato, once more went to war against Carthage. In the third Punic War, Carthage resisted a Roman siege for two years, but was eventually defeated, and in 146 BC its territory was annexed as the province of Africa. Then, to ensure that its old rival would never again be a threat to Rome, the city was destroyed, its surrounding lands ploughed up, the furrows sown with salt, and its population sold into slavery. Roman hegemony now spread along the Mediterranean to Sicily, Sardinia, Spain, and Tunisia. Rome became involved in several wars with the Macedonians; Rome's status as a Mediterranean superpower was now confirmed.

PUNIC WARS

First War, 264–241 BC

- controlled by Rome, 264 BC
- controlled by Carthage, 264 BC

Second War, 218–201 BC

- added to Carthage by 218 BC
- conquered by Rome by 201 BC
- Scipio's campaign, 218–210 BC
- Roman campaign against Macedonia, 216–211 BC
- Hannibal's campaign, 216–203 BC
- Hasdrubal's campaign, 208–207 BC
- Mago's campaign, 205–203 BC
- battle

Third War, 149–146 BC

- annexed by Rome by 121 BC

ROME—FROM REPUBLIC TO EMPIRE

During the last two centuries BC, Rome became the dominant military and political power in the Mediterranean, consolidating itself as an empire, although it was only at the end of that period that the title of emperor was adopted under Octavian. The rise of the Roman empire was brought about by military conquest and growing economic wealth, and the concomitant rise of a series of powerful generals who jostled for power in an attempt to become single ruler, thus pushing the republic toward dictatorship during the last century BC.

These military dictators were: Sulla (138–78 BC), Pompey (106–48 BC), and Julius Caesar (100–44 BC). Sulla established himself as dictator of Rome with absolute power in 82 BC, when he defeated all political opposition. He later abdicated in 79 BC, and a struggle for succession took place between younger rivals, most famous of whom was Pompey, who engaged in a series of campaigns in Spain in the 70s BC. Pompey would reach the height of power in the following decade.

Julius Caesar, the conqueror of Gaul and member of the Triumvirate. After many campaigns, he appointed himself perpetual dictator. He was assassinated after only a month on March 15, 44 BC.

In the meantime, Julius Caesar was appointed governor of northern Italy and southern France in 59 BC; he invaded Gaul and led two reconnaissance operations to Britain in 55 and 54 BC. Caesar defeated Vercingetorix, leader of the Gallic confederacy, at the battle of Alesia in 52 BC. Caesar could now turn his attention to seizing supreme power in Rome itself.

Caesar crossed the Rubicon in 49 BC, leaving the boundary of Cisalpine Gaul to march south against the senatorial party and occupy Rome. Then he marched against Pompey, his chief rival, engaging his forces in combat, first at Dyrranchium, then at Pharsalus in Thrace, forcing Pompey to take flight into Egypt, where he was murdered. Caesar achieved supreme

ALESIA, 52 BC

▙▟	Celtic fortifications
▪	Vercingetorix's positions
→	Celtic attack
⇢	Celtic retreat
—	Roman wall
○	Roman redoute
◄	Roman position

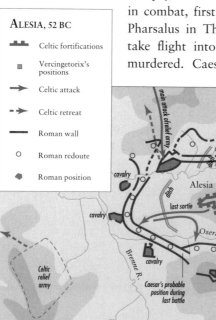

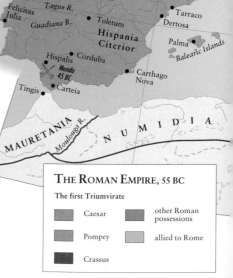

THE ROMAN EMPIRE, 55 BC

The first Triumvirate

■ Caesar	■ other Roman possessions
■ Pompey	■ allied to Rome
■ Crassus	

Rome

- aqueduct
- wall

1 Templum Jovi Capitolini
2 Comitium with Curia Hostilia
3 Basilica Aemilia
4 Tabularium
5 Basilica Julia
6 Forum Julium

power as master of Rome after defeating the army of Pompey's sons at the battle of Munda (45 BC) but was himself assassinated the following year. Further civil wars broke out, eventually culminating in Octavian's seizure of supreme power over the whole Roman world by defeating the armies of Anthony and Cleopatra at the battle of Actium in 31 BC. By this victory Octavian won acceptance from both the Senate and the Roman people at large, and in 27 BC, he was granted the title of Augustus with full support from the military, and the elimination of all political rivals in the Senate. He would be granted the status of god on his death.

PART III: LEGACY OF ROME

The Roman empire had a lasting influence on European history. Rome was noted not only for its excellent army, which acted as the main guarantor of the empire, but also for its cultural and intellectual achievements. Its language, Latin, has provided the foundation of the Romance languages: Italian, French, Castillian, Catalán, Galego, Portuguese, and Romanian. Latin served as the language of European diplomacy, until it was replaced by French, in the early eighteenth century. It was also the main instrument of scholarly activity in parts of Europe until the nineteenth century, and served as the language of the Christian religion well into the twentieth century. The literature of Rome, alongside the language, has been the mainstay of traditional European education well into the twentieth century.

The ruins of Roman settlements and works can be found from Britain to the deserts of Syria, from the Rhine to the upper Nile and Asia Minor. One of Rome's legacies, its laws, have inspired and influenced many European and non-European legal systems. Furthermore, despite the earlier persecution of Christians, Constantine the Great adopted the faith at the time of the battle of Milvian Bridge in 312; and under Theodosius, Christianity became the religion of state in 395. Christianity has remained, despite barbarian invasion, the dominant faith in most of Europe today.

The architects and planners in the cities achieved exceptional standards in street planning, buildings, central heating, aqueducts, dams, plumbing, and sewage disposal. Rome's roads were crucial both to communications and to Rome's military needs across Europe and into Asia Minor and the Middle East. Long and straight, the lines of these roads have provided the foundation for many roads still in use today.

Rome had dominated the Mediterranean, both politically and militarily, during the last two centuries BC, and under Octavian (Augustus), Rome was transformed into an empire by the end of the first century BC. Augustus gave Rome strong centralized government, so that Rome could prosper, stimulated by wealth and trade and an economic and political shift westward from Greece, Egypt, and Asia Minor. For the first two centuries AD Italy flourished, as is demonstrated by the remains of great buildings, jewelry, and other luxurious artifacts that archaeologists have unearthed from time to time.

Under Augustus, the northern Iberian peninsula was conquered, and the Danube became the frontier in the east. These conquests would continue throughout the first and second centuries, under Trajan (98–117) to Marcus Aurelius (168–180). Nevertheless, the second century became one of relative stability and consolidation; the period of great and gradual expansion came to an end.

The golden age of Rome came with the Antonines: Antonius Pius (138–161) and his adopted son Marcus Aurelius (168–180). During this period, Rome reached its greatest geographical limits. The Pax Romana now spread from the Atlantic to the Persian Gulf, with an almost stable frontier, with outbreaks of fighting in Asia against the Parthians and Persians, while the provinces were firmly controlled and protected within the *limes*, or frontier line, from Hadrian's

Wall to the Danube Delta.

Gradually, in the third century, Rome entered into a period of steady decline, with the exception of the reign of Diocletian (285–305), who introduced a series of reforms, restoring efficiency to government and laying the foundation of an empire in the east, which would last into the mid fifteenth century. By the late third and early fourth centuries, the eastern and western parts of the empire were growing apart and were confronted by different problems. Failure to defend the west against barbarian attack at the beginning of the fifth century was caused by the economic and social weaknesses of western Roman society. Large areas of the west were rural and underdeveloped, and wealth lay in the hands of a few overmighty landowning families. By contrast, in the east, wealth was based upon trade in the cities around the Mediterranean, which had prospered in a climate where a more egalitarian society had developed; the gentry in the east, unlike their western counterparts, provided well-educated civil servants for the administration in Constantinople. Likewise, the rural peasantry was more independent than their western peers, who had more or less become serfs.

After the reign of Diocletian, the Roman army began to suffer from manpower shortages, which led to the employment of barbarian troops as *foederati*. Whereas the barbarian element in the eastern army was about 28 percent, after the battle of Adrianople in 378, it was as high as 60 percent in the western army. This led to a situation in which a Germanized army faced Germanic invaders in the west, whereas in the east, the army could draw upon Asia Minor for its manpower.

The Visigoths crossed the Danube frontier in 376 and advanced upon Italy. The Vandals marched into Gaul and Spain between 406 and 409. Rome was sacked in 410 by the Visigoths and later in 455 by the Vandals and in 493 by the Ostrogoths. In the meantime, the Burgundians settled along the middle Rhône valley after 430. Nevertheless, rather than being organized military campaigns, the barbarian invasions should be seen as great waves of economic migration, from the underdeveloped north to the rich lands around the Mediterranean. The conquering tribes were often divided against each other, and their leaders wanted to become Roman and were quite prepared to desert their fellow tribesmen in order to attain this. The barbarian invasions greatly changed lifestyles in the west. By the late fifth century, most of the western provinces were virtually lost to the empire.

In the sixth century, Justinian tried to reunite the eastern and western portions of the empire, inspired by the ideal of a Christian Roman empire with the Mediterranean Sea at its epicenter. Although he reestablished Roman control over those Germanic peoples who had settled in Italy, France, Spain, and North Africa, Justinian can nevertheless be described as the last true Roman emperor, and his reign (527–656) marks the end of the Late Roman period and the beginning of the Byzantine empire, which, built upon its Roman foundations, would last until 1453.

Many attempts were made to emulate the power of ancient Rome, but nearly all failed, and none lasted as long. The iconography of military achievement, such as the triumphal arch, was easier to copy. Above is the original plan for the Arch of Triumph in Paris. Begun by Napoleon in 1806, it was not completed until 1836.

Imperial Rome

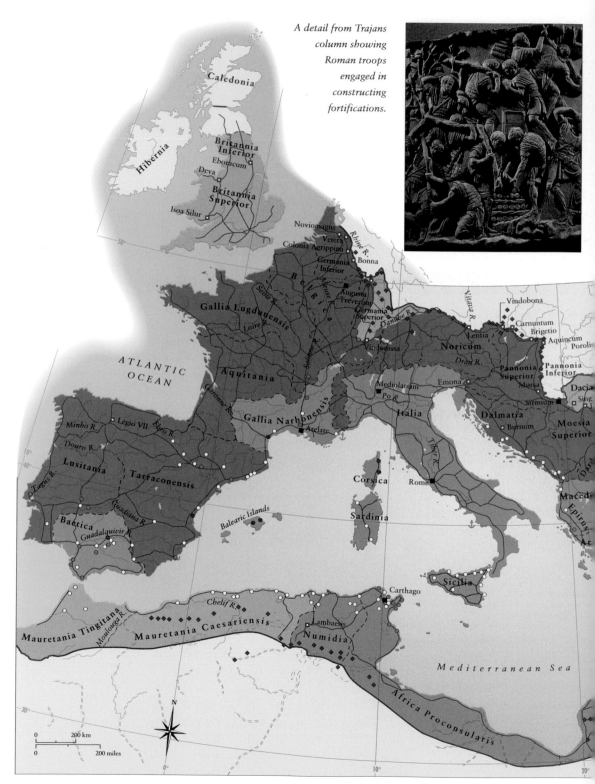

A detail from Trajans column showing Roman troops engaged in constructing fortifications.

Caledonia

Hibernia

Britannia
Inferior
Eboracum

Deva

Britannia
Superior

Isoa Silur

Noviomagus

Vetera
Colonia Agrippina
Germania
Inferior
Bonna

Rhine R.

Belgica

Augusta
Treverum
Germania
Superior

Danube R.

Vitava R.

Vindobona

Carnuntum
Brigetio
Aquincum
Poroli

Seine R.

Gallia Lugdunensis

Loire R.

Vindomissa

Noricum

Lentia

Pannonia
Superior

Pannonia
Inferior

Dacia

Sing

ATLANTIC
OCEAN

Aquitania

Drau R.

Mursa

Sirmium

Garonne R.

Gallia Narbonensis

Arelate

Mediolanum

Po R.

Emona

Italia

Dalmatia

Burnum

Moesia
Superior

Minho R.

Légio VII

Ebro R.

Douro R.

Lusitania

Tarraconensis

Corsica

Rome

Tiber R.

Macedo

Epirus

Lagus R.

Baetica

Guadiana R.

Guadalquivir R.

Balearic Islands

Sardinia

Ar

Mauretania Tingitana

Moulouga R.

Chelif R.

Mauretania Caesariensis

Lambaesis

Numidia

Carthago

Sicilia

Mediterranean Sea

Africa Proconsularis

N

0   200 km

0   200 miles

30°

50°

10°

40°

10°

10°

20°

Octavian's victory at the battle of Actium in 31 BC ended both the Civil Wars and the Roman republic. Octavian was crowned as the first emperor and renamed Augustus; his reign, from 27 BC to AD 14, was one of relative calm, stability, and peace, and Rome began to prosper once more.

Augustus provided Rome with strong, centralized government, made up from a cross-fertilization of elements taken from the republican period amalgamated with the concept of monarchical power. Although the Senate continued to function, Augustus, as *princeps,* or first citizen, held supreme power through his control of the government. As a result power was handed on, spanning a long line of emperors until the last quarter of the fifth century. Despite the fact that Roman emperors were absolute autocrats, and worshiped as gods, the legions' eagles continued to retain the legend SPQR (Senatus Populusque Romanus, the Senate and People of Rome).

Under Augustus, northern Spain was brought under Roman control, and in the Alps and Balkans the frontier was extended northward to the Danube River. However, in spite of attempts to expand the German frontier to the Elbe River, the *limes* was pulled back to the Rhine, where it would remain

> "As the Emperor Antonius, Rome is my city and my country; but as a man I am a citizen of the world."
> *Antonius,*
> Meditations

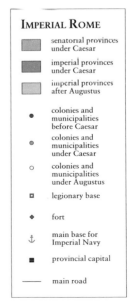

IMPERIAL ROME

- senatorial provinces under Caesar
- imperial provinces under Caesar
- imperial provinces after Augustus
- ● colonies and municipalities before Caesar
- ◉ colonies and municipalities under Caesar
- ○ colonies and municipalities under Augustus
- ▫ legionary base
- ◆ fort
- ⚓ main base for Imperial Navy
- ■ provincial capital
- —— main road

A Roman funerary relief of the 2nd century AD, showing a tavern scene and a delivery of more wine, gives a good impression of daily life across the empire.

until the empire began to crumble four centuries later.

Interspersed between the reigns of two of Rome's most unpopular and notorious emperors, Caligula (37–41) and Nero (54–56), came that of the Emperor Claudius (41–54). Claudius' great achievement was the invasion and occupation of Britain in 43. Southern Britain was almost completely subjugated when the last serious revolt, led by Boudicca, queen of the Iceni, was crushed in 60–61. By the end of the first century, most of the island would be under Roman control, although under Hadrian (117–138) the Romans eventually consolidated their position in Britain by withdrawing to the defensive frontier running across northern Britain, from Bowness to Wallsend, and known later as Hadrian's Wall. With this act, and the establishment of the German frontier on the Rhine and Danube, the great period of expansion came to an end.

The first and second centuries would be marked by four great emperors: Trajan (98–117), Hadrian (117–138), Antonius Pius (138–161), and Marcus Aurelius (168–180). Trajan mastered Dacia, in present-day Romania, by defeating its powerful ruler, Decabalus, in two wars between 101 and 102 and in 105. In 114, he turned his attentions eastward against the Parthians, conquering Armenia and later occupying Mesopotamia by 116, although he would be forced to abandon southern Mesopotamia in 117.

The golden age of Rome, known as the Antonine period, came with Antonius Pius and his adopted son Marcus Aurelius.

During the reign of Antonius, wars were fought in the northern British Isles, resulting in the building of the Antonine Wall, to the north of Hadrian's Wall, between the Clyde and the Forth. Likewise wars were fought in Mauretania and on the Danube frontier, while the Parthians were deterred in the east.

The greatest geographical extent of the empire, and the apex of Roman achievement, was realized during the reign of Marcus Aurelius, after which decline set in. The Pax Romana spread from the Atlantic to the Persian Gulf, with fighting in Asia against the Parthians and Persians, while the provinces were firmly controlled and protected within *limes* (frontier lines) from Hadrian's Wall to the Danube Delta, which was far away from the center of the empire. This meant garrison life for the Roman army, with static rather than mobile armies, engaged in defensive warfare carried out from large fortified camps, smaller forts, frontier posts, and watchtowers.

"Would that the Roman people had but one neck!"
Gaius Julius Caesar Germanicus-Caligula

Providing the provinces with adequate protection was a major preoccupation of the empire. A large proportion of the army was based on or close to the frontiers, with strongly constructed defensive works, like this stretch of Hadrian's Wall in northern Britain. It was built between AD 122–126 and was maintained until around AD 383.

DIOCLETIAN–THE EMPIRE REORGANIZED

DIOCLETIAN, THE EMPIRE REORGANIZED

▢ dioceses of the Prefecture of Gallia	▢ dioceses of the Prefecture of Illyricus, Italia and Africa	▢ dioceses of the Prefecture of Orient

— Western and Eastern Roman Empires border, 395

— province border

- - - diocese border

XII	Britannia	VI	Macedonia	I	Egypt
XIII	Gallia	VII	Dacia	II	Orient
XIV	Seven Provinces	VIII	Pannonia	III	Pontica
XV	Hispania	IX	Italia Annonaria	IV	Asia
		X	Italia Suburbicaria	V	Thracia
		XI	Africa		

N

0	200 km
0	200 miles

Diocletian, emperor between 285 and 305, is most remembered for having restored efficient government to the Roman empire after the troubled third century, during which time it had been weakened by internal faction and continuous attacks from external enemies. He temporarily reestablished the decaying empire in the west and laid the foundation of the Byzantine empire in the east. It was during his reign that the last persecution of the Christians took place.

When Emperor Numerian was found dead in camp, during a campaign against the Persians, Diocletian was acclaimed emperor by his soldiers in 284. However, Diocletian's power base lay only with his army in Asia Minor, so he had to achieve power, first by putting down a revolt in Pannonia, and then by the decisive battle against Numerian's brother and co-emperor, Carinus, near Sirmium (Belgrade) on the confluence of the Morava and Danube Rivers. As a

result, Diocletian became master of the Roman empire in 285, first as caesar (junior emperor), and then a year later, as augustus (senior emperor).

Given the vastness of empire, with disturbances on all the frontiers, Diocletian decided to share his throne with his friend Maximian in 286, thus dividing the empire administratively; Maximian was installed in Milan and granted the west, while Diocletian took responsibility for the east, and based himself in Nicomedia, where he could keep watch on the Persian frontier.

In 293, power was divided yet again with two other colleagues, Galerius and Constantius, who were appointed to the rank of caesar. This relationship, known as the Tetrarchy, was bonded by marriage and strengthened by the belief that like Jove and Hercules, Diocletian and Maximian no longer were mere *princepes*, but emperors and gods *(domini et dei)*. The empire took on the aspects of a theocracy, with Diocletian and Maximian exercising autocratic power based upon "divine right" and surrounding themselves with all the pomp and circumstance that would later become the hallmark of Byzantine imperialism.

The empire was still troubled by threats from external enemies. Maximian had to fight Carausius, who had declared himself emperor of Britain and reigned for nearly ten years before Constantius I reconquered Britain in 296. At the same time, revolts and disturbances had to be put down in Mauretania, the Danubian regions, and Egypt. No sooner had Diocletian reconquered Egypt in 296, than he had to turn his attention to Syria, which had been invaded by Narses, King of Persia, in 297. Galerius eventually won Syria back for the empire, so that the Tigris River became the eastern border of the empire.

Diocletian's vast administrative, military, judicial, fiscal, and monetary reforms led to firm government, and a centralized and absolute monarchy, that witnessed the growing specialization of administrative work and a concomitant increase in the number of bureaucrats.

Diocletian's first task was to restore civil order to the empire by taking the army out of politics in a bid to improve internal security, so that the governors of the provinces no longer held any military authority. This meant putting an end to the constant threat of insurrection by powerful provincial governors, who had undermined the empire throughout the previous half century.

The provinces were then reorganized into twelve larger administrative units called dioceses. The army was also reorganized and traditional discipline reintroduced along with a reduction of military service to twenty years and moves toward greater efficiency and increasing the number of troops. Diocletian also introduced agricultural and building programs and combated the inflationary financial crisis by levying taxes on a proportional basis, by fixing wages, establishing maximum prices and by introducing monetary reform, which included a return to sound gold and silver coinage.

Sick through overwork, Diocletian abdicated in 305, being the only Roman emperor to do so voluntarily. He retired to his birthplace in Split, present-day Croatia, where he constructed a stone-built palace, where he spent his last days until dying almost unnoticed, in 316.

In this fresco from a villa near Pompeii, a woman of rank plays her cithara. She may well look concerned, after Diocletian's reform—she and thousands like her would be governed not from Rome, but from four regional centers. Diocletian's principal residence was at Nicomedia in Asia Minor.

ENEMIES AT THE GATES

While Angles, Saxons, and Jutes crossed the North Sea and invaded Britain from 450, other Germanic peoples migrated from southern Scandinavia into Germany, pressured by an increasing population and deteriorating climatic conditions.

By 300, the Goths reached the lower Danube and the Franks the middle and lower Rhine. About 370, the Goths divided into the Ostrogoths, in a kingdom east of the Dniester on the shores of the Black Sea, and the Visigoths, who inhabited an area from the Dniester to the Danube. Another group, the Vandals, settled along the Danube. Mounting demographic pressure occasioned wars with the Romans, and in 375, a momentous event occurred: Huns from central Asia attacked the Ostrogoths, causing immense fear and dislocation among the German tribes. In 376, the Visigoths sought the protection of Rome and were allowed to settle in imperial Moesia, where they were converted to Arian Christianity.

In the west, Germanic war bands continued to migrate into the empire. The empire, as in the past, absorbed them, granting them "federate" status; in return, they agreed to perform a role in imperial defense, mostly aimed at preventing further of their relatives from entering, settling, or raiding the empire. In reality however they ruled over the areas and people they were supposed to defend, forming kingdoms, power centers in their own right. Rome's taxation income fell, and its ability to control its new allies and its own destiny declined.

This mosaic shows Bishop Ambrosius of Milan. High-ranking Christian clerics like him had immense power. In 390 Ambrosius even succeeded in making Emperor Theodosius do public penance.

GERMANIC KINGDOMS

In 395, the Visigoths renounced their allegiance to Rome, invaded Greece, and then migrated to Italy. Meanwhile, the Vandals entered France (406) and invaded Spain (409). After the Visigoths sacked Rome (410), they crossed the Pyrenees into Spain, where they fought the Vandals. Under their leader, Gaiseric, the Vandals moved to North Africa (429), defeated the Romans, and captured Carthage (439), making it the capital of a Vandal kingdom. Gaiseric's fleets raided Sicily, Sardinia, and Corsica and in 455 entered Rome and looted it for two weeks before moving east to ravage Greece and Dalmatia, forcing Emperor Zeno to recognize Gaiseric and make peace (476).

In Spain, the Visigothic kingdom embraced most of the Iberian peninsula and part of Provence with its capital at Toulouse. King Theodoric I died fighting Attila at Châlons (451) in alliance with Rome. King Euric declared the independence of Rome but introduced aspects of Roman civilization and codified a collection of German and Roman law. Visigothic kingship's elective nature ensured internal instability, and although reducing a Suevi kingdom in north Portugal (469), the Visigoths were threatened by the Franks, whose king, Clovis I, defeated them at Vouillé (507) and took most of Provence, confining the Visigoths to Spain. When the Huns attacked Europe, they conquered many Ostrogoths, compelling them to join Attila in his French raid. The defeat at Châlons freed the Ostrogoths, and they settled in western Hungary, northern Croatia, Serbia, Slovenia, and eastern Austria, where they were joined by the king who had fled the Roman empire during the Hun invasion. Under Theoderic, the Ostrogoths invaded Italy (488), killed Odoacer, the first barbarian ruler of Italy, and supplanted him. Theoderic used the Roman civil administration and economy, and Roman culture influenced the Germans, but the latter's Arian Christianity caused conflict with the Catholic Romans. Eventually, Visigothic power was destroyed (555) by the Byzantine empire. Other Germans settled near Lake Geneva, extending down the Rhône Valley. This Burgundian kingdom lasted from 443 to 534, finally being subjugated by the Franks. These Franks, who became Roman allies, established a kingdom north of the Loire. When Rome retreated, the Franks under Merovingian Clovis I became the most successful Germans, defeating the Alemanni, the Burgundians, and the Visigoths in Provence. In 496, Clovis was converted to Christianity, commencing a special link between the Frankish monarchy and the papacy.

An engraved bronze plaque of a horseman, often used as a symbol by wandering Germanic tribes. Lombard, 7th century, from Stabio in Switzerland.

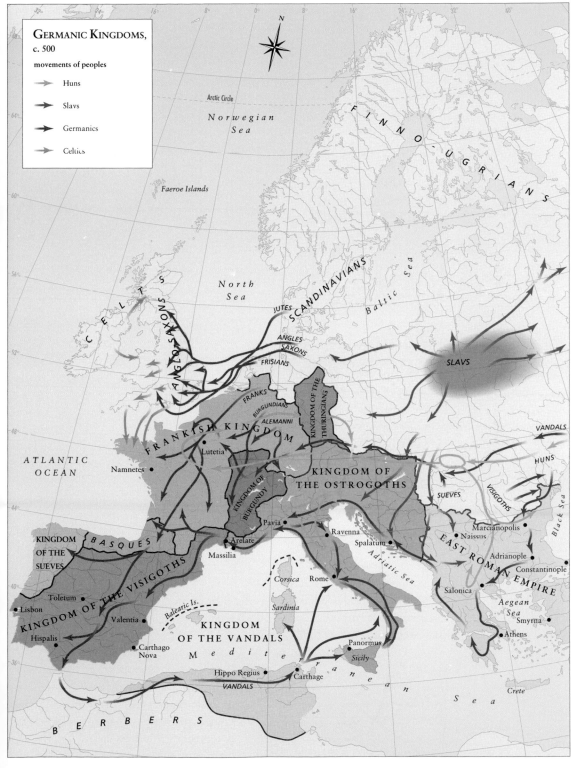

GERMANIC KINGDOMS,
c. 500

movements of peoples

→ Huns

→ Slavs

→ Germanics

→ Celtics

THE EMPIRE IN THE EAST

In 324, Emperor Constantine chose the old Greek settlement of Byzantium, which lay on the Bosphorus, as the site for a new city that would become the capital of the Roman empire in the east. As Constantinople—the city of Constantine—it served as a crossroads between Europe and Asia, opening up trade links between the Aegean, the Mediterranean, and Asia Minor, to the Middle and Far East. Although the eastern part of the empire, or *pars orientalis,* was more densely populated and had greater economic resources than the west, the two parts of the empire held together in the fourth century, due to the reforms of Diocletian. The empire remained one and indivisible.

This detail of a mosaic shows Justinian I, 483–565, who was Byzantine emperor from 527. He recovered North Africa from the Vandals, southeast Spain from the Visigoths, and Italy from the Ostrogoths, largely owing to the skills of General Belisarius.

The two main external pressures came from a rival empire in Persia and from the Germanic tribes from the north. As with Diocletian, it was probably because the main threats to the empire came from the Danube and the eastern frontiers that Constantine chose to take control of the eastern half of the empire, leaving his co-emperor to rule in the west. The problems in the east gravitated around the conflict between eastern Rome and the Sassanian empire over the control of Syria, Palestine, and Egypt.

Justinian is noted for the administrative reforms of the imperial government, for a concern for rooting out administrative corruption, and for the codification of laws, which are known as the Codex Justinianus, which formed the basis upon which later Byzantine codes would be built.

Justinian was inspired by the ideal of a Christian Roman empire that would be restored to its old boundaries and dominate the Mediterranean world, by re-establishing Roman control over the Germanic peoples who had settled in Italy, France, Spain, and North Africa. The Vandals in North Africa were defeated by Justinian's general, Belisarius, in 533. Belisarius proceeded to fight against the Ostrogoths in the Italian Peninsula and the islands of the western Mediterranean.

These were finally conquered by Narses in 555. Meanwhile, a bridgehead was established in southeastern Spain, although most of the Iberian peninsula, southern France, and Gaul would remain in the hands of the Visigoths and other Germanic tribes.

In the east the Persian-Sassanid king Chosroes I invaded Mesopotamia, northern Syria, and Byzantine Armenia in 540. Belisarious led counteroffensives in 541 and 542. The expensive military campaigning dragged on until 562, when a fifty-year truce was negotiated. On the northern frontier the imperial territories of Thrace, Dacia, and Dalmatia were confronted by attacks from Bulgar, Slav, and Avar invaders. Despite the building of forts and defense works, the invaders were neither assimilated nor were they repulsed. The problems of the Balkans would be left to Justinian's successors.

> "We have good hope that God will allow us to reconquer the lands of the old Roman empire which have been lost through indolence."
> *Justinian*

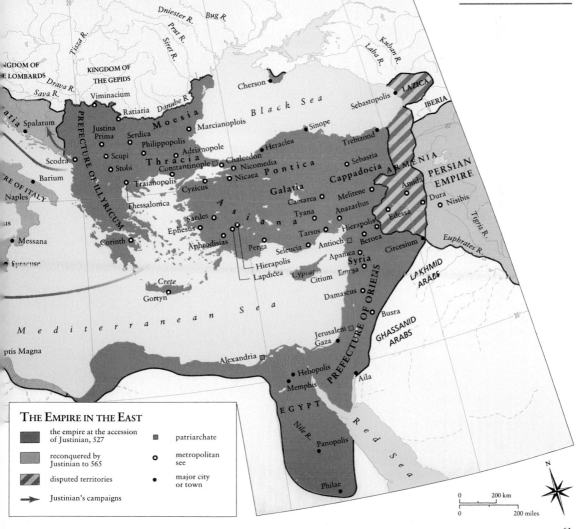

THE EMPIRE IN THE EAST

- the empire at the accession of Justinian, 527
- reconquered by Justinian to 565
- disputed territories
- Justinian's campaigns
- ▪ patriarchate
- ◦ metropolitan see
- • major city or town

PART IV: CHRISTIAN EUROPE

The European mental condition prior to the fall of the Byzantine empire in 1453 was pervaded by a hankering after the perceived glories of Roman empire, and the overwhelming spirit and influence of religion and faith.

Religion dominated every activity of life, both personal and political. The popularity of pilgrimages may be placed alongside the missionary activities throughout Europe, with the mass conversions of peoples and the spreading of the Gospel by "fire and sword." Ascetic hermits in isolation contrasted with the

rise of collective monastic orders in the tenth century. Along with a belief in miracles and millenarianism came the superstitious fear of purgatory and the eternal fires of hell and damnation. Organized and centralized religion brought a sense of unity to western Christendom, powered by the universal usage of the Latin in both worship and legal procedure. Linked with the religious mood of the times was the growing cleavage between western Christendom and the Byzantine empire. Latin Christianity and Orthodoxy grew further apart and completely broke with the Schism of 1054, so that east and west would both go their own ways.

The Carolingian empire reinforced the power of both church and state, with obligatory tithes, the banning of pagan ceremonies, the death penalty for the murder of priests, and a move toward centralizing political power. The link between the pope and the western emperor was established with the coronation of Charlemagne in 800. This action meant that there would be a Catholic emper-

This 15th century French illustration shows the Turkish fleet and army laying siege to Constantinople in 1453.

or in the west, independent of Byzantium, emphasizing once again the increasing separation between east and west. The existence of two empires sounded the death knell of the ideal of a universal empire. From this time on, the pope would always crown the emperor. In the eleventh and twelfth centuries, there arose the whole issue of the Investiture Controversy, which might have been the single most important issue of the central Middle Ages, for both the contemporary and long-term effect it had upon Europe, especially with regard to the Italian and German lands.

The Europe of the Middle Ages was also defined by external events and threats, especially those of the Vikings, the Magyars, the Mongols, and the Turks. The Vikings would exploit the internecine strife of Charlemagne's successors, raiding the coasts and rivers of Europe; eventually this threat receded due to a combination of military preparedness and the Vikings themselves becoming settlers. The Magyars, beaten at the battle of Lechfeld in 955, were forced to retreat to the Pannonian plain, which helped establish Otto I of Saxony's claim to supremacy as emperor over the German princes.

In the meantime, medieval European polity was based upon feudalism, the relationship or contract between a superior to a vassal, arising from the holding of lands in *feud* or in *fief*, a system by which land was held and protection offered in return for services, such as homage, obedience, duty, and military service. There developed a whole hierarchical system of contracts, with individuals being tied to their masters and in turn having their own vassals, each with their own privileges and rights. Even the pope and the emperor were the vassals of God, with the serfs at the bottom of the ladder, laboring on the lord's *demesne* for so many days a year, fixed by local custom.

Later, during the twelfth-century renaissance, feudal society would be supported by the concept of "chivalry"—a code of knightly honor and gallantry based upon the understanding and practice of "courtesy," loyalty, and bravery. This meant a respect for women and support for those weaker than oneself, along with obedience to one's lord, the protection of the church, and the obligation to go to war against the infidel.

Throughout Europe the process of institutionalized Christianity continued. The first monastic order, centered on reforms of Benedictine rule, was founded at Cluny in Burgundy in 910. A network of over three hundred monasteries was created by the middle of the twelfth century. The more austere Carthusian Order, based upon silence, contemplation, and closed cells, was founded in 1084 by St. Bruno at Chartreuse, and in 1098 the Cistercian Order was established at Citeux in Burgundy.

It can be said that the Saxon kings Henry II "The Fowler" (918–936), founder of the Saxon dynasty, and his son, Otto I "The Great" (936–973) were the successors of the Carolingian empire. Under Otto, the crown developed stronger links with the church, which became a pillar of the monarchy. The monasteries would act as centers of imperial power throughout the German duchies. By conquering the Italian lands and acquiring the imperial title, Otto recovered Germany from the anarchy of the late Carolingian period. His control of the papacy, whereby all popes had to swear allegiance to the emperor, and his dreams of reestablishing government in Rome, through his grandson Otto II (980–1002), meant that the German empire was the true successor to that of Charlemagne, and would maintain a prominent position in Europe until the death of Frederick II in 1251, despite the impact of the Investitures Struggle between the empire and the papacy.

Otto had restored the empire, which would last until 1804, when the Holy Roman empire became the Austrian empire, when some of its territories fell under the threat of Napoleon's expanding French empire.

In the meantime, the Byzantine empire reached its political and cultural apogee in the late ninth and tenth centuries, under the emperors of the Macedonian dynasty. Constantinople's economic strength and its trade with the east continued to flourish, despite the growth in importance of some Italian maritime cities. Furthermore, Byzantium's links with Kievan Rus along the "Water Road" were increasing. The Byzantine empire also benefited from the existence of a highly developed civil service and an efficient system of provincial government. It even looked as though the Byzantines might themselves recapture the

Holy Places. Certainly at the beginning of the tenth century nobody would have entertained the idea that Byzantium would one day have to rely upon Latin crusaders to achieve this.

The situation in the Balkans was slightly different in that the Slavs were assimilated into the Balkans, although in the short term this meant the cities were isolated from the surrounding Balkan countryside. Gradually the Slavs fell under the military and political control of Byzantium and began to reach out for the fruits of Byzantine culture they so much admired. Ever since the development of an alliance between the papacy and the Frankish rulers in the eighth century, the Church of Rome and that of Constantinople had tried to win the Slavs for their particular part of the Christian Church. Serbia, Bulgaria, and Russia would come under the influence of the patriarchate of Constantinople, while Croatia would fall under the influence of western Christendom, through the intermediary of Hungary.

The Orthodox faith spread throughout southeastern Europe, particularly through the missionary activities of Saints Cyril (827–869) and Methodius (825–884), whose main achievements in the history of the Balkans were the invention of Slavonic scripts, Glagolitic and Cyrillic, and the spread of the Old Church Slavonic language, which became the main intermediary for transmitting Byzantine civilization to Bulgarians, Serbs, Romanians, and Russians. The main task of Basil II was to dominate the northern part of the Balkan peninsula. During his reign the Byzantine empire was prosperous and expanding, and it could not afford to tolerate the power of the Bulgarian state on its frontier. Basil aimed for the control of the Macedonian mountains to consolidate the northern part of the peninsula. He downgraded the patriarchate of Ohrid and blinded 14,000 Bulgarians at the Kleidion pass in 1014. According to Obolensky, he left one in every hundred with one eye so that he could guide his comrades back to the Bulgarian tsar. From the second half of the eleventh century western Europe entered a period of "reform and revitalization," while the Byzantine empire began a period of "irreversible decline."

Setbacks in Byzantine fortunes would come toward the end of the eleventh century, with the Norman occupation of Sicily in 1071; the threat of the Seljuk Turks in Asia Minor, who that same year had routed a Byzantine army at the battle of Manzikiert; the Pechenegs laying Constantinople to siege; and the arrival of the First Crusade in 1095.

Pecheneg pressure on Byzantium had been stimulated by events in Russia, when in 1036 Yaroslav had inflicted a defeat upon them, putting an end to their dominion over the steppes and forcing them to aim toward the Byzantine empire. Byzantium's links with Kievan Rus had been growing throughout the ninth century, through trade along the Water Road and the supply of military services to the emperor in Constantinople. In the tenth century, with paganism on the decline everywhere, Kievan Rus was becoming isolated. Eventually, Christianity was adopted in 988 by Vladimir (980–1015). The conversion had been politically inspired as a pragmatic necessity to end Russia's isolation and also to stimulate trade, thus introducing stronger Byzantine influences to Russia.

Nevertheless, the process whereby the country experienced long and bitter quarrelling and infighting among the princes, on the death of each Grand Prince, exhausted Russia's resources. Trade was disrupted, and people fled certain areas or invited foreign intruders for their protection. In many ways this contributed to the downfall of the Kievan state, and the situation was exploited by the Tatars in the second half of the thirteenth century.

Meanwhile, in the eleventh century, the West witnessed the rise of wealthy, well-defined cities and urban societies, with their artisans' guilds and merchant associations. Alongside the formation of a new class, the burghers, was the rise of trade. Trade across the North Sea was based upon English wool, with key trading centers established in Bruges and Ghent. In the Mediterranean the control of trade gradually passed from Constantinople to Genoa and Venice, the latter becoming the key trading center between east and west, while in Germany Lübeck and Hamburg became important trading centers on the Baltic.

The Crusade was first launched by Pope Urban II at the synod of Clermont in 1095, with an appeal to all Christians to win back Jerusalem from the Turks. There would be a variety of Crusades, one of the most curious, the Albigensian Crusade in twelfth-century Provence, was launched by Innocent III on the grounds of heresy and in response to their censure of the corruptions of the papacy. The Albigensians were dualist gnostics, who believed that only spiritual things belonged to God and that all things physical were of the Devil. If the western church had its Albigensians, so the Orthodox Church attempted to wipe out the Bogomils and Patarenes in the Balkans, especially in Bosnia and Bulgaria.

Conflict between Christians and Muslims was not just confined to the Byzantine eastern frontier, nor was it just a concern of the Latin Crusaders, for it also affected Spain, much of which had fallen to the Moors in the eighth century. The Christian Reconquista of Spain began in 1085, when the Muslim city of Toledo fell to Alfonso VI of Castle-Leon, followed by the capture of Valencia by El Cid. So began four centuries of conflict between Christian and Muslim for control of the Iberian Peninsula. Already by the end of the thirteenth century, with the seizure of Cordova (1236), Seville (1248), and Murcia (1266), the bulk of the Iberian Peninsula was in Christian hands.

Growing prosperity in Europe led to a desire for knowledge that resulted in an increase in scholarship and book production. Along with a growth in libraries came the spread of monasteries and the rise of the universities as centers of secular learning, the first at Bologna in 1088, then Paris c. 1150 and Oxford in 1167. Scholars gathered to hear the teachings of William of Malmesbury, Geoffrey of Monmouth, Adelard of Bath, and others, while medical schools and law facilities were established at Salerno, Montpellier, and Bologna. The classical texts of many scientific and philosophical writers had been preserved by the Arabs; these were retranslated into Latin and spread throughout western Christendom.

THE EMPIRE OF CHARLEMAGNE

This reliquary bust of Charlemagne, the man who became the first Holy Roman emperor, is from the cathedral treasury at Aachen.

Charlemagne, son of Pepin, who usurped the last Merovingian king, became sole king of the Franks in 771. His long reign was spent at war, amassing lands in what became a "Christian empire." As early as 772, he commenced the Saxon wars, which lasted until 804. During this conquest, the Saxons' sacred wood, the Irminsul, was destroyed and their nobility baptised en masse. The Christianization of the Saxons developed through the activities of bishoprics at Verden, Bremen, Paderborn, and Hamburg. A Saxon March was established to keep the Danes in check. Meanwhile, Charlemagne invaded the Kingdom of Lombardy, annexed it, and assumed its crown (774), thereby placing the papal states under Frankish protection, since Lombardy had been devouring papal lands. The Duchy of Spoleto south of Rome was also acquired in 774. In 778, the Duchy of Bavaria was absorbed, and Charlemagne continued the Bavarian policy of establishing tributary marches among the Slavic Sorbs and Czechs. The remaining power confronting the Franks in the east were the Avars, but they were destroyed by a combined Franko-Bulgarian attack (796), and Charlemagne acquired further Slav areas, including Bohemia, Moravia, Austria, and Croatia. His onslaught on the Umayyad Muslim Caliphate in Spain achieved limited success, but a buffer Spanish March was established (795, and enlarged in 812) as a shield against a possible Muslim power revival. Charlemagne had built a mighty empire, and in 800, Pope Leo III crowned him emperor, recognizing and formalizing political realities that all Christians inhabiting Europe, except the British Isles, owed allegiance to Charlemagne. His position was recognized by the Byzantine emperor Michael I by the 812 Treaty of Aix-la-Chapelle in exchange for Istria, Venice, and Dalmatia.

Charlemagne placed his power and prestige in the service of Christianity. He encouraged monasteries and cathedrals to maintain schools and invited to his court scholars and writers from Ireland, England, Spain, and Italy. Alcuin of York, later Abbot of St. Martin's of Tours, standardized writing, which aided improvements in teaching and helped revive Latin. These processes were useful in the copying of manuscripts of surviving classical works. The church benefited from a better-educated clergy and scholarship, and authors flourished; Einhard wrote his *Vita Karoli Magni*. Charlemagne utilized bishops and abbots as agents of government and established a more permanent royal capital at Aix-la-Chapelle, where his Palatine Chapel was consecrated. The emperor attempted to introduce vassalage as a system of government, and the frontier marches comprised several counties as a means of controlling the tributary tribes inhabiting them. A major flaw in the empire was its personalized nature, and Charlemagne's decision to divide his territories among his three sons was frustrated by only one surviving him. Louis the Pious continued the scheme, and the Frankish empire was finally fragmented into three parts by the Treaty of Verdun (843). The descendants of Carolingian royal agents tended to identify with their localities, stressing a movement toward feudalism. The empire was weakened by a minimalist administration and was seriously damaged by Viking raids, which had begun during Charlemagne's lifetime.

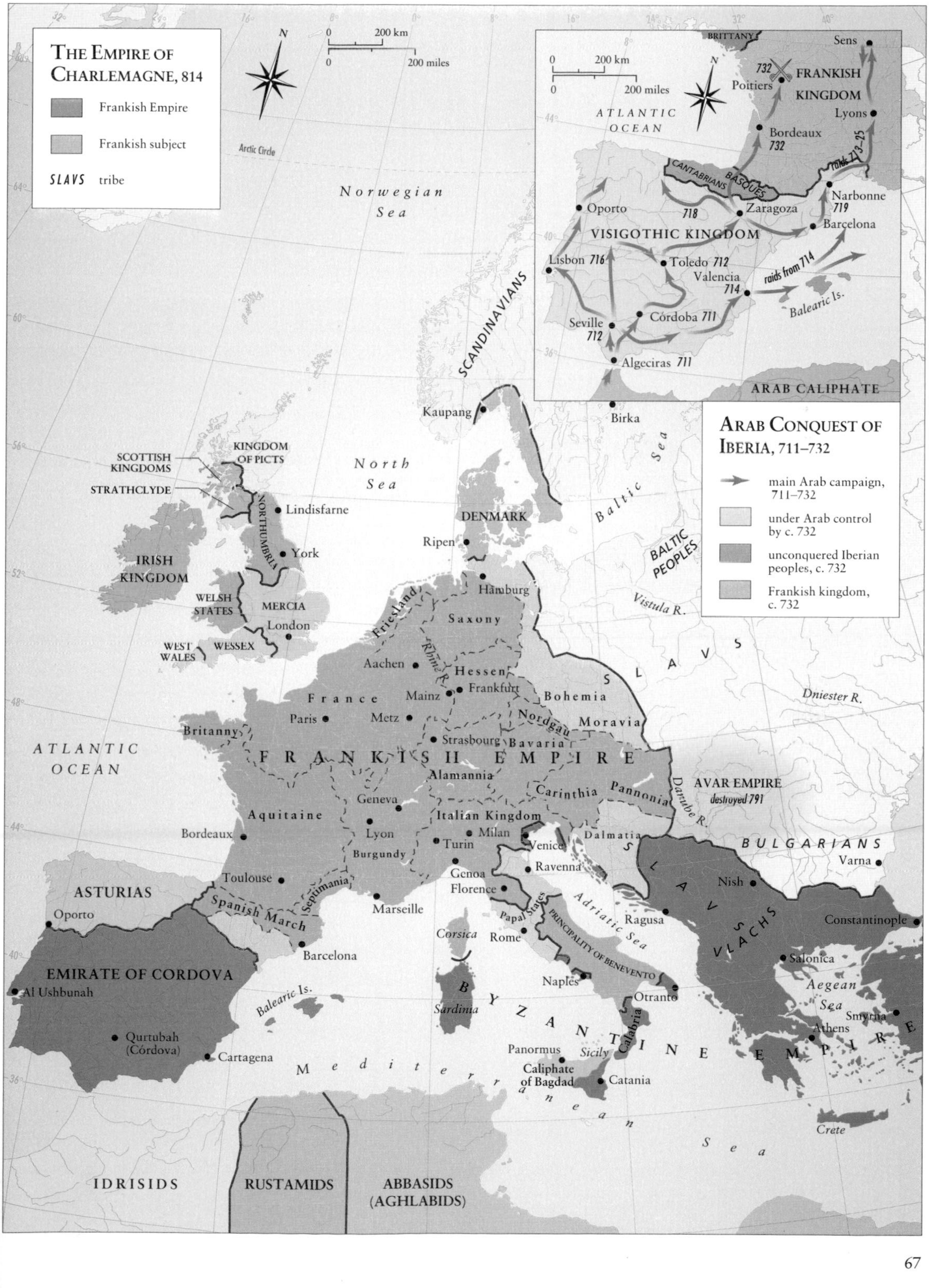
THE EMPIRE OF CHARLEMAGNE, 814
Frankish Empire
Frankish subject
SLAVS tribe
0 200 km
0 200 miles
Arctic Circle
Norwegian Sea
North Sea
SCANDINAVIANS
Kaupang
Birka
KINGDOM OF PICTS
SCOTTISH KINGDOMS
STRATHCLYDE
NORTHUMBRIA
Lindisfarne
York
IRISH KINGDOM
WELSH STATES
MERCIA
London
WEST WALES
WESSEX
DENMARK
Ripen
Hamburg
Baltic Sea
BALTIC PEOPLES
Vistula R.
SLAVS
Dniester R.
Friesland
Saxony
Rhine R.
Aachen
Hessen
Frankfurt
Mainz
France
Paris
Metz
Bohemia
Nordgau
Moravia
Strasbourg
Bavaria
Britanny
FRANKISH EMPIRE
Alamannia
Carinthia
Pannonia
Danube R.
AVAR EMPIRE destroyed 791
ATLANTIC OCEAN
Aquitaine
Geneva
Italian Kingdom
Lyon
Milan
Burgundy
Turin
Venice
Dalmatia
Bordeaux
Ravenna
BULGARIANS
Varna
Genoa
Toulouse
Septimania
Florence
Nish
ASTURIAS
Spanish March
Marseille
Adriatic Sea
Papal States
Ragusa
Constantinople
Oporto
Corsica
Rome
PRINCIPALITY OF BENEVENTO
VLACHS
Barcelona
Salonica
EMIRATE OF CORDOVA
Naples
Al Ushbunah
Balearic Is.
Otranto
Aegean Sea
Sardinia
BYZANTINE EMPIRE
Calabria
Smyrna
Athens
Qurtubah (Córdova)
Panormus
Sicily
Cartagena
Caliphate of Bagdad
Catania
Mediterranean Sea
Crete
IDRISIDS
RUSTAMIDS
ABBASIDS (AGHLABIDS)
ARAB CONQUEST OF IBERIA, 711–732
main Arab campaign, 711–732
under Arab control by c. 732
unconquered Iberian peoples, c. 732
Frankish kingdom, c. 732
BRITTANY
Sens
732
Poitiers
FRANKISH KINGDOM
Lyons
ATLANTIC OCEAN
Bordeaux 732
raids 725
CANTABRIANS
BASQUES
Narbonne 719
Oporto
718
Zaragoza
Barcelona
VISIGOTHIC KINGDOM
Lisbon 716
Toledo 712
Valencia 714
raids from 714
Balearic Is.
Córdoba 711
Seville 712
Algeciras 711
ARAB CALIPHATE

FIRE AND SWORD

The relative peace and security established during the rule of the Carolingians ensured that most of western and east-central Europe was protected from attack. The spread of Christianity under the impetus of missionaries from Ireland and the enforced conversion at the point of the sword in places like Saxony aided the growth of churches and religious communities. Their wealth added to that of merchant settlements proved an attractive target to attacks from three marauding groups: Muslims from North Africa, Vikings, and Magyars. The Muslim raids were a continuation of Islamic conquest. Sicily was occupied by 827, the victorious Aghlabids from Tunisia moving into the Balearics, attacking Sardinia and Corsica and establishing bases in southern Italy. One group, from either the Emirate of Cordoba or Tunis, used Fraxinetum in Provence as a permanent base to penetrate southern Europe. Overall, the Muslims robbed, ransomed, or raided Italian monasteries and towns, including Rome, and the Aghlabid fleet reigned supreme in the central Mediterranean. Further expansion was prevented by the Byzantine empire's reviving its fleet and reducing the Italian bases, together with the disintegration into civil war in the Muslim states of Spain and North Africa. In the the east, Arabs captured Crete, keeping it from 827 to 861, and shared control of Cyprus. Arabs plundered Thessalonica (904) and defeated a Byzantine expedition to Crete (911).

The Magyars comprised a different type of threat. Arriving in the Danube plains in the 890s, these nomadic horsemen raided with extreme mobility and speed, plundering in turn northern Italy, Germany, and France (c. 899–955) and terrorizing as far afield as Constantinople. Difficult to combat, the Magyars were rarely vulnerable except in mountains and at river crossings. The Saxon emperor Henry I defeated them at Riade (933) in Thuringia, while his son, Otto I, crushed them at Lechfeld in 955. Thereafter, the Magyars, under Geza and Stephen I, becoming Christians, settled what was to become a strong Hungarian state. The Vikings possessed seaborne mobility, descending on unsuspecting coastlines and sailing up rivers. Although Viking activity appeared essentially violent, these raiders could also be colonists. Bases were established in Ireland (Dublin, 841) by Norwegians who ravished Ireland and parts of Britain; Danish Vikings settled what became known as the Danelaw in England and settled Normandy in France. Vikings penetrated the Mediterranean, while others colonized the Orkneys, Shetlands, Faroes, and Iceland, and reached Greenland and the Americas. Swedish Vikings crossed the Baltic and sailed down the Dvina-Dnieper River complex to the Black Sea, while others reached the Volga and Caspian Sea. Establishing colonies at Novgorod and Kiev, these Varangians challenged Khazar control of the Constantinople–Black Sea trade. Eventually, they founded the Kievan Rus state but were absorbed by the Slavs and subjected to Orthodox Christianity. By 1000, the Magyar, Muslim, and Viking scourges had practically ceased. However, the raids and conquests had two major results. First, the far-flung Viking network established new interlocking trade routes, and second, the weaknesses shown by Frankish and Byzantine leadership saw a devolution of power to local lords for defense purposes, leading to the rise of feudalism.

FIRE AND SWORD, c. 910

→ Viking invasions

→ Viking invasions

→ Magyar invasions

→ Abbasids invasions

▨ permanent Scandinavian settlement

Norwegian Sea

Arctic Circle

FINNIC PEOPLES

Hladir

NORWAY

Kaupang

Staraya Ladoga (Aldeigjuborg)

Uppsala

SWEDEN

Birka

Novgorod (Holmgard)

North Sea

DENMARK

Lund

Roskilde

Baltic Sea

BALTIC PEOPLES

KIEVAN RUS

KINGDOM OF ORKNEY

IRISH KINGDOMS

Dublin

NORTHUMBERLAND

York

Hedeby

Bremen

SLAVS

Kiev

Cork

WELSH STATES

WESSEX

London

Aachen

Cologne

Rhine

Cracow

Frankfurt

Baycux

Paris

EAST FRANKISH KINGDOM (GERMANY)

Lorch

Nitrava

HUNGARY

Orleans

Mosapurc

PECHENEGS

ATLANTIC OCEAN

WEST FRANKISH KINGDOM (FRANCE)

Besançon

UPPER BURGUNDY

Milan

Danube R.

Presov

Bordeaux

Lyon

LOWER BURGUNDY

Genoa

KINGDOM OF ITALY

Venice

CROATIA

Nish

Constantinople

Bayonne

Avignon

Serbia

BULGARIA

Corunna

NAVARRE

Nice

PAPAL STATES

Adriatic Sea

Philippopolis

LÉON

ARAGON

Fraxinelum

Barium

Thessalonica

Adrianople

Oporto

MUSLIM STATES

Barcelona

Corsica

Rome

BYZANTINE EMPIRE

Aegean Sea

Smyrna

Toledo

Tarragona

Naples

Balansiyah

Sardinia

Pr. of Benevento

EMIRATE OF CORDOVA

Balearic Is.

Panormus

Ishbiliyah

Ibn Hafsun (autonomous)

Cartagena

Mediterranean

Sicily

Chandax

Sétif

Tunis

Crete

IDRISIDS

RUSTAMIDS

ABBASIDS (AGHLABIDS)

Kairawan

Malta

Sea

Tripoli

EMPIRE AND PAPACY

The German conquest of Italy in the tenth century and the acquisition of the imperial title demonstrate that of all the lands of Europe, Germany had recovered first from the anarchy of the late Carolingian period and that the Saxon kings Henry II "The Fowler" (918–936) and his son Otto I "The Great" (936–973) were the true successors to the Carolingian empire. Henry conquered Italy in a series of campaigns between 951 and 972, and was crowned as Holy Roman emperor in 962, by Pope John XII. Otto ordered that every pope should swear allegiance to the empire. Later his grandson Otto II (980–1002) even dreamed of establishing his government in Rome, in an attempt to return to the idealized glories of Roman *imperium*.

The Saxons and their successors, the Salian and Hohenstaufen dynasties, maintained imperial predominance by regaining control over the royal demesnes within each duchy and by breaking each duke's control over the church within his land. The transhumance court, continually on the move throughout the German lands and northern Italy, enabled the emperor to enforce his will even further, and led to an increasingly closer relationship between the empire and the church, which became a pillar of the monarchy and an instrument of the crown.

In the meantime, a rift arose between emperor and pope over who had the ultimate God-given authority over western Christendom. Known as the Investiture Controversy, this centered upon the pope's right to invest or crown the emperor and the right of lay rulers to grant ecclesiastical officials the symbols of their authority. In 1059, in an attempt to extract the papacy from the control of the emperor, Pope Nicholas II had given orders that in future all papal elections should be carried out by the College of Cardinals. The Investiture Controversy really began in 1075, when Pope Gregory VII (1073–1085) claimed supreme legislative and judicial power within Christendom, with the right to depose any prince, and excommunicated five of the emperor's officials. As a reaction, the emperor, Henry IV (1050–1106), supported by the northern Italian bishops, ordered the imperial bishops to excommunicate the pope; Gregory VII in turn excommunicated the emperor and declared him deposed. Subsequent rebellion by the German barons, and the dwindling of his support, forced Henry to seek penitence by crossing the Alps in winter in 1077 at Canossa, where he stood barefoot and in rags for four days, begging the pope's forgiveness. Despite this, Gregory would be forced to excommunicate Henry again in 1080, leading to war between the empire and the papacy. Gregory appealed for help to Robert Guiscard, the Norman duke of Apulia and Calabria, who marched on Rome and rescued Gregory in 1085. In the meantime, Henry, backed once again by the German bishops, appointed Clement III as an "antipope" in Gregory's stead.

Pope Innocent III (1198–1216), building upon the earlier reforms, had an exalted view of the papacy in Christendom and increased both the power and prestige of the church and the papacy, based upon the right of the pope to approve or reject elections to the imperial throne. Innocent III excommunicated Otto IV (1182–1218) for having invaded Sicily in 1210 and supported the election of Frederick II Barbarossa to the imperial throne in 1212. A truce between pope and emperor would be established later with the Concordat of Worms in 1122.

Baltic Sea

KINGDOM OF DENMARK

Prussia
1231 won by Teutonic knigts

North Sea

County of
Holstein
Oldenburg
Lübeck
Hamburg
Ratzeburg
Mecklenburg
Slavinia

Duchy of Pomerania
1181 imperial fief

Friesland

Bremen
Verden
Duchy of
Saxony
Osnabrück
Minden
Detmold
Nijmegen
Paderborn
Hildesheim
Goslar
Magdeburg
Halberstadt

March of
Havelberg
Brandenburg
Brunswick

Gniezno

KINGDOM OF POLAND

Utrecht

Duchy of
Lausitz
*1158 joined
to Empire*

Duchy of
Silesia
1163 imperial fief

Brabant
Duisburg
Dortmund
Cologne
Aachen
Remagen
Mühlhausen
Naumburg
Merseburg
Meissen

Opol
and
Ratibor
*1163 imperial
fief*

Bruges
Antwerp
Flanders
Duchy of
Lower Lorraine
Hainault
Cambrai
Liege
Landgravate of Thuringia
Altenburg

March of
Meissen
Neisse

Oberwesel
Trier
Mainz
Frankfurt
Gelnhausen
Bamberg
Eger
KINGDOM OF GERMANY
Prague
KINGDOM OF BOHEMIA
Olomouc
March of Moravia

Reims
Verdun
Metz
Toul
Kaiserslautern
Trifels
Speyer
Weissenburg
Strasbourg
Worms
Würzburg
Franconia
Nuremberg

Troyes
Heilbronn
Esslingen
Hohenstaufen
Ulm
Eichstatt
Regensburg
Freising
Duchy of Bavaria
Passau
Augsburg
Duchy of
Austria
Linz
Vienna
Bratislava
Esztergom

KINGDOM
OF
FRANCE
Duchy of Swabia
Duchy of Upper Lorraine
Besançon
Basle
Zurich
Constance
Innsbruck
Munich
Salzburg
Chiemsee
Seckau
1156 imperial fief
Budapest

KINGDOM
OF
HUNGARY

County of
Burgundy
Solothurn
Fribourg
Bern
Lausanne
Geneva
Sitten
Chur
Disentis
Brixen
Duchy of
Carinthia
Gurk
Lavant
Graz
Duchy of
Styria

Lyon
Vienne
Tarentaise
Savoy
Aosta
Ivrea
Como
Bergamo
Trent
Vicenza
Padua
Treviso
Grado
Patriarchate
of Aquileia
Aquileia
March of
Carniola

KINGDOM
OF
BURGUNDY
1033 joined to Empire
Valence
Die
Viviers
Embrun
Saluzzo
Turin
Novara
Vercelli
Lodi
Milan
Brescia
Verona
Mantua
March of
Verona
Venice

Arles
Avignon
Digne
Asti
Tortona
Alessandria
Piacenza
Parma
Modena
Ferrara
Comacchio
Ravenna
Rimini

Provence
Aix
Marseilles
Nice
Fréjus
Genoa
Luna
Emilia
Bologna
Romagna
Fano

Toulon
Pisa
Florence
Siena
Duchy of
Spoleto
Perugia
Camerino
Spoleto
Ancona
March of Ancona

KINGDOM OF ITALY

Adriatic Sea

Corsica

Sutri
Patrimony
of St Peter
Rome
Tivoli
Anagni

KINGDOM
OF SICILY
*1194 conquered
by Henry VI*

Tuscany

Mediterranean Sea

N

0   100 km
0   100 miles

Sardinia

THE EMPIRE AND THE PAPACY	
▬	Empire border, 1152
	Kingdom of Germany
	Kingdom of Italy
	Kingdom of Burgundy
	Kingdom of Bohemia
	imperial land in Italy
▨	Hohenstaufen demesne land
◪	Welf demesne land
	ecclesiastical land
●	archidiocese
○	diocese
■	Lombard League town, 1167

THE CRUSADES

Pope Urban II at the Council of Clermont on November 27, 1095, proclaiming the First Crusade and calling on the knights of christendom to liberate the holy city of Jerusalem.

"In all the streets and squares of the city, mounds of heads hands and feet were to be seen. People were walking quite openly over dead men and horses."
Raymond of Aguilers, eyewitness of the capture of Jerusalem

The Crusades were a series of military expeditions, most carried out between 1095 and 1270, with the essential, though not exclusive aim of freeing the Holy Land from Islam. In the eleventh century, Europe experienced a religious revival that stimulated the growing popularity of pilgrimages to the Holy Sites, which were controlled by the Muslim Seljuk Turks, who were also threatening the Byzantine empire.

It was against this background that the First Crusade was launched in 1095 by Pope Urban II at the Council of Clermont; it would serve as the prototype of the crusades that were to follow, the object being to assist the Byzantine empire in its struggle against the Seljuk Turks. Although armies were raised by knights, such as Bohemond, Hugh of Vermandois, and Robert of Flanders, the First Crusade was as much a pilgrimage as a Holy War, with indulgences being offered to pilgrims on their journey toward the Holy Sepulchre. Antioch was taken by Bohemond in 1098, after a siege lasting many months, and Jerusalem fell to the Crusaders in July 1099; its Muslim and Jewish inhabitants were put to the sword. The kingdom of Jerusalem was founded by Baudoin in 1100, alongside a loose federation made up of the principality of Antioch and the counties of Edessa and Tripoli. These were defended by a line of "Crusader" castles along the Palestinian littoral.

The fall of Edessa to the Turks in 1144 resulted in the Second Crusade, led by Louis VII, king of France, and the emperor Conrad III. When their forces arrived in Syria, instead of retaking Edessa, they laid siege to Damascus in 1148, but failed to take it. The ensuing defeat froze relations between the Crusader states and Europe for decades.

With the fall of Jerusalem to Saladin in 1187, a Third Crusade was called by Pope Gregory VII and led by the kings of France and England, who traveled by sea, joining Frederick II, who had taken the land route. Cyprus was taken and Acre put to siege by Richard the Lion Heart; although he failed to capture Jerusalem and was obliged to treaty with Saladin in 1192, he secured access for European pilgrims to the Holy Sites for a period of five years.

The Fourth Crusade was launched by Pope Innocent III, retaking Egypt, but it was diverted when the Crusaders took the Hungarian town of Zara for the Venetians as recompense for their sea journey. When the Crusaders eventually arrived in Constantinople in 1204, they captured the Byzantine capital, and in league with the Venetians founded the Latin empire, which lasted for sixty years and seriously weakened the Byzantine empire, thus ending any possible reconciliation between the Orthodox and Latin churches.

In 1215, the king of Hungary set out for Acre, launching the Fifth Crusade. In 1218, the king of Jerusalem, Jean de Brienne, invaded Egypt and put the port of

Damietta to siege; however, his subsequent march on Cairo ended in disaster in 1221.

The Sixth Crusade was launched in 1223 by Pope Honorius III in support of an expedition led by Emperor Frederick II, who would later be excommunicated for his procrastination. The Sultan eventually gave up Jerusalem, Bethlehem, and Nazareth to Frederick and signed a ten-year truce in 1229.

The Seventh Crusade, originated in 1239, was led by the King of Navarre and the Duke of Burgundy. Nevertheless, Jerusalem fell once again to Muslim forces. St. Louis then led a campaign against Egypt; he captured the town of Damietta in 1249 and marched on Cairo, captured in 1250.

Antioch fell in 1268, which resulted in an Eighth Crusade, led by the king of France, who attacked Tunis, but was killed during the siege in 1270, his army subsequently being forced into retreat.

There would be other Crusades, even into the fifteenth century, which tended to be more anarchic in character, the result of popular outbursts of enthusiasm.

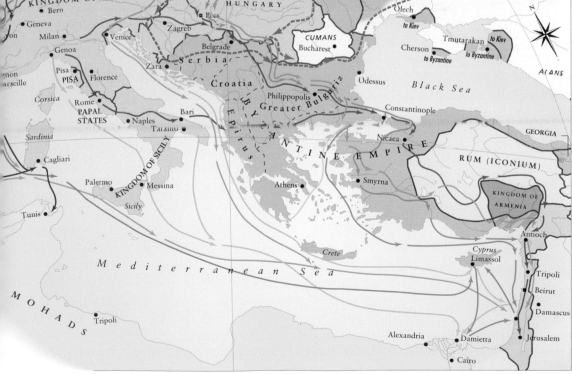

THE CRUSADES

religion

- Latin (Catholic) Christian
- Greek (Orthodox) Christian
- Armenian Christian
- Muslim

route of crusades

- First Crusade, 1094–99
- Second Crusade, 1146–49
- Third Crusade, 1189–92
- Fourth Crusade, 1202–04
- Fifth Crusade, 1228–29
- Sixth Crusade, 1248–54
- Seventh Crusade, 1228–29
- Mongol invasion, 1240–41
- battle

RUSSIA AND THE TATAR INVASIONS

The Tatars (or Mongols), moving westward from the heart of Asia, had a huge impact upon the histories of both Russia and Europe. A nomadic, Turkic people, the Tatars lived in the general area of modern-day Mongolia. They were united by Temujin (Genghis Khan) whose grandson, Batu Khan, following up on an earlier reconnaissance in force, led a lightning winter campaign against the northern Russian principalities with a large force in 1237 and subjugated the Rus and their neighbors in the west. This was the only successful winter invasion of Russia in recorded history.

First they defeated the Volga Bulgars, moving on to Vladimir Suzdal, and destroying its wealthy towns. In 1239, due to internecine princely disputes, the Rus princes failed to form a united front, enabling the Tatars to overrun southwest Rus. They sacked Kiev and hundreds of other settlements in the process. By 1240, all Rus resistance had virtually ceased, and the Tatars were able to turn their attentions on Poland and Hungary. Although the Tatar conquest of northern Rus was part of a larger scheme, the conquest of Europe, they were unable to penetrate Europe because of internal disputes following the death of the Great Khan Ogedei in 1241. Nevertheless, the Mongol conquest of all of northern and central Asia and eastern Europe made a strong impression in western Europe and successive missions, such as that of John of Pian de Carpine who, in 1245, would set out to the Golden Horde in an attempt to convert them to Christianity, leaving us with rich descriptions of their travels.

The Tatar conquest of Rus forced many principalities to submit to the hegemony of the "Golden Horde" (The Great Mongol empire). Only Novgorod, Pskov, and several lesser principalities would escape the "Tatar yoke," which technically would last until 1480. Yet, although the Tatars eventually converted to Islam, they remained tolerant of other religions and allowed the Russians to pursue Orthodoxy and to maintain their association, along the "Water Road,"with Constantinople and the Byzantine empire.

From their capital at Sarai, the Tatars held nine principalities in their power. Tribute was exacted from all inhabitants, irrespective of status and class. The leading cities, centers of culture, were destroyed. Yet the Tatars also initiated a population census, and had a considerable impact upon the Russian language. They also influenced military developments, especially cavalry tactics, which along with discipline and strategic coordination explained their successes on the battlefield.

The Tatars eventually withdrew to the steppes, restricting their intervention in the interior of Rus to punitive expeditions and the collection of taxes. Their ultimate defeat did not end their influence; their invasion would deeply affect Russia's future political, social, and economic development, particularly by cutting Rus off from the rest of Europe. They also left an indelible imprint upon Muscovite life and society; the seeds of the "Russian Question" still are very much in evidence today, whereby Russia moved from a collectivity of independent principalities to an absolutist autocracy and from a system of diffused landholdings to the concentration of land in the hands of an autocrat.

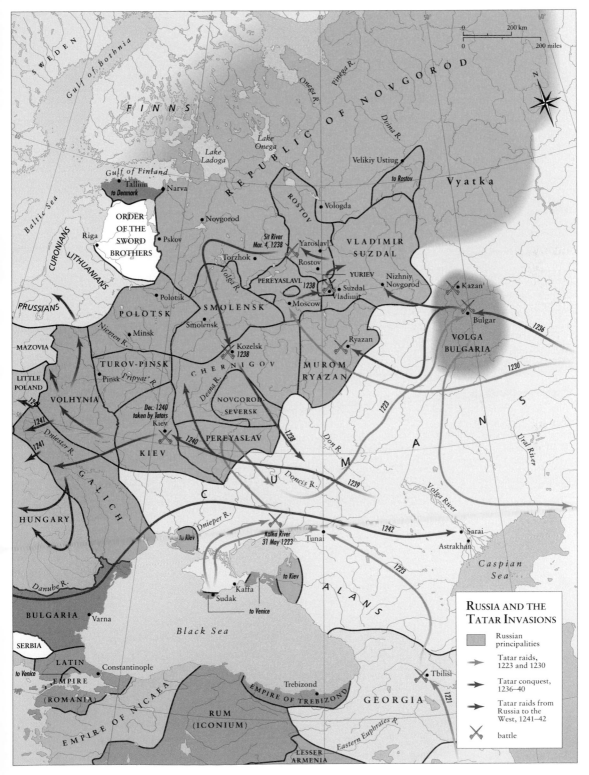

SWEDEN

Gulf of Bothnia

F I N N S

Lake Onega

Lake Ladoga

Baltic Sea

Gulf of Finland

Tallin
to Denmark • Narva

R E P U B L I C O F N O V G O R O D

Onega R.

Pinega R.

Dvina R.

Velikiy Ustiug

V y a t k a

to Rostov

• Vologda

ORDER OF THE SWORD BROTHERS

Riga • • Pskov

CURONIANS

LITHUANIANS

• Novgorod

R O S T O V

Sit River
Mar. 4, 1238 ✗

Yaroslavl ✗
Rostov

VLADIMIR SUZDAL

PRUSSIANS

Polotsk •

P O L O T S K

• Minsk

Niemen R.

Volga R.

Torzhok •

PEREYASLAVL
1238 ✗

Suzdal •
Vladimir ✗

YURIEV

Nizhniy
Novgorod

✗ Kazan'

MAZOVIA

SMOLENSK

Smolensk •

Moscow •

✗ Bulgar

VOLGA BULGARIA

1236

LITTLE POLAND

TUROV-PINSK

Kozelsk ✗
1238

Ryazan ✗

1230

VOLHYNIA

Pinsk •
Pripyat' R.

C H E R N I G O V

Desna R.

MUROM RYAZAN

1223

C U M A N S

Ural River

1241

Dec. 1240
taken by Tatars
Kiev ✗

NOVGOROD-SEVERSK

1238

Don R.

Volga River

Dniester R.
1241

KIEV

1240

PEREYASLAV

Donets R.

1239

• Sarai

G A L I C H

to Kiev

Dnieper R.

Kalka River
31 May 1223 ✗

Tunai •

1242

Astrakhan •

HUNGARY

1223

Caspian Sea

Danube R.

to Kiev

A L A N S

to Kiev
• Kaffa

BULGARIA

• Varna

Sudak •

to Venice

Black Sea

SERBIA

LATIN EMPIRE (ROMANIA)

Constantinople

to Venice

Trebizond •

✗ Tbilisi

1221

GEORGIA

EMPIRE OF NICAEA

EMPIRE OF TREBIZOND

RUM (ICONIUM)

Eastern Euphrates R.

LESSER ARMENIA

RUSSIA AND THE TATAR INVASIONS

Russian principalities

→ Tatar raids, 1223 and 1230

→ Tatar conquest, 1236–40

→ Tatar raids from Russia to the West, 1241–42

✗ battle

0 ____ 200 km

0 ____ 200 miles

N

THE FALL OF CONSTANTINOPLE

"It was his purpose to make Constantinople the most powerful and self-sufficient city in all respects, enjoying its previous level of attainment in terms of power, wealth, reputation, sciences, arts and all other affairs and fine accomplishments, and in the quality of the buildings and monuments set up for the public good."
Kritovoulos
on Mehmet II's rebuilding of Constantinople

The capture of Constantinople by the Crusaders during the Fourth Crusade in 1204 led to the creation of the short-lived Latin empire, which in turn accelerated the economic and political decline of the Byzantine empire, in favor of the Venetians, who were keen to destroy their main commercial rival in the Mediterranean. By the time that the Byzantines reestablished power in 1261, the Venetians and Genoese had begun to play a greater part in the political and economic life of the Byzantine empire.

By the fifteenth century, the empire, riven by civil war, was much reduced in territorial size, to the city of Constantinople itself and the adjacent province of Roumelia, the Aegian coast, and a few cities in Asia Minor. Byzantium had become heavily dependent upon Italian merchant colonies, while much of its territory in the Balkans lay in the hands of the kingdoms of Bulgaria and Serbia. By the mid fourteenth century, Byzantium, a shadow of its former glory, could no longer defend itself. Its army had been reduced to several thousand men by the time that the Ottomans had begun making inroads into Thrace from Asia Minor.

In 1355, the Ottomans took possession of the Dardanelles, and during the 1370s, they captured Adrianople, Macedonia, and northern Greece, decisively defeating the disunited Serbian armies, led by Prince Lazar, at the battle of Kosovo in 1389.

Constantinople was put to siege in 1422 by Sultan Murad, a siege that the Byzantines would endure until May 29, 1453, when Sultan Mehmet II's troops stormed the city walls after a bombardment that lasted for a whole month. The city was pillaged and sacked, its citizens massacred, raped, or put to flight. The great church, Hagia Sophia, was converted into a mosque. The Byzantine empire ceased to exist.

The fall of Constantinople enabled the Ottomans to dominate the straits and the southern shores of the Black Sea. They were now able to advance through the Balkans to the Pannonian plain, where Hungary now became the main European power to confront the Ottoman expansion.

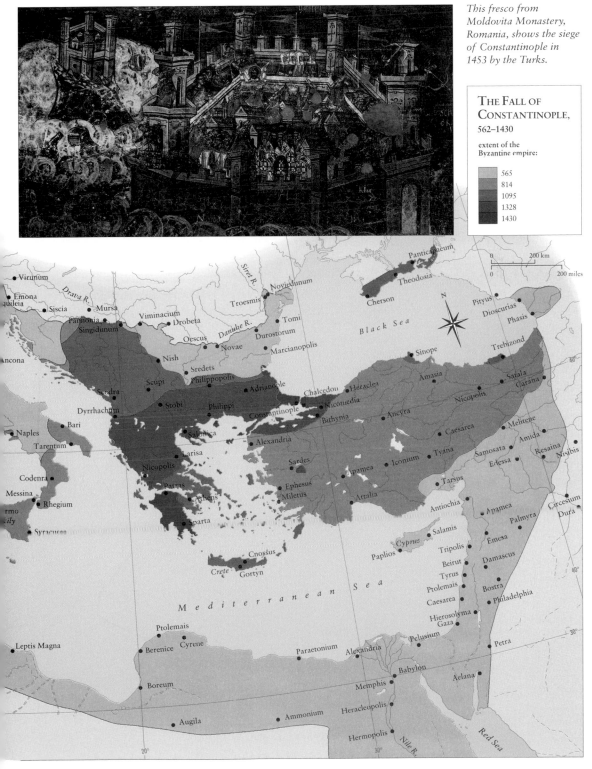

This fresco from Moldovita Monastery, Romania, shows the siege of Constantinople in 1453 by the Turks.

THE FALL OF CONSTANTINOPLE, 562–1430

extent of the Byzantine empire:

- 565
- 814
- 1095
- 1328
- 1430

77

RECONQUEST AND UNIFICATION OF SPAIN

"Once you know that the Spanish Church is being continually worn down by such a succession of disasters and by so many deaths of the sons of God as a result of the oppression of the pagans, we believe that not one of you will lie low."
Pope Calixtus II, proclaiming a Crusade in Spain, April 2, 1123

Weaknesses within the ruling family of the Caliphate of Cordoba and internal clashes between various Berber and Arab factions fragmented Muslim Spain into a series of emirates. The tiny Christian kingdoms of Leon, Navarre, Aragon, and the county of Barcelona eventually united into two states: Leon was linked with Castile in 1037 under Ferdinand I, while Aragon achieved union with Barcelona (Catalonia) in 1118. The recognition of its independence by the pope in 1179 strengthened Portugal against Leon's ambitions. The monarchs were aided in their efforts by orders of knights that were established to fight the Muslims. A major Arab defeat in 1212 at Los Navas de Tolosa led to rapid capture of Cordoba (1236), Valencia by Aragon (1238), Murcia (1243), Seville (1248), Cadiz (1262), and the Algarve by Portugal (1250). Castile now controlled over half of the Iberian Peninsula, hemming in Portugal to the west and Aragon to the east. Granada remained the last Arab state in Spain and enjoyed a period of cultural brilliance under the Nasrid dynasty that endured until 1492. Portugal and Aragon channeled their energies elsewhere. Using the seapower of the Cataláns, Aragon captured the Balearic Islands (1228), and seized Sicily (1282), and Sardinia was incorporated in 1320. Aragonese power reached its apogee in 1442, when Alfonso V conquered the kingdom of Naples. The Portuguese experience was different. Diniz, the Farmer King, encouraged agriculture, aided by Cistercian skill; founded the first Portuguese university at Coimbra; and was responsible for the development of a navy. In 1294, he signed a commercial treaty with England to which Portugal permanently allied itself by the Treaty of Windsor (1386).

The impact of the reconquest was felt in other areas. The centralization of church influence was seen in the economic exploitation of Jews, the infringement of rights of converted Moors (Moriscos), and the growth of the Inquisition. The crown took over the orders of knights, lest they become too rich and powerful. The country became extremely religious, the process being accelerated by the marriage of the Catholic monarchs, Isabella of Castile and Ferdinand II of Aragon (1469). The conquest of Grenada in 1492 saw the expulsion of Jews and

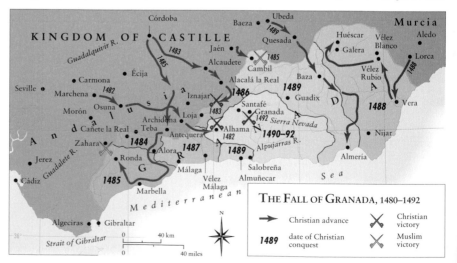

THE FALL OF GRANADA, 1480–1492

→ Christian advance ✕ Christian victory

1489 date of Christian conquest ✕ Muslim victory

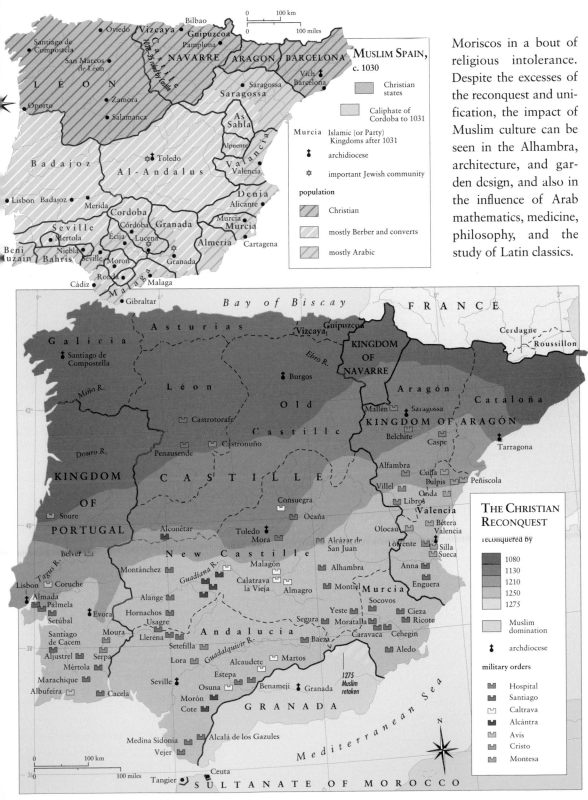

Moriscos in a bout of religious intolerance. Despite the excesses of the reconquest and unification, the impact of Muslim culture can be seen in the Alhambra, architecture, and garden design, and also in the influence of Arab mathematics, medicine, philosophy, and the study of Latin classics.

THE TIES OF TRADE

The expansion of the western European economy maintained itself during the medieval period until curtailed by the Black Death. Before this slump, developments in shipbuilding (the Hansa cog), the opening up the Baltic hinterland by the Teutonic knights, a newly awakened European demand for Middle Eastern goods, and the growth of the Genoese and Venetian trading fleets, all allowed a web of trade routes to penetrate Europe and link together areas of textile production, with markets being established in fairs such as that at Antwerp, which became the mercantile metropolis of western Europe. In the Baltic, German merchants established a union between Lübeck and Hamburg, and in 1252 they signed advantageous commercial treaties with Flanders (Bruges). An alliance was made, eventually numbering eighty-five members. Known as the Hanseatic League, and its mercantile interests obtained full or partial control of trade between Germany and the coastal towns of eastern England. Although the members sought to destroy piracy and foster safe navigational techniques, they established trading bases, monopolies, and commercial enclaves (kontore) in foreign towns such as Bergen in Norway, the Steelyard in London, and Novgorod in Russia. This protectionist policy aroused considerable opposition and occasional warfare with rival towns. The goods traded were rich and varied including textiles, metals, salt, fish, grain, wine, and luxury items. The league's strength was eventually reduced by the growing power of non-German Baltic states: the Union of Kalmar between the Scandinavian kingdoms (1397) and that between Lithuania and Poland (1386), together with the rise of Muscovy.

An illustration from the Hamburg City Charter of 1497, reflecting the seaport and its trades. In 1510 Emperor Maximilian I made Hamburg a free imperial city.

Trade in the Mediterranean benefited from the gradual ebb of Arab power. The Spanish Reconquista, the Crusades, and the Pisan-Genoan liberation of Corsica and Sardinia left trade falling into the hands of the city-republics of Genoa, Venice, and Pisa. Genoa and Venice grew wealthy and powerful with the carrier business during the Crusades, and grew knowledgeable about the Levant. Chief items of trade were oriental silks, brocades, and other textiles, ivory, perfumes, and especially spices; these were exchanged for wool and other European goods from the network of cities in northern Italy, Germany, and Flanders. Genoese forts and trading posts spread through the eastern Mediterranean, the Aegean, and the Black Sea, causing intense rivalry with the growing enterprise of Venice. In 1284, a victorious war with Pisa brought Genoa the islands of Corsica, Elba, and Sardinia (until 1326). Genoa was internally weakened by bitter rivalry between competing families. A final blow occurred in 1380, when the Genoese fleet fell into Venetian hands, and the city became dependent thereafter on France or Milan. Venice then became the most important naval and trading power, partly due to its geographical position between the Alpine passes and Byzantium and to its port and fleet of galleys. During the Fourth Crusade, Doge Enrico Dandolo managed to secure a commercial empire when Venice and the Crusaders partitioned Byzantium. This empire included Crete and parts of Euboea, with sundry forts and trading posts on the Greek mainland. Control of the Dalmatian coast through Ragusa and occasional rule over Corfu ensured a thriving trade, as did the acquisition of Cyprus.

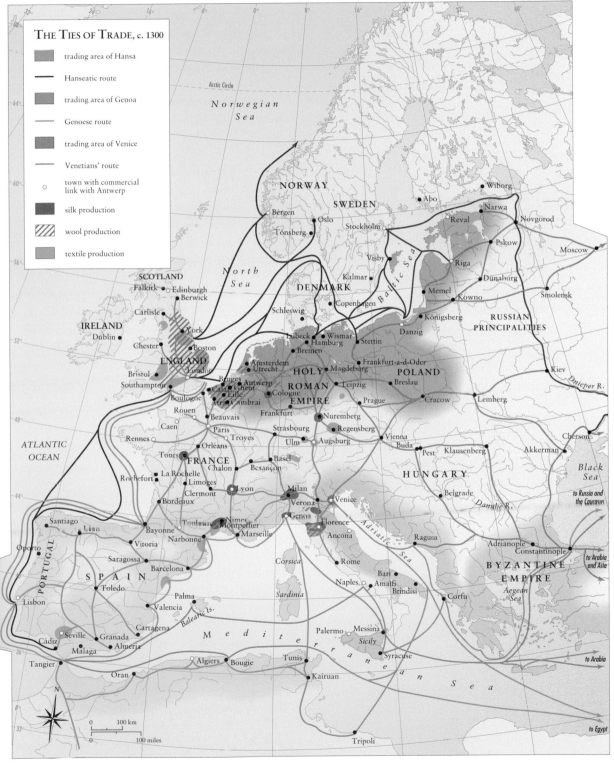

THE TIES OF TRADE, c. 1300

- trading area of Hansa
- Hanseatic route
- trading area of Genoa
- Genoese route
- trading area of Venice
- Venetians' route
- ○ town with commercial link with Antwerp
- silk production
- wool production
- textile production

Norwegian Sea

Arctic Circle

NORWAY

SWEDEN

Bergen
Oslo
Tönsberg
Stockholm
Visby

Åbo
Wiborg
Narwa
Reval
Novgorod
Pskow
Moscow
Riga
Dünaburg
Memel
Smolensk
Kowno
Königsberg

RUSSIAN PRINCIPALITIES

North Sea

SCOTLAND
Falkitk
Edinburgh
Berwick
Carlisle

IRELAND
Dublin
Chester
York
Boston

DENMARK
Schleswig
Copenhagen
Kalmar
Lübeck
Wismar
Hamburg
Stettin
Bremen
Danzig
Breslau
Cracow
Lemberg
Kiev

Dnieper R.

ENGLAND
London
Bristol
Southampton
Boulogne
Rouen
Caen
Rennes

Amsterdam
Utrecht
Bruges
Antwerp
Ghent
Calais
Lille
Arras
Cambrai
Beauvais
Paris
Troyes
Orleans

HOLY ROMAN EMPIRE
Cologne
Magdeburg
Frankfurt-a-d-Oder
Leipzig
Prague
Frankfurt
Nuremberg
Regensberg
Strasbourg
Ulm
Augsburg
Vienna
Buda
Pest
Klausenberg

POLAND

Cherson
Akkerman

Black Sea

ATLANTIC OCEAN

FRANCE
Tours
Chalon
Besançon
Basel
Lyon
La Rochelle
Limoges
Clermont
Bordeaux
Rochefort

Milan
Verona
Genoa
Venice
Florence
Ancona

HUNGARY
Belgrade
Ragusa

Danube R.

to Russia and the Caucasus

Adriatic Sea

Adrianople
Constantinople

BYZANTINE EMPIRE

to Arabia and Asia

Santiago
Lugo
Bayonne
Toulouse
Nimes
Montpellier
Marseille
Narbonne
Vitoria
Saragossa
Barcelona
Oporto
Lisbon

PORTUGAL

SPAIN
Toledo
Palma
Valencia
Cartagena
Balearic Is.

Corsica
Rome
Sardinia
Naples
Bari
Amalfi
Brindisi
Corfu

Aegean Sea

Seville
Granada
Almeria
Malaga
Cadiz
Tangier
Oran

Algiers
Bougie
Tunis
Kairuan

Palermo
Messina
Sicily
Syracuse

Mediterranean Sea

to Arabia

to Egypt

N

0   100 km
0   100 miles

Tripoli

PART V: NEW DIRECTIONS

The period between the late fifteenth century and the middle of the seventeenth century witnessed a number of new directions in European culture, politics, and society. The main themes in this period were the development and spread of humanist thought; reform theology; scientific discovery; and overseas exploration. Although this period has traditionally been interpreted as one of great change, it had much that was in common with the late medieval world, whereby magic, astrology, miracles, witchcraft, and superstition prevailed in the thoughts and beliefs of many people against a background of the harshness of winter, vagrancy, plague, famine, disease, and the ravages of war with their attendant scourges of pillage, rape, torture, and destitution. A man or woman could be hanged, burned, or broken on the rack or wheel for giving voice to heretical ideas.

The key issues confronting people in the late fifteenth century revolved around faith, superstition, witchcraft, and the Devil. Everything revolved around the idea of a life after death. How could one avoid purgatory and the eternal fires of hell? There was an interaction between religion, magic, alchemy, and the rise of technical and scientific methods and discovery.

The Renaissance and Reformation were both a reaction against the authority and control of a corrupt church and a superstitious society, aided by the rise of the cities and an increase in trade and technical progress—a scientific revolution that presaged the eighteenth-century Enlightenment.

The whole issue of Reformation and Counter-Reformation has to be put into the context of being a movement, almost a revolution, that kicked against all accepted doctrine, ideas, and belief systems in Europe at the time. The Reformation was primarily a religious dispute that took place at a time when religion totally occupied people's lives. Nobody in society could escape from religion, which was an all-pervasive phenomenon that permeated every level of society. Yet although a religious dispute in its origins, the Reformation was soon hijacked by politics and more worldly issues.

The structure of European society at the time that the medieval world was "waning" (to paraphrase Huizinga) was portrayed as a transcendental hierarchy that descended from God, to his angels, to the pope, the Holy Roman emperor, the kings, their queens, the princes, lords and ladies, merchants and seamen, down to the serf or peasant cultivating his master's land. Nevertheless, if we look more closely at some of the secular art at the beginning of the sixteenth century, we might perceive how the times were changing. The artist Holbein, for example, in a series of woodcut prints entitled *Dance of Death,* illustrated a new mood. Despite the hierarchy in society, from pope to peasant and prince to beggar, one thing linked them all: death—death the leveler; with the portrayal of death, enticing prince, beggar, and the common man. But where to: Heaven, Purgatory, or Hell? If life as experienced on earth was transmogrified into a long and weary vale of tears, deeper thought was given to the afterlife, which could be the individual human being's recompense for so much earthly suffering. This problem of securing a place in Heaven, through piety and good works, or by buying a papal indulgence to expiate one's sins, lay at the heart of religious and social life, which would result in strife for more than a century, a strife that would not really end until the Treaty of Westphalia of 1648, bringing to an end the bloody and destructive Thirty Years' War.

Toward the end of the Middle Ages, the church had been in a state of crisis. It was rotten from top to bottom. There had been the fourteenth-century crisis of the Avignon captivity of the pope, followed by the Great Schism, when there were two, even three rival popes. After the Council of Constance (1414–1418), the bishops struggled with the pope to turn the church into a limited, instead of an absolute monarchy. Spiritually there was corruption and venality. A succession of popes in the fifteenth century and the early sixteenth century failed to reform.

Could the church have reformed itself without a schism? The very fact that Pope Paul III was obliged to call the Council of Trent in December 1545 highlighted the need for the so-called Counter-Reformation, or Catholic response to the Reformation, and was an admission by the church that reform was needed from within. The Council of Trent defined doctrines, introduced ecclesiastic discipline, and reformed abuses within the Catholic Church, while strengthening the authority of the pope. The problem for the Catholic Church was that Pope Paul III (1534–1549) was acting twenty-eight years too late. The reforms that came were too late to alter the course of schism within western Christendom.

In the meantime, in 1534, a new religious order, known as the Society of Jesus, or the Jesuits, was founded by Ignatius Loyala (1491–1556); the Jesuits both reinvigorated Catholic Europe and won back many areas that had gone over to Protestantism. The Jesuits spread education and led missions to the "New World," converting the indigenous non-Christian populations of the Americas, Africa, and Asia. In the meantime, the Inquisition, originally founded in Spain in 1478, had been reactivated by Pope Paul III in 1547, with the intention of extirpating heresy.

The Reformation took place at a time when the princes of the Holy Roman empire were consolidating their own territories in a process that established the modern principality and witnessed the decline of the feudal system.

A tremendous amount of power was consolidated in the princes' hands. They acquired territory through marriage, conquest, or the exchange of distant territories. Crucial to this were developments in the judicial and financial systems, so that instead of being able to appeal to a wider authority, external to the principality, members of the clergy or nobility who went before the courts were obliged to appeal to their own prince. This increased the prestige of the prince, whose wealth grew through a more efficient system of tax collection and the ending of tax exemptions and local privileges.

The end of the fifteenth and the beginning of the sixteenth centuries were also a great period for the founding of universities. Seventeen had been founded in Germany in the space of a century. The German lands had a better record for university building than any other part of Europe. This was because every local prince wanted a university in his city. The universities attracted scholars and teachers at a time when there was a tradition of the wandering scholar who would

Henry VIII, king of England from 1509 to 1547, is mostly remembered for marrying six wives in a determined attempt to provide for the succession.
The pope had refused to recognize Henry's original divorce from his first wife. This led after 1532 to a total break with the papacy and Henry declaring himself head of the Church of England.

move from one university to another, spreading the latest knowledge.

Hand in hand with the expansion of universities was the German Renaissance and the rise of Humanism. Humanism was a new attitude, a new intellectual movement, which from an intellectual standpoint witnessed the move away from the medieval world and medieval scholasticism, and would become the basis of the western European education system well into the nineteenth century. Without the Humanists it is argued that there could have been no Reformation. Desiderius Erasmus (1466–1536), Sir Thomas More (1478–1535), Ulrich von Hutten (1488–1523), and Philipp Melanchton (1497–1560) are typical examples of the new school of Humanism, and many historical works repeat the old formula that "Erasmus laid the egg that Luther hatched."

Humanism and its pietistic Christian version, the *devotio moderna,* was an intellectual movement that flourished in advanced urban centers. The new city-states and university towns, the wealthy commercial centers and ports, such as Rotterdam and Antwerp, that were part of the new northward shift in trade and commerce from the Mediterranean provide the backdrop to the development of a "German" or northern Renaissance in opposition to its Italian counterpart.

Humanists were scholars who studied and taught the humanities—grammar, rhetoric, history, poetry, and moral philosophy. Humanism was man-centered rather than God-centered. The work of the humanists was based upon writings and studies in Latin, and to a lesser extent in Greek, concomitant with the discoveries, rediscoveries, and new developments of the Renaissance.

The humanists used the works of Latin and Greek authors, emphasizing the role of the individual and the individual conscience, essential prerequisites to the coming Reformation. A key theme to their work was a belief in the dignity and nobility of man. This was summed up in the words of Shakespeare's Hamlet, written at the end of the sixteenth century: "What a piece of work is man! How noble in reason! How infinite in faculty! In form, in moving, how express and admirable! In action how like an angel! In apprehension how like a god!"

There was a further break with medieval scholasticism, with a movement away from the contemplative life toward a life of action. Rather than spend their lives in monastic libraries and cells in deep religious contemplation, they moved toward an involvement in diplomacy, legal work, and producing works on political theory.

That man could master his environment, independent of outside authority and as a complete individual in his thirst for all knowledge, was something of a progressive phenomenon in the mentality of the age as it tried to break free from the mental strictures of the Middle Ages. Yet ironically the Renaissance looked backward as it moved forward: back to the ideals of the classical age of Greece and Rome. It had started in Italy and spread out, but hardly touched those territories of Europe that had been occupied by the Ottoman empire or Moscow, once again widening the cleavage between east and west.

Likewise, from a religious point of view, there was a move away from the abstractions of theology, and its attendant superstitions, such as indulgences, relics, and pilgrimages, toward the problems of leading a good Christian daily life, where man's faith and his knowledge and understanding of theology should be based upon the authority of the scriptures and a direct relationship with God, through Christ. There was, with Humanism, a new belief that the individual now had a direct relationship with God, based upon faith, and that there was no need to have a priest who acted as intermediary in worship and confession. These ideas were crucial to the Reformation.

Perhaps the greatest innovation in the late fifteenth century was that of printing. Printing provided the means of spreading the new religious, political, philosophical, and technical ideas by reaching a wider audience. Printing has been described by G. R. Elton as a "new weapon." Without printing there would have been no Reformation, a limited spread of Humanism, and certainly a delay in technical and scientific transformation. Thirty years after Luther, professor of theology, had nailed his ninety-five theses (or arguments) to the church door at Wittenberg, printing presses had helped spread the ideas of the Catholic counter-reformation, so that all camps, political, cultural, religious, and intellectual, would gain from its services.

The period was not only one of self-discovery through a different view of the position and role of mankind that initiated access to confessional difference, but also a period of the discovery of new lands—new worlds. The great voyages of discovery by Cabot, Columbus, Magellan, Vespucci, and others posed navigational problems that acted as a further stimulus to scientific progress. In turn, the development of "Europe overseas" was only made possible by improvements in shipbuilding techniques. Improved compasses allowed for dead-reckoning in navigation. The work of astronomers made it possible to calculate accurately the latitude of vessels at sea—the problem of longitude, based upon accurate chronometers, would not be solved until the eighteenth century. One of the biggest bonuses to navigation was an improvement in cartography, of which Mercator's chart of 1569 allowed for the curvature of the earth, making it possible to plot a course at sea by drawing straight lines between two points.

The scientific revolution arose from the growing self-confidence, individualism, and rediscovery of ancient texts that had all been stimulated by Renaissance Humanism, the logic of Protestant ideas, and the rise of capitalism alongside the rise of urbanism and the changing social conditions of the sixteenth and first half of the seventeenth century. The spirit of scientific inquiry was afoot, based upon evidence and the realization that man's view of the universe and his place in it had been completely reshaped. The key areas of development were in navigation, which stimulated the exploration and conquest of the Americas and the development of trade routes to India; astronomy, through the discoveries of Nicolas Copernicus (1473–1543) and Galileo (1564–1642); mathematics, logic, and physics through the works of René Descartes (1596–1650), Blaise Pascal (1623–1662), and Benedict Spinoza (1632–1677); all of these developments paved the way for the Enlightenment. By the middle of the seventeenth century, educated Europeans were living in a different mental world from their counterparts at the beginning of the sixteenth century.

OTTOMAN THREAT

The continuous struggle between Islam and the Byzantine empire, with interventions by western Crusaders, changed in emphasis during the fourteenth century, following the unification of Turkic tribes under able leaders from the Osmanli dynasty.

The Dardanelles were captured in 1355, when Osman's son, Orkham, landed in Gallipoli. Thrace was overrun, and in the 1370s, Adrianople, the northern part of Greece, and Macedonia were occupied. The Serbian nobility, led by Prince Lazar, were heavily defeated at the battle of Kosovo in June 1389, and by the end of May 1453, Constantinople fell to Sultan Mehmet II.

Now based upon the "Sublime Porte" at Constantinople, the Ottoman empire gradually spread through the Balkans and into the Pannonian Plain of Hungary. The Hungarians were defeated at the battle of Mohacs in 1526, and by 1529 Sultan Suleiman II attacked Vienna with an army of 250,000 men, although the Ottoman armies were obliged to abandon the siege after three days of violent fighting, withdrawing into Hungary and Romania.

The whole of the Balkans fell under Ottoman control until the nineteenth century. Croats and Serbs (the Prekocani), exiled north of the Sava and Danube Rivers, would act as frontier

troops protecting Christendom and the Holy Roman empire from further Ottoman incursions.

In turn, during the next hundred years, the Austrians and Hungarians gradually drove the Ottomans back, although in the 1670s, the Ottomans struck back, putting Vienna to siege in 1683, only to be driven off by Polish troops.

Ottoman success was not just predicated upon military prowess and organization, but also upon Ottoman diplomacy and a policy of tolerance toward non-Muslims, whereby Christian princes and nobles, such as Vlad Tepes of Transylvania or Marko Kraljevic of Serbia, were employed in the Ottoman service because they feared the potential spread of Habsburg power more than that of the Ottomans. Likewise, the Sublime Porte developed trade with the peoples around the Mediterranean coast, taking over from the Merchants of Marseille, Venice, and Dubrovnik (Ragusa).

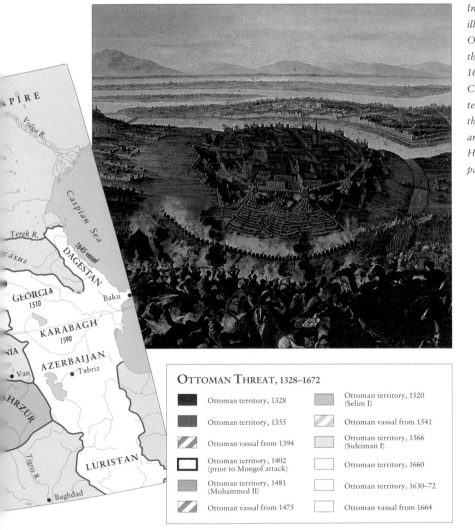

In this 17th century illustration, the Ottoman army reaches the gates of Vienna in 1689; meanwhile the Christian states had temporarily set aside their individual interests and in 1684 formed a Holy League under papal sponsorship.

OTTOMAN THREAT, 1328–1672

- Ottoman territory, 1328
- Ottoman territory, 1355
- Ottoman vassal from 1394
- Ottoman territory, 1402 (prior to Mongol attack)
- Ottoman territory, 1481 (Mohammed II)
- Ottoman vassal from 1475
- Ottoman territory, 1520 (Selim I)
- Ottoman vassal from 1541
- Ottoman territory, 1566 (Suleiman I)
- Ottoman territory, 1660
- Ottoman territory, 1630–72
- Ottoman vassal from 1664

PROTESTANT REFORMATION

The Protestant Reformation took place at a time of transition in the late fifteenth and sixteenth centuries. Change was fueled by both a heightened religious awareness, and the spread of the *devotio moderna;* and by the Renaissance, which boosted the interests of princely power and also led to greater intellectual curiosity, spread through humanism, whose key practitioners were Erasmus of Rotterdam and Sir Thomas More. In the background lay economic and social change engineered by a rising merchant and artisanal class and by the process of urbanization.

People began to question the role and nature of the Universal Church, which had grown corrupt and had become open to abuse and scandal.

Humanism demanded an improvement in scholarship and a break from non-biblical superstition and an independent-mindedness that underpinned the concept of personal salvation that, in terms of worship, did not demand the intermediary role of a priest between the individual and God. In the meantime, various lay social forces militated against an end to church taxation, for better standards of religious practice and duty. Anticlericalism came to a head in the German lands when Martin Luther, outraged by Cardinal Tetzel's sale of papal indulgences, nailed his ninety-five theses to the door of All Saints Church in Wittenberg in October 1517.

The Reformation gave support to the rise of centralized and absolutist states with Luther, the Swiss reformer Huldrich Zwingli (1484–1531), and the Frenchman John Calvin (1509–1564) acting as the main proponents of reform against other forces, such as the Anabaptist and millenarian movements.

Anticlericalism and a hatred of church abuse was particularly strong in Germany. Politically the princes, imperial knights, and city councils wanted to curtail the powers of the Holy Roman emperors Maximilian I and Charles V, and the papacy. Church property was seized, and Protestant churches became subordinate to temporal rulers, a feature that would particularly benefit the monarchy in England, especially during the reign of Henry VIII.

In a failed attempt to unite the Protestant movement, Philip of Hesse tried to bring Luther and Zwingli together, where unity would only stumble upon their different interpretations of the Mass.

A new wave of Protestantism began with John Calvin, whose ideas spread from Geneva at the beginning of the 1540s into France, the Netherlands, the German lands, and parts of eastern Europe, notably Poland and Transylvania.

Protestant political leaders formed the Schmalkaldic League in February 1531 in defense of Protestantism, and fought against Emperor Charles V in the war of 1546–1547. Charles V was never able to control the influence and spread of Protestantism in the Holy Roman empire, nor the political, economic, and social forces behind it, since his hands were always tied by external demands: his wars with the French Valois dynasty; the Ottoman Turks, and his need to control Spain and the Spanish Netherlands within the Holy Roman empire.

By the Treaty of Augsburg in September 1555, the decision was reached that subjects of each territory should follow the religion of the local prince according to the policy of *Cuius regio eius religio.* By this time, almost 40 percent of Europeans accepted some version of "reformed" theology.

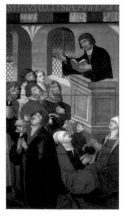

On this altarfront from Torslund in Denmark, a stronghold of the Protestant faith, Martin Luther preaches to the converted.

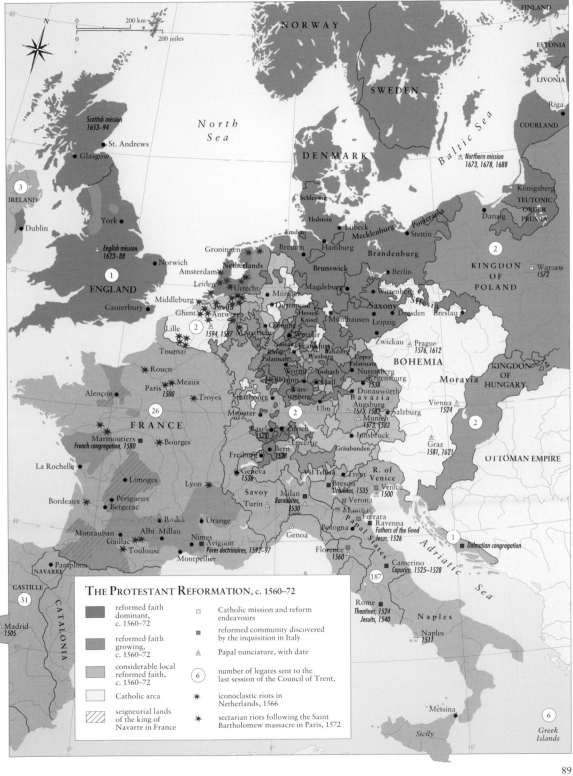

THE PROTESTANT REFORMATION, c. 1560–72

▮ reformed faith dominant, c. 1560–72	▫ Catholic mission and reform endeavours
▮ reformed faith growing, c. 1560–72	▪ reformed community discovered by the inquisition in Italy
▮ considerable local reformed faith, c. 1560–72	Ⓐ Papal nunciature, with date
▯ Catholic area	⑥ number of legates sent to the last session of the Council of Trent,
▨ seigneurial lands of the king of Navarre in France	✳ iconoclastic riots in Netherlands, 1566
	✴ sectarian riots following the Saint Bartholomew massacre in Paris, 1572

HABSBURG RULE

The Netherlands, after refusing to carry the taxation demands of the Spanish crown, rose in revolt in 1568. The leaders of the revolt established the Union of Utrecht in 1579, which created the United Provinces. After a savage struggle, Dutch independence was eventually recognized in 1648.

"To God I speak Spanish, to women Italian, to men French, and to my horse–German." *Charles V,* Holy Roman emperor (1519–58), king of Spain (1516–56), and founder of the Habsburg dynasty

A dynasty of German origins, the Habsburg monarchy ruled over a period of six centuries between 1278 and 1918. In 1278, Rudolph of Habsburg acquired the Duchy of Austria, and with time his family would become the leading dynasty in central Europe. In 1438, Albert of Habsburg, who had recently been crowned king of Hungary, was elected Holy Roman emperor, and that title would remain in his family's possession until 1806. In the fourteenth century the Habsburgs had gained Carinthia, Carniola, Tyrol, Istria, and Trieste. As a single political entity the collection of territories that made up the Habsburg empire was a dynastic creation that would never be linked to one single nation, nor bound together by geography. The Habsburg empire would therefore become multinational in its makeup. Marriage, rather than conflict, gradually became the key to Habsburg expansion, and through a series of marriages the dynasty acquired Burgundy in 1477, Bohemia in 1526, and Croatia in 1527. Throughout the sixteenth and seventeenth centuries the Habsburgs confronted two enemies: externally the threat of Ottoman Turkish expansion, while internally Habsburg power and authority were weakened by the rise of Protestantism. Whereas the Turks never managed to take the Habsburg capital of Vienna, despite the sieges of 1529 and 1683, the Protestant Reformation continued to undermine imperial power from within, culminating in the widespread chaos and destruction throughout much of central Europe during the Thirty Years' War (1618–1648).

Meanwhile in Spain Archduke Philip, son of Emperor Maximilian (1486–1519), had married Juana of Castile in 1496; they became king and queen of Castile in 1496. They were succeeded by their son Charles of Ghent, who became the ruler of the Netherlands on his father's death, then Charles I of Spain (1516 and 1556). Three years later in 1519, as Charles V, he was elected Holy Roman emperor, on the death of Emperor Maximilian.

Under Charles V, Burgundy was one of the richest imperial territories, ruled by his aunt Margaret of Austria between 1509 and 1530, and then by his sister Mary of Hungary between 1531 and 1555. Although Charles faced revolts in the Netherlands that were motivated by grievances over heavy imperial taxation, especially the revolt of 1539, worse would follow under his son and successor, Philip II (1555–1598), during whose reign there began an eighty-year-long conflict between 1566 and 1648, culminating in Dutch independence. Whereas Charles had mostly based his policy in the Low Countries upon a spirit of compromise, Philip made few concessions to Dutch local sentiments, privileges, and confession. Worse, because he spoke neither French or Dutch, and ruled from Madrid, the Dutch saw him as a Spanish king and therefore an alien, unlike his father, who had been born in the region.

In the meantime, under Cortés and Pizzaro the Americas had been conquered; yet despite the enormous wealth enjoyed by the Habsburgs from the Spanish Americas, all would be squandered on Charles's European projects and wars.

Charles's inheritance proved to be an impossible task; no sooner did one problem appear to have been resolved than another one arose. In Germany he had to confront the rise of princely power, posited upon the spread of the Protestant Reformation. He was constantly caught between the threats of the Protestants, the Turks, and the French. In 1556 he abdicated; the Habsburg empire was divided into two, with his brother Ferdinand inheriting the Holy Roman empire and his son, Philip, inheriting Spain and its possessions in the Low Countries, the Italian lands, and the Americas.

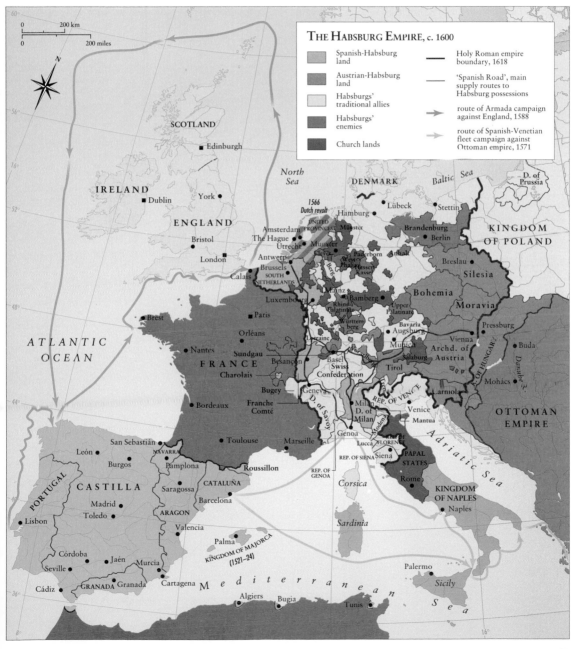

THIRTY YEARS' WAR, 1618–1648

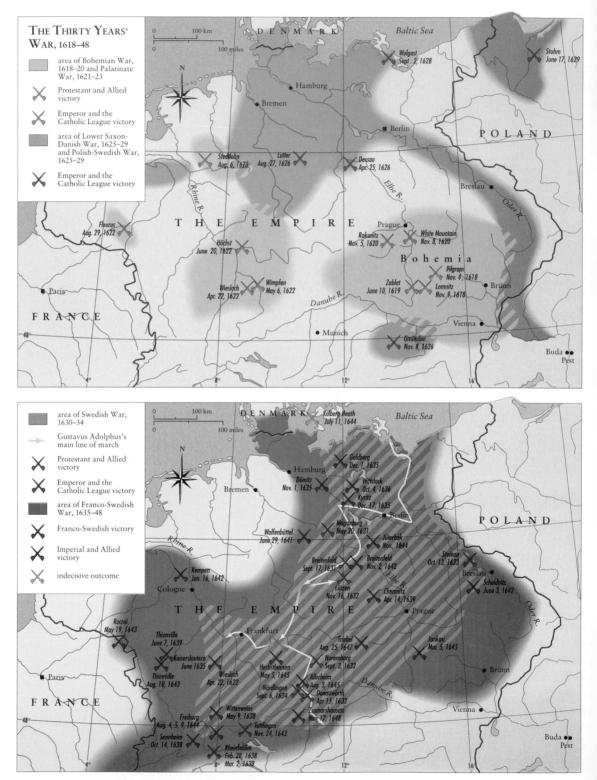

THE THIRTY YEARS' WAR, 1618–48

- area of Bohemian War, 1618–20 and Palatinate War, 1621–23
- ✕ Protestant and Allied victory
- ✕ Emperor and the Catholic League victory
- area of Lower Saxon-Danish War, 1625–29 and Polish-Swedish War, 1625–29
- ✕ Emperor and the Catholic League victory

- area of Swedish War, 1630–34
- → Gustavus Adolphus's main line of march
- ✕ Protestant and Allied victory
- ✕ Emperor and the Catholic League victory
- area of Franco-Swedish War, 1635–48
- ✕ Franco-Swedish victory
- ✕ Imperial and Allied victory
- ✕ indecisive outcome

This war, or series of wars, was perhaps the most costly seen in Europe, with great human suffering, pillaging, and decline in population and trade, simultaneously with a general economic recession. The Thirty Years' War(s) served as the decisive phase in the struggle between Protestants and Catholics, which began in Bohemia in 1618, and spread to almost the whole European continent by the middle of the 1630s. The Thirty Years' War can be divided into five phases: the Bohemian War (1618–1620), in which the Imperial armies, under Tilly, invaded Bohemia from Austria and decisively defeated the Protestant Bohemian rebels at the battle of White Mountain in November 1620; the Palatinate War (1621–1623), with fighting to the west of the Rhine, in which Spain and the United Provinces (the Netherlands) renewed the Eighty Years' War, which had begun with the Revolt of the Netherlands in 1567; the Danish War (1624–1629), in which Tilly drove the Danes out of northwest Germany and Wallenstein occupied Pomerania and Mecklenburg, opening up the Baltic to the empire with the capture of the Hanseatic League ports of Wismar and Rostock; the Swedish War (1630–1635), when Gustav Adolf of Sweden, taking over the Protestant leadership

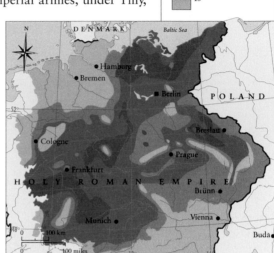

POPULATION CHANGE, 1618–48

estimated percentage of population decrease due to war and plague:

66
33
15

no data

from Denmark and with Cardinal Richelieu's support from France, invaded Germany, destroyed Magdeburg, and defeated Tilly at Breitenfeld and then Wallenstein in 1632 at Lützen (where Gustav Adolf was killed in battle); and finally the Franco-Habsburg War (1635–1648). Richelieu and his successor, Mazarin, in a risky strategy broke the Spanish encirclement of France and thus strengthened the French frontiers in coordination with the Dutch. With France's Swedish allies securing central and southern regions of the empire, the French largely concentrated on Spanish armies, culminating in the great victory at the Battle of Rocroi in the Ardennes in 1643, effectively ending Spain's military capabilities.

Peace negotiations began in 1638, ending in the Treaty of Westphalia (1648), which established the political frontiers of central Europe for over 100 years and the political and religious fragmentation of "Germany," thus preventing the emperor from turning "Germany" into an absolute monarchy based upon the principles of the Counter-Reformation. Some historians have seen in these wars a struggle that established a bipolar cleavage in Europe between two different cultures, the one characterized by the Counter-Reformation, absolutism, persecution, and the Inquisition; the other by Protestantism, free institutions, civil society, religious toleration, and the development of free-enterprise culture. This bipolar cleavage might well reflect perceived differences between east-central Europe and western Europe, which continue to impact on contemporary thinking and attitudes at the end of the second millennium.

EXPANSION OF RUSSIA

Under Ivan IV, "The Terrible" (1533–1584), Muscovy developed into a centralized, autocratic state, building upon the achievement of Ivan III "The Great"
and by weakening the power of the
boyar aristocracy. From the beginning
of the sixteenth century, Muscovy
steadily began to increase

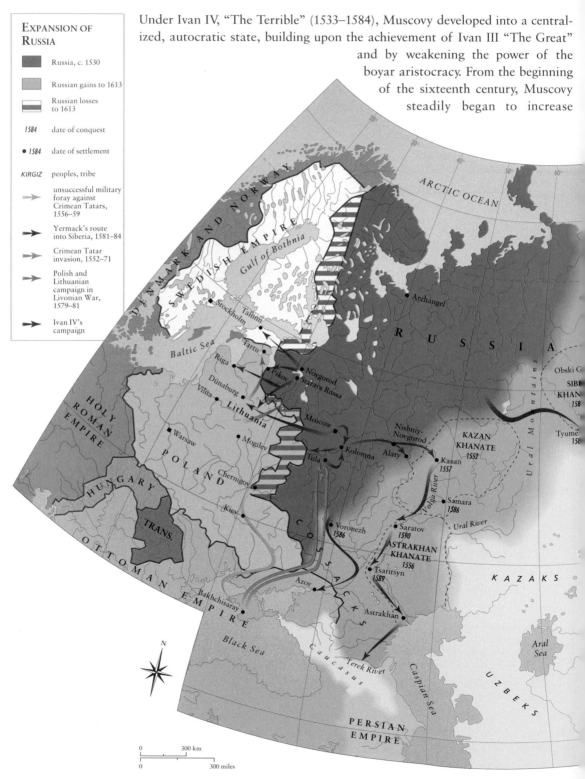

EXPANSION OF RUSSIA

Russia, c. 1530

Russian gains to 1613

Russian losses to 1613

1584   date of conquest

● *1584*   date of settlement

KIRGIZ   peoples, tribe

→ unsuccessful military foray against Crimean Tatars, 1556–59

→ Yermack's route into Siberia, 1581–84

→ Crimean Tatar invasion, 1552–71

→ Polish and Lithuanian campaign in Livonian War, 1579–81

→ Ivan IV's campaign

pressure on the Tatar Kazan Khanate and the Astrakhan Khanate, bringing the bulk of the Volga basin, as far as the Caspian Sea, under the control of Ivan by 1556. These victories opened the way to Siberia and the east.

Further expansion eastward would come in the early 1580s, when the Cossack Yermack conquered western Siberia. Meanwhile, with the establishment of a defensive line of fortresses centered on Tula, Ivan decided to go on the defensive against the Tatars in the east. He then turned his attentions westward to the Baltic, by attacking the Livonian knights in 1558 in an area equating with present-day Latvia and Estonia. This attack soon developed into a major conflict with Denmark, Sweden, Poland, and Lithuania, which would last for a quarter century. Ivan's initial successes turned to defeat when Poland gained most of Livonia in 1582, and Russia lost its territory in the Gulf of Finland and west of Lake Ladoga, including the cities of Yam, Kaporia, and Karelia (Kexholm) to Sweden in 1585.

Ivan IV "the Terrible" ruled Muscovy with a violent and sometimes unbalanced hand. His victims were not only members of the nobility but also members of his family, including his eldest son, whom he killed in a fit of rage.

Whereas Russian expansion in the east had been successful, greatly expanding the size of Russia, Ivan's efforts in the west had turned to humiliating defeat. Access to the Baltic had been denied, nevertheless Russia was able to benefit from the discovery of a new route to the White Sea that had been opened up by English explorers and merchants in the 1550s. The port of Archangel was subsequently founded in 1584 on the mouth of the Dvina River.

On the death of Ivan IV in 1584, Boris Godunov acted as regent to Ivan's weak son Fyodor I, until the latter's death in 1598. Godunov continued to advance into Siberia, while waging a successful campaign in the northwest, thus winning back territory on the eastern Baltic coast, which Ivan had previously lost to Sweden during the Livonian War.

FRENCH DESIGNS

Louis XIV, king of France from 1643 to 1715. After 1661 he assumed absolute power, declaring "L'état c'est moi" ("I am the state").

"Every time that I fill a high office, I make one hundred men discontented and one ungrateful."
Louis XIV, known as the *Sun King*

Louis XIV symbolized the reassertion of royal power and divine right when he assumed power in 1661. The development of absolutism as an idealized political system coincided with the French struggle for European hegemony. However, any attempt at achieving ascendancy was predicated upon a reformed and strengthened France. The monarchy grew stronger by using royal agents *(intendants)* and the *Conseil du roi,* but at the expense of institutions traditionally checking royal power, the Estates-General and the Paris Parlement. The Gallicanization of the church, together with an assault on Jansenists and Huguenots, centralized religion, making the church a powerful instrument of state. The crown extended control over the economy through rules and regulations and Colbert's mercantilism. Académies (Académie Française), providing the environment for artists and writers like Poussin, Racine, and Corneille, were established to promote standards in the arts and sciences. The army was reorganized by Le Tellier and Louvois. The new France was epitomized by the building of Versailles, an expression of power, might, and authority. The centralizing absolution, combined with large natural resources and a population of twenty million, gave Louis XIV an excellent base for a carefully orchestrated foreign policy. His military objectives were limited and aimed at the security of France's frontiers. Weak borders, even protected by Vauban's fortresses, could readily be invaded through the Spanish Netherlands, Lorraine, and from Italy. The thought that Habsburg possessions might be united (Spain and Austria encircling France) was a nightmare. Louis's foreign policy comprised various means: legal argument over the réunions to obtain Alsace, Lorraine, Flanders, and Franche Comté; diplomacy resulting in the purchase of Dunkirk from England (1662); the use of subsidies to secure an alliance (1672–Sweden against the Dutch); and aggressive combat in the War of Devolution, fought to successfully acquire several towns in the Spanish Netherlands and the Franche Comté in 1668, and that against the Dutch Republic in 1672. The first ended in the Treaty of Aix-la-Chapelle, whereby Louis retained towns in the Spanish Netherlands such as Oudenarde, Courtrai, and Ath; in 1670, France occupied Lorraine. The Franco-Dutch War engendered an anti-French coalition, including the Dutch, England, Austria, Spain, and Brandenburg, which forced the Treaties of Nymwegen (1678). France lost certain towns in the north but finally won Franche Comté. By now, Louis had achieved more secure frontiers, and he was arguably at the height of his power. Two further wars dominated Louis's reign. The French seizure of Zweibruck and Strasbourg (réunions) occasioned the War of the League of Augsburg. This anti-French League was fought both in Europe and overseas colonies. The following Treaty of Ryswick (1697) compelled France to surrender most of her gains since 1678, but she retained Alsace and Strasbourg. The outbreak of the War of Spanish Succession (1702) again generated a large anti-French coalition. The Treaties of Utrecht (1713–1715) ended the long war, and France managed to acquire Barcelonnette, thereby securing her Italian border. Taken together, Louis's wars secured French frontiers, but their cost was enormous and a burden on the French people.

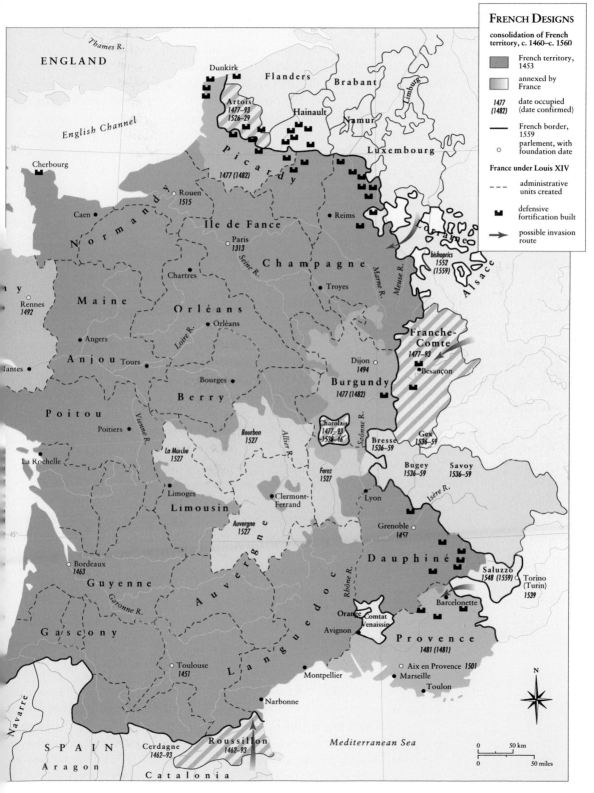

FRENCH DESIGNS

consolidation of French
territory, c. 1460–c. 1560

French territory,
1453

annexed by
France

1477   date occupied
(1482)   (date confirmed)

———   French border,
1559

○   parlement, with
foundation date

France under Louis XIV

- - - -   administrative
units created

defensive
fortification built

→   possible invasion
route

ENGLAND

Thames R.

Dunkirk

Flanders   Brabant

English Channel

Artois
1477–93
1526–29

Hainault   Limburg

Namur

Luxembourg

Cherbourg

P i c a r d y

Lorraine

bishoprics
1552
(1559)

Caen

Rouen
1515

Reims

Alsace

Normandy

Ile de Fance

Paris
1313

Champagne

Chartres

Seine R.

Troyes

Marne R.

Meuse R.

Rennes
1492

Maine

Orléans

Orléans

Loire R.

Franche-
Comte
1477–93

Angers

Anjou   Tours

Bourges

Berry

Dijon
1494

Besançon

Nantes

Poitou

Poitiers

Vienne R.

La Marche
1527

Bourbon
1527

Allier R.

Burgundy
1477 (1482)

Charolais
1477–93
1538–16

Saône R.

Bresse
1536–59

Gex
1536–59

La Rochelle

Forez
1527

Bugey
1536–59

Savoy
1536–59

Limoges

Limousin

Clermont-
Ferrand

Lyon

Isère R.

Bordeaux
1463

Guyenne

Auvergne
1527

Grenoble
1457

Dauphiné

Saluzzo
1548 (1559)

Torino
(Turin)
1539

Garonne R.

Auvergne

Rhône R.

Barcelonette

Gascony

Languedoc

Orange

Comtat
Venaissin

Provence
1481 (1481)

Navarre

Toulouse
1451

Avignon

Aix en Provence *1501*

Marseille

Toulon

N

Montpellier

Narbonne

SPAIN

Cerdagne
1462–93

Roussillon
1462–93

Mediterranean Sea

0   50 km

0   50 miles

Aragon

Catalonia

THE BALTIC BALANCE

After 1660, the Baltic region enjoyed an extended period of peace. Monarchs concentrated upon French ambitions and warfare and the conflict between Habsburgs and Ottomans. Sweden had achieved great power but now faced the problems of matching her limited economic and population resources with the responsibilities of governing and defending her recently acquired territories, thereby turning her into a "subsidy-hunting power." Russia was relatively backward and focused her foreign policy on the Black Sea, while Poland was weakened by the magnates' *liberum veto*, devastated by war, and intent on rebuilding the economy and developing her Baltic trade. Brandenburg-Prussia was to be drawn into French conflicts, while Denmark was internally reforming under an absolute monarchy and was too weak to confront Sweden. Nevertheless, all the old causes of resentment remained to be solved. Denmark sought to eradicate the threat of Holstein-Gottorp, the duchy straddling the south of Jutland that was allied to Sweden. Furthermore, Danish statesmen dreamed of regaining Scania to control the Sound and destroy Sweden's maritime hegemony. Brandenburg harbored jealousy of Swedish control of the Oder River in western Pomerania and resentment over loss of custom revenue from a 1653 treaty with Sweden. Brandenburg had designs on much of the Baltic littoral, Poland was eyeing Livonia, and ultimately Russian ambitions in the Gulf of Finland would conflict with Swedish interests.

A Swedish ship sails into action against the combined fleets of Russia and Poland at the Battle of Oland, in the long struggle to dominate the Baltic.

In this situation, Sweden became dependent on French subsidies and was obliged to invade Brandenburg in 1675; her defeat at Fehrbellin by a force half her size was a severe blow to Sweden's military prestige and a portent for the future. When Denmark invaded Scania and defeated the Swedish Navy at Kjöge Bay (1677), Sweden was lucky to have Louis XIV intervene in the peace treaties, whereby Sweden kept all her empire, even western Pomerania, just captured by Brandenburg. Despite a number of vicissitudes in Swedish-Danish relations, Sweden managed to avert war, changed her political system into an absolute monarchy, and reformed the army, allowing her to defend her army without French subsidies, essential since Louis was now an ally of Denmark. By 1700, foreign affairs once again dominated the region, with Peter the Great of Russia seeking outlets in the Baltic and allying with Saxony/Poland, and Denmark against Sweden. Charles XII of Sweden began the Great Northern War with an attack on Denmark and then crushed the Russians at Narva. Despite his brilliance as a general, by 1713 the forces ranged against him proved too much. Onslaughts by Denmark, Russia, Prussia, and Hannover were destroying the empire, and Charles XII's death at Frederickshald in 1718 further weakened the Swedish position. Finally, British-French diplomacy helped achieve the peace treaties at Stockholm (Hannover, Prussia) and Nystadt (Russia). Hannover gained Bremen and Verden, Brandenburg won Further Pomerania, and Russia received Karelia, Ingria, Livonia, and Estonia. Russia was now the leading power in the Baltic but chose not to become dominant, having interests outside the Baltic. Franco-British interference was to ensure that there would be no successor power in the Baltic.

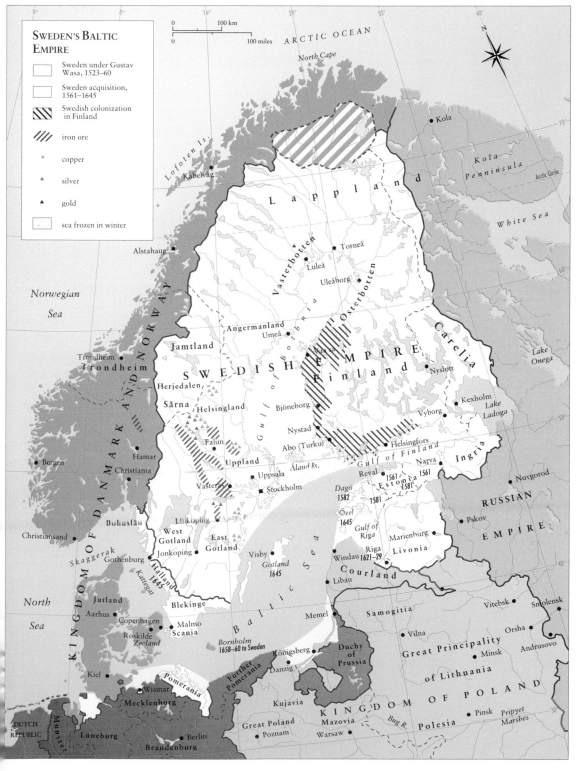

SWEDEN'S BALTIC EMPIRE

Sweden under Gustav Wasa, 1523–60

Sweden acquisition, 1561–1645

Swedish colonization in Finland

iron ore

copper

silver

gold

sea frozen in winter

ARCTIC OCEAN

North Cape

Kola

Kola Penninsula

Arctic Circle

Lofoten Is.

Kabelvåg

Lappland

White Sea

Alstahaug

Torneå

Luleå

Uleåborg

Vasterbotten

Norwegian Sea

Österbotten

Carelia

Trondheim

Angermanland

Umeå

Wasa

SWEDISH EMPIRE

Finland

Nyslott

Lake Onega

Jamtland

Helsingland

Björneborg

Vyborg

Kexholm

Lake Ladoga

Herjedalen

Särna

Falun

Nystad

Abo (Turku)

Helsingfors

Ingria

Bergen

Hamar

Christiania

Uppland

Åland Is.

Gulf of Finland

Narva

RUSSIAN

Uppsala

Reval

1561

Novgorod

Vasteras

Stockholm

Estonia 1561

1581

EMPIRE

Dagö 1582

1581

Boushän

Llikoping

Ösel 1645

Pskov

Christiansand

West Gotland

East Gotland

Visby

Gotland 1645

Gulf of Riga

Marienburg

Livonia

Jonkoping

Windau 1621–29

Riga

Gothenburg

Courland

Libau

Vitebsk

Smolensk

Jutland

Memel

Samogitia

Orsha

Andrusovo

Aarhus

Copenhagen

Malmo

Scania

Vilna

Minsk

North Sea

Bornholm 1658–60 to Sweden

Königsberg

Duchy of Prussia

Great Principality

Roskilde

Zeeland

Danzig

of Lithuania

Kiel

Pomerania

Further Pomerania

Kujavia

of POLAND

Pinsk

Pripyet Marshes

Wismar

Great Poland

Mazovia

Bug R.

Polesia

DUTCH REPUBLIC

Lüneburg

Mecklenburg

Berlin

Poznam

Warsaw

Brandenburg

KINGDOM OF DANMARK AND NORWAY

Baltic Sea

Blekinge

Halland 1645

Kattegat

Skaggerak

Bohuslän

PART VI: THE IDEA OF STATE

The Battle of Edgehill in October 1642, during the English Civil War, was a seven-year struggle that culminated with the overthrow of the monarchy, completed by public execution of King Charles I in January 1649.

During the seventeenth, eighteenth, and nineteenth centuries, the European peoples sought to construct modern states based upon more than a royal household and court. States developed into a broad spectrum of institutions—political, legal, military, and administrative—to regulate society. These new states sometimes came to acknowledge or claim to represent their people politically. The inhabitants of each state developed their own explicit identities, which reduced or eliminated differences among them but distinguished them from peoples governed by other states. Societies were transformed economically by changing modes of production, maritime trade routes, and other means of distribution, leading to different concentrations of wealth. Institutions of state had to govern during these developments and were often influenced by diverse social classes or dominant elites. The historical formation of modern states was accompanied by a number of important processes. All states claimed to be democratic, even if they were not, and most peoples attempted to broaden the political consensus and to limit arbitrary or absolute rule. Changing economic organizations developed the commercialization of agriculture and investment in capitalist endeavors, and the growth of industrial societies was eventually dominated by the factory system. States and the societies they governed felt themselves to possess a unique common identity based on cultural, linguistic, religious, historical or other factors, such as loyalty to a particular constitution. In sum, these were "nation-states" despite the existence of centrifugal ethnic groups such as Bretons in France, Basques in Spain, and the chaos of east and central Europe. Governments also presided over societies showing a diversified class system, which could threaten national unity. Class was the preeminent socioeconomic form in societies industrializing under capitalist economic conditions. Hence, class and class antagonism possessed major political importance. Assuming that the state favors the interest of one class above others, then dominated and exploited classes might seek change through democratic means or by violence. Socialist states have claimed to eradicate class divisions by acting in the interest of one class to destroy class differences. Hence, class conflict can result in events like the 1917 Russian Revolution, or, to a lesser extent, aspects of the 1789 French Revolution. Such events involve the state's exercising control on behalf of all people over the capitalist economy in order to socialize it. Therefore, all modern states are characterized by democratization, industrialization, nationalism, class tensions, and socialism.

While most European states were moving toward the alleged centralized efficiency of absolutist monarchies, the system of estates of the realm or parliaments continued and developed in northwestern Europe, in the Low Countries and Great Britain. Both powers were great trading countries, the Low Countries taking first place. The rapid expansion of sea trade enriched enterprising citizens, both gentry and middle class, who were capable of playing a political role and defending their own interests, which often differed from the monarch or governing authorities. Several analysts have perceived a link between the Protestant Reformation and early capitalist industry and trade. R. H. Tawney in *Religion and the Rise of Capitalism* (1926) argued that individualism and the thrift of

Calvinist Protestantism nurtured industrial organization and an efficient work-force in northern Europe. He therefore moved and developed the ideas of Max Weber's *The Protestant Ethic and the Spirit of Capitalism*. This book argued that the ideological stage for the rise of capitalism had been prepared by Calvinist religious doctrines, especially predestination. Indeed, Weber thought that Roman Catholicism's hostility toward lending money for profit was contradicted by the Protestant conviction that wealth was a godly award bestowed upon the diligent and frugal. In the northern Low Countries, Protestantism took hold in areas resenting the fact that Roman Catholic Spain threatened traditional liberties. The Dutch Revolt protected local independence against central government, despite the dominant position of Holland among the seven provinces of the United Provinces. The new republic, whose existence was ratified by the 1648 Treaty of Westphalia, was an early form of liberalism and federalism. Legislative power was entrusted to each member province that appointed a jurist (pensionary) in charge of administration and a *stathouder*, the president of the province. Federal power was in the hands of the Estates-General, with delegates elected by the provincial estates. A Council of State controlled the army and exchequer. Mirroring local politics, a federal jurist (grand pensionary) and a *stathouder* were appointed. This situation was complicated by the grand pensionary, who was supported by leading merchants supporting autonomy for Holland confronting the *stathouder*, the Prince of Orange, who had the backing of the lower classes, peasants, and sailors, convinced Calvinists, who desired a firm, highly centralized state.

In Britain, tradition affirmed that the king was subject to the law, and he could not raise new taxes nor pass legislation without the consent of Parliament. When King Charles I, a convinced absolutist, confronted Parliament, imprisoned members, and ruled for eleven years without Parliament, revolution was assured. In the subsequent civil war, fought in England, Scotland, and Ireland, the king faced an alliance between a group of aristocrats and the prosperous middle classes. The latter were often innovating landlords, using experimental agricultural techniques and efficient business management, who were enclosing land and dispossessing small occupiers and cottagers, turning them into rural wage labor, the victims of agricultural capitalism. In the landlord's eyes, the king championed the old economic order, making him an obstacle to progress. Furthermore, support for the Roundheads, the Parliamentary Army, developed strongly among Calvinists and other dissenting sects, such as the Levellers. The Protestant faith was adopted by numerous middle class, artisan, and merchant families who saw in the monarch, the personification of Roman Catholicism, an old enemy recalling Tudor wars with Spain. The king's defeat in 1647 and his execution by a legally elected legislature in 1649 ushered in a Cromwellian republican dictatorship (the Commonwealth), ironically ruling with a truncated Rump Parliament, all ending in 1660. This first revolution, together with example of the United Provinces, showed Europe the possibility of creating republics; this demonstration of anti-absolutist politics was ignored. The Restoration's attempt to return to absolutism under Charles II and James II failed, leading to the second Glorious Revolution, when important aristocrats invited William of Orange to invade England in order to preserve English liberties by ousting his father-in-law. William's military success was rewarded by Parliament, deciding that England should be ruled by William and Mary. The subsequent Bill of Rights embodied several principles, including: the power of law superseded that of the king; Parliament had to annually consent to levying taxes, and Parliament decided monarchical succession. Now Britain had a state based upon constitutional monarchy. The liberal political attitudes in Britain and the United Provinces provided the climate for producing leading antiabsolutist thinkers such as Hobbes, Locke, and the Dutch jurist Grotius.

The 1789 French Revolution introduced a new type of state, producing a political earthquake, thereby undermining a Europe of absolutist states. A series of revolutionary ideas involving sovereignty of the people, republicanism, and several versions of democracy were offered to Europe and the world, sometimes on the point of a bayonet. France demonstrated that the state should act in the interests of the people, the nation at large; that rule by inherited privilege and lineage was immoral; and, that monarchy was evil and monarchs should be deposed, by violence if necessary. These novel ideas challenged dynastic rule, and developments within the revolution confronted states with notions of direct democracy and egalitarian economic policies. By 1791, the French state was constitutional, republican, representative, and essentially middle class. The Constitution included the separation of powers derived from Montesquieu's view of how the British constitution operated. Tom Paine, whose pamphlet *Common Sense* was so significant in the American War of Independence, became a member of the French legislature and wrote *The Rights of Man* (1791). This defense of the French Revolution became an analysis of discontent in Europe and a prescription for the sins of arbitrary government, including poverty, illiteracy, unemployment, and war. The book included radical ideas demanding popular education, poor relief, old age pensions, and public works for the unemployed. The original bourgeois Assembly eventually incorporated the *sans-culottes* (the urban poor) and was transformed into a direct democracy. Here, delegates to the Assembly were defined as mandate holders only and could be replaced at any time. Thus, the *sans-culottes* sought to extend forms of democratic control over the representative sate. The impact of war and the excesses of the Jacobin Committee of Public Safety led to a conservative countercoup, with stability being organized by the Directory, a small oligarchy dependent on military support. Its incompetence and financial mismanagement opened the way for an autocratic military dictatorship, achieved by Napoleon's coup d'état in October 1799. The resultant attempt to conquer Europe was eventually ended at the Battle of Waterloo in 1815.

After the ordeal of the Revolutionary and Napoleonic Wars, reason ordained that Europe would not return to the pre-1789 political and social status quo. A new means of keeping the peace through international arbitration was essential. Europe was to be reconstructed, based on the two principles of legitimacy and the balance of power. Legitimate sovereigns would have their lands returned and those remaining unclaimed–former republics (Genoa), free cities, or church principalities—would be distributed to maintain the balance of power. These achievements made by the Congress of Vienna (1815) would be guaranteed by a Concert of Europe, whereby monarchs would meet regularly to discuss common interests and generate policies to solve common problems. Congresses were held at Aix-la-Chapelle (1818), Troppau (1820), Laibach (1821), and Verona (1822). Monarchs were interested in curbing revolutionary movements, whether liberal or nationalist. The power of conservative monarchs to restrain these new ideas resulted in major confrontations on city streets across Europe in 1848, after which rulers had to be more flexible in order to survive. Great Britain wisely extended the franchise over a number of years, constantly widening the political consensus, but countries such as Russia and Austria-Hungary remained archconservatives. The tradition of congresses continued with the Congress of Paris (1856) ending the Crimean War and the Congress of Berlin (1878) concerning reorganization in the Balkans.

An unknown artist recorded this scene of unrest outside a factory gate in Vienna on March 13, 1843, in the same year such events were repeated many times across Europe.

A major event of the mid nineteenth century was the exercise in German state-building. The series of wars creating the German empire (1871) was predicated upon an alliance between German industrial and commercial interests linked to the Prussian state bureaucracy and its military and agricultural aristocracy (the alliance of iron and rye). However, despite the Kaiser's retention of some remnants of absolutism, the state was constrained within an identifiable legal framework. This Rechtsstaat established a constitutional monarchy, even if it was not accountable to the elected representatives in the Reichstag. The nature of class and political alliances in Germany differed from other countries. The accommodation of Prussian absolutism with capitalist industrialization was confusing. The authoritarian and patriarchal legacy of Bismarck saw a Kaiser's state bestowing sickness, old age, and disability insurance on a working class with its large Social Democratic Party, which also quite happily signed up for war in 1914.

Capitalist industrialization in Russia included an intense rural-urban drift where cheap and abundant labor fueled an industrial revolution. Rapid industrialization and urbanization swelled a working class that suffered severe hardships. The impact of war on an inflexible and dysfunctional tsarist autocracy allowed Lenin and the Bolsheviks to manipulate the proletariat and establish a dictatorship of the working class (1917). However, this rapidly turned into a dictatorship by the party over the working class, eventually succumbing to Stalin's dictatorship over the party itself. In the aftermath of war, Lenin allowed a degree of economic freedom through the New Economic Policy, while consolidating political control over the country and by banning factionalism within the party. The surge toward monolithic and totalitarian power was noted, aided, and abetted by Stalin who, as Commissar for Nationalities, carried out a bloodbath against his own Georgian people. Stalin's accession to power established a new style of dictatorship predicated upon economic planning, the purging of actual or potential dissidents, psychological terror, and the gulags. However, the application of force in all policies allowed the Communists to expand industry to such an extent that the Soviet Union had the capacity to bear the major burden of the Nazi onslaught during the Second World War.

ENGLISH CIVIL WAR

Below center: Cromwell at the head of his victorious cavalry after the battle of Marston Moor, in July 1644, a victory for the parliamentary forces that seriously weakened the Royalist cause in northern England.

Against the background of science and reason that arose from the Renaissance and Reformation, the causes of the English Civil War were those of a growing hostility to the Stuart monarchy, embodied in the persons of Charles I and his French wife, Henrietta Maria. This hostility was based upon: constitutional resistance to absolutist monarchy, posited upon the principle of the "Divine Right of Kings"; resistance against centralism from county and urban radicals and borough representation in Parliament; and Puritanism and contempt for Laudism—High Church innovations that supported the privileges of monarchy and the principles of clerical authority over the laity. In the background there lay a general fear that England would return to Catholicism. Along with the intellectual stimulus of the Renaissance and Reformation, with a simultaneous growth in science and reason, was the spread of lay education in England, which resulted in the rise of an independent-minded and self-confident social group often influenced by the rise of English Puritanism.

The real issue was the rivalry between Parliament and the absolutist monarchy with the rise of the gentry and professional classes in a socioeconomic revolution that was based upon social mobility, set against the weakening of the feudal aristocracy, the growth of capitalism in agriculture, trade, and industry, and a general increase in population.

When Charles raised his standard at Nottingham in August 1642, the two opposing armies were more or less equal in number, although the Royalists were superior in cavalry until the formation of the New Model Army in 1645.

ENGLISH CIVIL WAR,
1642–43

controlled by the king throughout the campaign of 1643

conquered by the king during the campaign of 1643

controlled by Parliament throughout the campaign of 1643

conquered by Parliament during the campaign of 1643

Eastern Association

The king's generals (Prince Rupert, Hopton, and Newcastle) were less able than those of Parliament (Pym, Fairfax, and Cromwell) in terms of organizational and fighting abilities. Furthermore, with time the aristocratic officers began to quarrel among themselves.

Charles could successfully fight a short war, but as the war developed, Parliament began to win the upper hand, maintaining support and power in the richer and more populous southeast of England, especially in London, while Royalist support mostly came from the north and west of England and from Wales. Parliament therefore held access to the chief ports, the sea, and the navy, thus maintaining an advantage over the Royalists, by maintaining an administrative center in London, good communications, and unified command. This position was enhanced by taxation, the availability of manpower, and a constant supply of war materials. The key to parliamentary success was the religious, puritanical fervor, discipline, training, and the development of a cavalry that became numerically superior with the creation of the disciplined and highly professional New Model Army.

The campaigns of 1642 brought small parliamentary gains in the northwest, but were countered by heavy losses in the southwest, so that it seemed certain that the king would win in 1643, until Parliament won the support of the Scottish Covenanters. Parliamentary victory at Marston Moor on July 2, 1644, followed by the overwhelming victory by the New Model Army at Naseby on June 14, 1645, ensured parliamentary success, although the war would continue for a further year and a half, with the king taking refuge with the Scots, only to be handed over as a prisoner of Parliament in January 1647.

The king would later escape from the army to the Isle of Wight, where he negotiated with the Scots, promising to establish Presbyterianism in England in return for their support. This led to the Second Civil War, more a series of royalist risings, backed by a Scottish invasion of England, which was repulsed by Cromwell. Charles was executed in January 1649.

The Third Civil War began in Ireland in 1649, when Cromwell suppressed a major rising of Catholics and Royalists at Drogheda and Wexford. Ireland was subjugated, and a subsequent rising in Scotland was put down at Dunbar in September 1650 and utterly routed at Worcester in September 1651, which resulted in Charles II's flight abroad. A republic had been created whose power extended throughout the British Isles until the monarchy was restored in 1660.

> "You have sat too long here for any good you have been doing. Depart, I say, and let us have done with you. In the name of God, go!" *Cromwell*, dismissing Parliament, April 1653

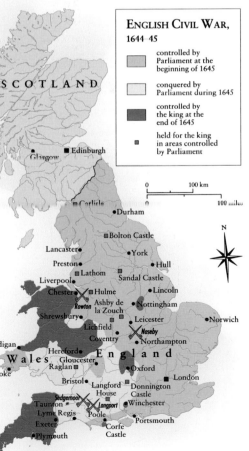

ENGLISH CIVIL WAR, 1644–45

controlled by Parliament at the beginning of 1645

conquered by Parliament during 1645

controlled by the king at the end of 1645

held for the king in areas controlled by Parliament

SCOTLAND

Glasgow • Edinburgh

Carlisle • Durham

Bolton Castle

Lancaster • York

Preston • Hull

Liverpool • Lathom • Sandal Castle

Chester • Hulme • Lincoln

Rowton • Ashby de la Zouch • Nottingham

Shrewsbury • Leicester • Norwich

Lichfield • Naseby

Cardigan • Coventry • Northampton

Hereford • Wales Gloucester • England

Pembroke • Raglan • Oxford

Bristol • Langford • Donnington Castle

Sedgemoor • House • London

Taunton • Langport • Winchester

Lyme Regis • Poole • Portsmouth

Exeter • Corfe Castle

Plymouth

0   100 km
0   100 miles

N

REPUBLICS OF TRADE

"The prodigious increase of the Netherlands in their domestic and foreign trade, riches, and multitude of shipping, is the envy of the present and may be the wonder of the future."
F. Charpentier, 1664

The Dutch revolt against Spain lasted from 1559 to 1648, but in effect Spain recognized the independence of the seven provinces in 1609. In a world of absolutist centralization, the Dutch republic emerged as a federation, each province retaining its sovereignty and local self-government, and was unique, basing its wealth on commerce and industry rather than agriculture. The republic's government was aristocratic, but the separate provinces were suspicious of the House of Orange, which provided necessary military leadership. Constant friction between *stathouder* and provinces resulted in a *stathouder*less period from 1650 to 1672. In a violent and insecure world, the republic soon came to blows with France (1672–1678 and 1689–1713) and England in three naval wars: 1652–1653, 1665–1667, and 1672–1674. Conflicts with England concerned trade after the English Commonwealth passed the 1651 Navigation Act, forbidding the Dutch from acting as transit merchants in English trade with Europe or overseas. During the final war, the Dutch gave full power to William III of Orange as *stathouder* to combat a Franco-British alliance. A major reason for Dutch survival was her trading interests, prosperity originally being dependent on links with the Baltic, France, and the Iberian peninsula.

The Dutch East Indies Company, constituted in 1602, established bases in India, Ceylon, and Indonesia, the major trading center being Batavia in Java. The European demand for spices and pepper allowed the monopolistic company to make huge profits when its fleet returned annually. Further wealth accrued from cessions of territory by native Javan Sultans, and on the other side of the world the West India Company, founded in 1621, traded in commodities and slaves. Taken together, the Dutch cities became the major entrepôts of Europe, especially Amsterdam and Rotterdam, which handled about 50 percent of world trade, while the Bourse at Antwerp was the center of the European money market. So significant was the republic in European politics that three major peace treaties were signed on its soil: Nymwegen, Ryswick, and Utrecht.

During this period, regarded as the Dutch Golden Age (1609–1713), a large measure of religious toleration allowed Calvinists, Lutherans, Roman Catholics, Anabaptists, and Jews to coexist in a stability that encouraged trade and the arts. Ideas were readily debated, and Hugo Grotius became the progenitor of international law, while Spinoza found peace to investigate philosophy and science. However, the Golden Age is mainly remembered for its painting, resting upon local patronage. The Flemish School developed, with Rubens and Van Dyck painting landscapes and seascapes, while the Dutch School, including Frans Hals, Vermeer and Rembrandt, created portraits and group paintings. Architecture, however, remained low key, except for the immense variety of roof gables.

The republic had relations with England other than war. In 1688, William II became King of England by virtue of his marriage to Mary II Stuart. Thereafter, Dutch internal affairs were managed by resident councilors, and arguably this led to stagnation through competition with the English East India Company and the cost of war, especially with France.

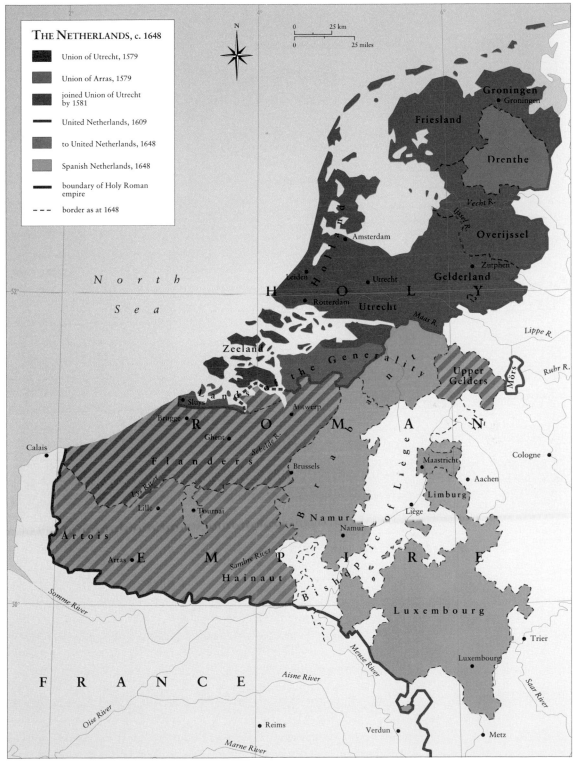

THE NETHERLANDS, c. 1648

- Union of Utrecht, 1579
- Union of Arras, 1579
- joined Union of Utrecht by 1581
- United Netherlands, 1609
- to United Netherlands, 1648
- Spanish Netherlands, 1648
- boundary of Holy Roman empire
- border as at 1648

N

0   25 km
0   25 miles

North

Sea

Groningen
• Groningen

Friesland

Drenthe

Vecht R.

IJssel R.

Overijssel

• Zutphen

Amsterdam

Leiden •

Utrecht •

Gelderland

H   O   L   Y

Rotterdam •

Utrecht

Maas R.

Lippe R.

Zeeland

the Generality

Upper
Gelders

Ruhr R.

Mörs

Lands

Sluys •

Antwerp •

R   O   M   A   N

Brügge •

Ghent •

Schelde R.

Brabant

Cologne •

Calais
•

Flanders

Lys River

Brussels •

Maastricht •

• Aachen

Lille •

• Tournai

Limburg

Bishopric of Liège

Liège •

Artois

B   Namur

N   M

Arras • E

Sambre River

P   I   R   E

Namur •

Hainaut

Luxembourg

F   R   A   N   C   E

Somme River

Aisne River

Meuse River

• Trier

Luxembourg •

Suar River

Oise River

• Reims

Verdun •

Marne River

• Metz

REVOLUTION IN FRANCE

This engraving by Carnavalet shows the execution of Louis XVI on January 21, 1793.

"L'immoralité est la base du despotisme comme la vertu est l'essence de la République."

"Wickedness is the root of despotism as virtue is the essence of the republic."
Maximilien Robespierre, Revolutionary leader

The French Revolution of 1789–1799 would fuel the main political and social forces of the nineteenth century: democracy, liberalism, socialism, and nationalism. It would result in a complete break with the feudal legal structure and the Ancien Régime.

Always open to controversial historical debate, causes of the French Revolution can be put down to demographic, economic, and social change in the eighteenth century. The failure of wages to keep pace with price rises and a recession from the 1770s were exacerbated by poor harvests in 1787 and 1788. In February 1787 efforts to reform the financial system and remove the budget deficit introduced by the king's ministers Calonne and Necker backfired and resulted in further resistance from the aristocracy who, in 1788, in the hope of protecting their own rights, called for an Estates-General, made up of the three estates, Clergy, Nobility, and the Third Estate, which met in Versailles for the first time since 1614.

Opposition from the middle-class representatives of the Third Estate would prove too strong, especially when they won the support of the Parish priests. Imbued by the ideas of the eighteenth-century *philosophes,* who advocated social and political reform, the Third Estate, led by Abbé Sièyes, established a National Assembly, La Constituante, on June 20, in the Jeu de Paume tennis court at Versailles, and demanded constitutional reform. The formation of a Committee of Public Safety, the creation of a National Guard, and the symbolic fall of the Bastille on July 14 turned revolt into revolution.

The subsequent Grande Peur, the great fear of unrest in the countryside, throughout the summer of 1789 led to revolutionary decrees, especially the Abolition of Feudalism and the Declaration of the Rights of Man.

Although the Revolution was not, in its origins, antimonarchical, and the Constituante had tried to establish a monarchical regime whereby executive and legislative powers could be shared with the king, the situation changed with the king's abortive escape from Paris to Varennes on the night of June 20, 1791. Fears that the Revolution was in danger were exacerbated by support for the monarchy from Austria, birthplace of Queen Marie Antoinette. On April 20, 1792, France declared war on Austria, as the Austrian emperor and the king of Prussia prepared a joint invasion, and marched on Paris, defeating revolutionary armies on their route, until they were turned back at the Battle of Valmy on September 20, 1792.

The royal family was imprisoned following an attack on their home in the Tuileries Palace. Louis XVI was guillotined on January 21, 1793. External threats were enjoined by a need for internal security; this led to further repression and to the Terror, especially under Robespierre. In the meantime the revolutionary armies continued to win battles abroad, occupying Belgium, the Rhineland, Savoy, and Nice by April 1793.

In the spring of 1793 a coalition between Austria, Prussia, and Great Britain led to further French defeats; then a year later the French defeated the Austrians at Fleurus and reoccupied Belgium (June 26, 1794). In the meantime Robespierre was overthrown on July 27-28, 1794 (Thermidor). After his execution the Republicans would return to the liberal principles of the Declaration of the Rights of Man.

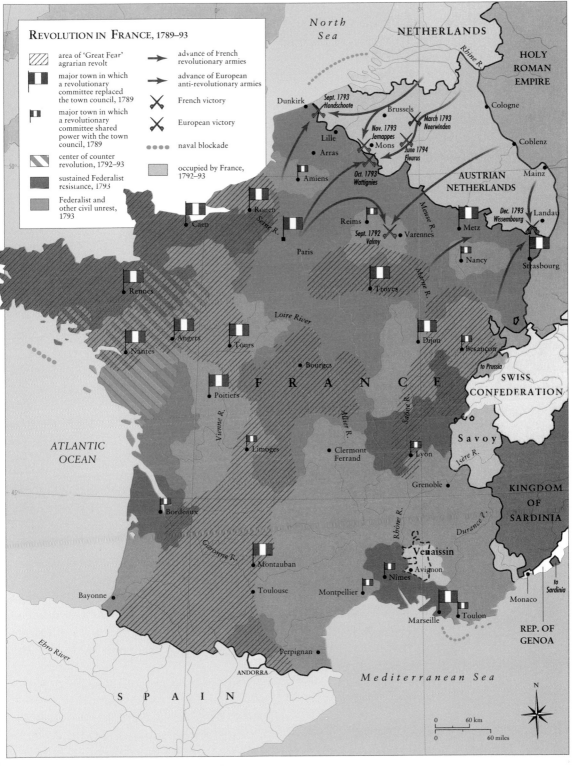

REVOLUTION IN FRANCE, 1789–93

- area of 'Great Fear' agrarian revolt
- major town in which a revolutionary committee replaced the town council, 1789
- major town in which a revolutionary committee shared power with the town council, 1789
- center of counter revolution, 1792–93
- sustained Federalist resistance, 1793
- Federalist and other civil unrest, 1793
- advance of French revolutionary armies
- advance of European anti-revolutionary armies
- French victory
- European victory
- naval blockade
- occupied by France, 1792–93

North Sea

NETHERLANDS

HOLY ROMAN EMPIRE

Rhine R.

Dunkirk

Sept. 1793 Hondschoote

Brussels

March 1793 Neerwinden

Cologne

Nov. 1793 Jemappes

Mons

June 1794 Fleurus

Coblenz

Lille

Arras

AUSTRIAN NETHERLANDS

Amiens

Oct. 1793 Wattignies

Mainz

Caen

Rouen

Seine R.

Reims

Meuse R.

Metz

Dec. 1793 Wissembourg

Landau

Paris

Sept. 1792 Valmy

Varennes

Marne R.

Nancy

Strasbourg

Rennes

Troyes

Nantes

Angers

Tours

Loire River

Dijon

Besançon

to Prussia

SWISS CONFEDERATION

Poitiers

Bourges

F R A N C E

Vienne R.

Allier R.

Saône R.

Savoy

ATLANTIC OCEAN

Limoges

Clermont Ferrand

Lyon

Isère R.

Grenoble

KINGDOM OF SARDINIA

Bordeaux

Rhône R.

Durance R.

Garonne R.

Montauban

Venaissin

Avignon

Nîmes

to Sardinia

Monaco

Bayonne

Toulouse

Montpellier

Marseille

Toulon

REP. OF GENOA

Perpignan

ANDORRA

S P A I N

Ebro River

Mediterranean Sea

N

0   60 km
0   60 miles

THE NAPOLEONIC EMPIRE

This painting by Ingres, presented to the citizens of Liège after a state visit, shows Napoleon Bonaparte, at age 34, first consul in 1803, striking the pose that was to become almost his hallmark, although it was also a common artistic convention in portraits of the period.

By 1812, Napoleon reached the height of his power. France had expanded into Catalonia, the Low Countries, to the Rhine, and acquired parts of Italy and the Illyrian provinces on the Adriatic. Buttressed by family members ruling lands such as Spain, Westphalia, Naples, and other allied countries, this edifice dominated all Europe except Great Britain. The Code Napoleon, a mixture of Germanic customary law and Roman law, was introduced into a number of European countries, a form of "judicial imperialism." Belgium still retains the Code, which also became the model for the civil codes of Quebec Province, Canada, and many other parts of the world, including the state of Louisiana.

Despite the apparent stability and coherence of the empire, its foundations were seriously undermined by various flaws. First, French territorial aggrandizement was predicated upon the humiliation of other countries. The Treaty of Pressburg (December 1805), preceded by Austria's defeat at Austerlitz, forced Austria to cede her Italian possessions to France; Tyrol and the Vorarlberg went to Bavaria, with a financial penalty of forty million francs. After being defeated at Wagram (July 1980), Austria, again victimized by the Peace of Schönbrunn, was compelled to cede her Dalmatian territories directly to France; western Galicia was divided between Russia and the Grand Duchy of Warsaw; further lands were added to Illyria, Salzburg to Bavaria, Austria looted of eighty five million francs in reparation payment, and the Princess Marie-Louise was constrained to marry Napoleon.

Second, the sanctions imposed on Austria were mirrored by the ill-treatment of Prussia. By the Treaty of Tilsit (July 1807) between France and Prussia, the latter lost half of her territories: those west of the Elbe were taken to form the new states of Berg and Westphalia. Also, Prussian Poland was seized to create the Grand Duchy of Warsaw. The large financial penalty and the reduction of the Prussian army to 42,000 men rubbed salt into the wounds.

The dual maltreatment of Austria and Prussia served to commence administrative and military reform in these countries while they waited for an appropriate time to rejoin the fray.

Third, the Continental System was designed by France to prevent Great Britain from trading with other European nations. Its various decrees (Berlin, 1806; Milan, 1807) generated a British blockade producing important economic and military results. In November 1807, Portugal's refusal to join the System resulted in a French incursion, initiating the Peninsula War. The eventual guerrilla warfare waged by Spanish patriots together with Wellington's campaigns seriously drained the French army's resources. The system excluded many imports from Europe, and when Russia withdrew in 1810, Napoleon attacked the tsar in 1812.

The problems encountered by a war on two fronts in Spain and eastern Europe occasioned new allied declarations of war, with Austrians, Prussians, Russians, and Swedes advancing across Europe, and an invasion of France. The total exhaustion of the Napoleonic imperial system and military resulted in an enforced abdication in April 1814.

THE NAPOLEONIC EMPIRE, c. 1812

ruled directly by Napoleon

ruled by members of Napoleon's family

dependent state

N

0   200 km
0   200 miles

Arctic Circle

Iceland

ATLANTIC
OCEAN

Faeroe Is.
to Denmark

Shetland Is.

Bergen

Christiana

SWEDEN

Stockholm

Åland Is.

Gotland

Gothenburg

Baltic Sea

Finland
1809 to Russia

Helsingfors

St. Petersburg

Novgorod

Revel

Riga

Smolensk

Vilna

RUSSIAN
EMPIRE

Scotland

Edinburgh

North
Sea

DENMARK – NORWAY
United until 1814

Copenhagen

Ireland

Dublin

UNITED KINGDOM
OF GREAT BRITAIN
AND IRELAND

Helgoland
1807–14 to Br.

Hamburg

Bremen

to Sweden

REP. OF
DANZIG

PRUSSIA

Königsberg
East
Prussia

Bialystok
1807 to Russia

Wales

England

Amsterdam

1807–10
to Fr.

1810 to Fr.

Antwerp

Hanover

Berlin

Brandenburg

WESTPHALIA

GR. DUCHY
OF WARSAW

Warsaw

London

Brussels

Cologne

Erfurt

Silesia

Cracow

Galicia

Ternopol
1809 to Russia

Channel Is.

Paris

Frankfurt

CONFEDERATION
OF THE RHINE

Bohemia

Prague

AUSTRIAN
EMPIRE

1812 to Russia
Bessarabia

Orléans

Tours

Munich

Vienna

Moldavia

FRANCE

Bern

HELVETIA

Styria

Buda
(Ofen)

Pest

Transylvania

occupied by Russia

Lyon

Geneva
1798–1814 to Fr.

Milan

Carinthia

Hungary

Banat

Bucharest

Bordeaux

Turin

ITALY

Venice

Illyrian Provinces

OTTOMAN

Belgrade

Wallachia

Bulgaria

Toulouse

Marseille

LUCCA

Tuscany

Florence

Adriatic Sea

EMPIRE

Sofia

Constantinople

Cataloña
1808–13 to Fr.

Oporto

Barcelona

Corsica

Papal
States

Rome

MONTENEGRO

Macedonia

Aegean
Sea

Madrid

Balearic Is.

Minorca
1798–1802 to Br.

SARDINIA

NAPLES

Naples

Corfu
1807–14 to Fr.

Thessaly

SPAIN

Athens

Lisbon

PORTUGAL

Gibraltar
to Spain

Ceuta
to Spain

Oran

Algiers

Bona

Mediterranean   Sea

Tunis

SICILY

Palermo

Malta
1798 to Fr.
1800 to Br.

Ionian Is.

occupied by Britain

Crete

MOROCCO

ALGERIA

Tunisia

THE CONGRESS OF VIENNA

"It will be the province of ministers abroad, to inculcate in all quarters the importance of union, to the preservation of peace for which the powers have for so long and so gloriously contended, and to keep down as far as possible the spirit of local intrigue which has proved no less fatal to the repose of states than the personal ambitions of their sovereigns."
Viscount Catlereagh in a letter to the British ambassador to Vienna

With Louis XVIII restored to the French throne and Napoleon safely en route to Elba, peace was concluded between the Great Powers and France, with the signing of the First Treaty of Paris in May 1814. The congress was, therefore, an attempt by the Great Powers of Europe to make a constructive agreement for peace. Despite having been the enemy of the other European states, France was included in the Congress, because the other powers wanted to emphasize that normal relations between the French government and the rest of Europe had returned with the restoration of Louis XVIII. The idea was not to weaken Louis's position by humiliating France, which meant that France would be allowed to maintain the frontiers of 1792, although France would not recover her lost colonies. Nevertheless, France maintained Guadeloupe and most of her possessions in the West Indies and could maintain all her trading stations and commercial interests in India and fishing rights in the St. Lawrence and off Newfoundland. France had to reduce the size of her army, but was not required to disarm. France also had to surrender claims to territories conquered in Germany, Italy, Switzerland, and the Low Countries.

The Congress of Vienna was held between September 1814 and June 1815, and continued throughout the Hundred Days (March–June 1815) that followed Napoleon's return to France. It was signed on June 9, 1815.

Every state of Europe was represented, including the papacy, with the notable exception of the Ottoman empire. The decisions of the Congress were dominated by the Great Powers, whose chief representatives were Castlereagh and Wellington (Britain); Metternich and Gentz (Austria); Alexander I, Capodistrias, Nesselrode, and Stein (Russia); Hardenberg (Prussia); and Talleyrand (France).

The terms of the Second Treaty of Paris were harsher (November 20, 1815). France was offered her 1789 frontiers, and lost parts of Belgian territory and most of Savoy. France also had to return the art treasures that had been looted during the Napoleonic Wars and pay a war indemnity of 700 million francs and allow the allies to garrison her fortresses for five years.

The general principle of balance of power had been that the Great Powers should obtain the territory, or its equivalent, that each had held in 1805. Only Russia would obtain more by gaining a large part of Poland, including Warsaw, which British and Austrian opinion felt upset the balance of power.

Prussia gained Polish territory, half of Saxony and the Province of the Rhine. British interests concerned the creation of a central European bloc to provide security against French and Russian ambitions, leaving Austria as the dominant power in central Europe for the next fifty years and allowing Britain to relinquish her continental commitments. Austria gained Venetia and recovered Lombardy in Italy and became effective head of the German Federation.

Holland and Belgium were united into one short-lived kingdom, under Dutch rule. Britain would retain Helgoland, Malta, Mauritius, Trinidad, St. Lucia, Tobago, and the Cape of Good Hope and Ceylon, also gaining a protectorate over the Ionian Isles in the eastern Mediterranean.

The Congress of Vienna settled the peace of Europe for the next fifty years. It was a historical bridge between one period and another.

EUROPE AFTER THE TREATY OF VIENNA

— German Confederation

N

0   200 km

0   200 miles

Iceland
to Denmark

*Norwegian
Sea*

Arctic Circle

Finland

Faeroe Islands
to Denmark

Scotland

Edinburgh

*North
Sea*

Copenhagen

DENMARK

Baltic Sea

RUSSIAN
EMPIRE

IRELAND
Dublin ▪

GREAT
BRITAIN
England

London ▪

Wales

Hamburg

Amsterdam ▪

NETHERLANDS

Brussels ▪

HANNOVER

PRUSSIA

Berlin ●

Warsaw ●

REPUBLIC OF
CRACOW

ATLANTIC
OCEAN

Paris ▪

Loire R.

FRANCE

NEUCHATEL

BADEN

BAVARIA
Stuttgart ●
WURTTEMBERG

SAXONY

Prague ●

Vienna ▪

Buda ● ▪ Pest

Cracow ●

Hungary

AUSTRIAN EMPIRE

Transylvania

Danube R.

Moldavia

SWITZERLAND

SARDINIA

LOMBARDY
VENETIA

Illyrian Kingdom

military frontier

Wallachia

Bucharest ●

PARMA

Genoa ●

MODENA

Zara ▪

Adriatic Sea

OTTOMAN EMPIRE

Montenegro ●

Oporto ●

PORT.

ANDORRA

MASSA AND
CARRARA

LUCCA

Corsica

Florence ▪
TUSCANY

Rome ▪

PAPAL
STATES

Madrid ▪

Lisbon ●

SPAIN

Balearic Is.

SARDINIA

Naples ▪

KINGDOM OF THE
TWO SICILIES

Sicily

*Ionian Islands
to Great Britain*

*Aegean
Sea*

Athens ●

Gibraltar
to Great Britain

Algiers ▪

Tunis ▪

Mediterranean

Sea

Crete

MOROCCO

ALGERIA

TUNIS

STATE UNIFICATION

Prince Otto Eduard Leopold von Bismarck, prime minister of Prussia (1862-1890) and Chancellor of the German empire from 1871 until his resignation in March 1890.

In Germany and Italy, cultural unity provided a basis for political movements to unify a number of separate states into a larger whole. Existing small states Prussia and Piedmont-Sardinia were instrumental in achieving unification. Bismarck and Cavour were probably motivated more by the interests of their respective states than nationalism. Napoleon III favored a powerful Prussia in northern Germany and promoted Piedmontese expansion to include Lombady-Venetia, Parma, Modena, and Romagna within an Italian federation under papal presidency. This alliance, aimed at destroying Austrian power in Italy, triggered a war whereby the Franco-Piedmontese armies crushed the Austrians.

In June 1860, Garibaldi took a band of volunteers to Sicily. Historians debate his relationship with King Victor Emmanuel of Piedmont, who could have prevented the campaign. Garibaldi's success caused Cavour to invade the papal states, to prevent Garibaldi's invading Rome (garrisoned by France since 1848) to prevent French or Austrian intervention. The halting of Garibaldi at the Volturno was followed by plebiscites resulting in the union of Sicily, Naples, Umbria, and the

GERMAN UNIFICATION, 1815–71

- Prussia, 1815
- border of German Confederation, 1815
- Prussia gains by 1867
- border of North German confederation, 1867
- German states joining the confederation in 1871
- border of German empire, 1871
- German confederation invades Denmark, 1864
- Prussia invades Austria, 1866
- Prussia invades France, 1870
- battle

Marches of Ancona with Piedmont, leading to the proclamation of a united Italy at Turin in 1861. In 1866, Italy acquired Venice following a Prussian alliance against Austria, and after Prussia defeated France (1870), Italy entered and annexed Rome, confining the pope to Vatican City.

Prussian expansionism was based upon the policy of joining together her territorial blocs. In 1843, the German customs union was created, within which Prussia gained economic dominance. When Bismarck became chancellor (1862); a new realpolitik was introduced. In 1864, Austria and Prussia invaded Denmark over the Schleswig-Holstein Question and in 1865 took over the two duchies, with Prussia receiving Lauenburg. The victory preceded a war between Prussia and Austria in 1866 over Holstein and Prussian proposals reforming the German Confedration. The defeat of Austria and her German allies allowed Prussia to annex most opposing states north of the Main River and to form the North German Confederation. After Prussia defeated France (1870) and the annexation of Alsace-Lorraine, the south German states joined the Confederation to create the German Reich (1874).

Count Camillo Benso di Cavour was an army officer before he turned to politics, serving as prime minister of Piedmont in 1852 until 1859 and again in 1860 until 1861. He secured foreign support for the idea of Italian unity.

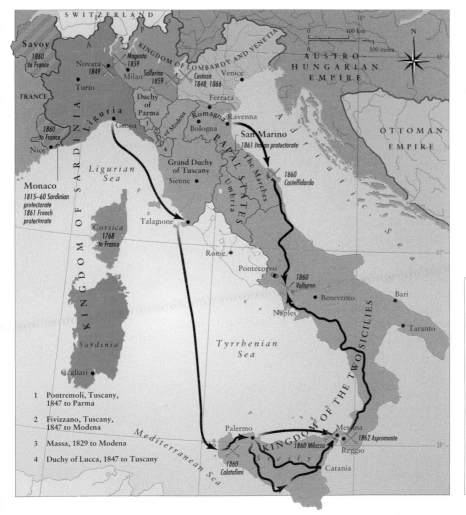

1 Pontremoli, Tuscany, 1847 to Parma

2 Fivizzano, Tuscany, 1847 to Modena

3 Massa, 1829 to Modena

4 Duchy of Lucca, 1847 to Tuscany

UNIFICATION OF ITALY, 1859–1870

- Kingdom of Sardinia, 1815
- annexed to Kingdom of Sardinia, 1859
- annexed to Kingdom of Italy, 1860
- annexed to Kingdom of Italy, 1866
- annexed to Kingdom of Italy, 1870
- → route of Victor Emmanuel II, 1860
- → route of Garibaldi's Thousand, 1860
- ✗ battle

THE RUSSIAN REVOLUTION

*"We will now
proceed with the
building of
socialism."
Vladimir Ilyich
Lenin*

The Russian revolutions of 1917 and their legacy have had a tremendous impact upon both European and world history, politics, and belief systems in the twentieth century. It was not the successive military setbacks on the eastern front during the First World War that resulted directly in the February Revolution but rather the deteriorating economic conditions within Russia. In the meantime, inflation grew against a background of war profiteering, corruption, and government instability. Yet, although the events of February 1917 were initially brought about by industrial unrest, it was the soldiers' refusal to fire on the crowds that turned the demonstrations into a revolt. Against a background of growing discontent, representatives of the Russian elite brought about the abdication of the tsar at Pskov on March 15, 1917, in a failed attempt to stem the drift toward revolution. Meanwhile, the liberals of the Duma (Parliament) took temporary control of the country, establishing a provisional government under Prince Lvov, and later Alexander Kerensky; from the beginning this was weakened by sharing power with the Soviets.

In the eight months that followed, the provisional government introduced a number of reforms, but was hampered by its concern to continue the war with Germany. Furthermore, the provisional government was not a legitimately elected body, and its position was weakened by its failure to establish a democratically elected Constituent Assembly. Ultimately it would be discredited by the failure of the Kerensky offensive in June, which provided yet another example of Russian strategies, being constantly subordinated to the war aims of her allies.

Although the Bolsheviks played no role in the February Revolution, and suffered setbacks following the preemptive July coup; by the end of summer, their popularity was enhanced in the key urban centers by their role in the abortive Kornilov affair, and their demands for: "Peace, bread, and land." Lenin returned to Russia on October 10, as Kerensky, Prince Lvov's successor, faced growing opposition from the Petrograd Soviet.

In a climate of growing anarchy it became clear that the provisional government could neither continue the war nor finish it, and in October 1917, Lenin and the Bolsheviks seized power in Petrograd with relatively little loss of life. The Bolsheviks arranged a cease-fire with the Germans, and in March 1918, peace proposals were negotiated between Russia and Germany at Brest-Litovsk.

Lenin returned from exile in Switzerland after the February revolution in 1917, leading the Bolshevik Revolution of the following November. He became the first leader of the new Soviet state, dying in office in 1924.

The civil war that ensued was also a war of foreign intervention in which Russia's former allies, Britain, the United States, and France, shifted their aims from containing the Germans on the eastern front to containing Bolshevism within Russia. The ravages of both the First World War and Civil War, in which between seventeen and eighteen million people lost their lives, were exacerbated by "War Communism," requisitioning, and famine, which led to peasant disturbances, and urban discontent in the winter of 1920–1921. The Bolsheviks crushed resistance, wiping out all opposition.

After Lenin's death on January 21, 1921, opposition to Trotsky led to a struggle for the overall control of the party. Stalin, with the help of Kamenev and Zinoviev, rose to power.

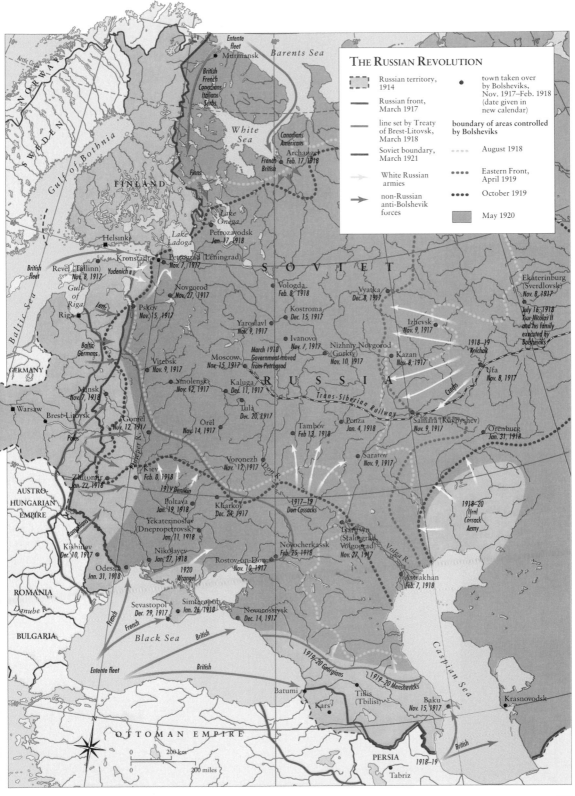

THE RUSSIAN REVOLUTION

- ⌐ ⌐ ⌐ Russian territory, 1914
- ▬▬ Russian front, March 1917
- ▬▬ line set by Treaty of Brest-Litovsk, March 1918
- ▬▬ Soviet boundary, March 1921
- → White Russian armies
- → non-Russian anti-Bolshevik forces

- ● town taken over by Bolsheviks, Nov. 1917–Feb. 1918 (date given in new calendar)

boundary of areas controlled by Bolsheviks
- ∙∙∙∙ August 1918
- ●●●● Eastern Front, April 1919
- ●●●● October 1919
- ▨ May 1920

NORWAY

SWEDEN

FINLAND

Barents Sea

British French Canadians Italians Serbs

Entente fleet

Murmansk

White Sea

Canadians Americans

Archangel Feb. 17, 1918

French British

Finns

Gulf of Bothnia

Lake Onega

Petrozavodsk Jan. 17, 1918

Lake Ladoga

Helsinki

British fleet

Revel (Tallinn) Nov. 8, 1917

Kronstadt

Yudenich

Petrograd (Leningrad) Nov. 7, 1917

S O V I E T

Ekaterinburg (Sverdlovsk) Nov. 8, 1917

July 16, 1918 Tsar Nicolas II and his family executed by Bolsheviks

Gulf of Riga

Lenin

Pskov Nov. 15, 1917

Novgorod Nov. 27, 1917

Vologda Feb. 8, 1918

Vyatka Dec. 8, 1917

Baltic Sea

Riga

Baltic Germans

Vitebsk Nov. 9, 1917

Yaroslavl Nov. 9, 1917

Kostroma Dec. 15, 1917

Ivanovo Nov. 1, 1917

Izhevsk Nov. 9, 1917

1918–19 Kolchak

GERMANY

Minsk Nov. 7, 1918

Smolensk Nov. 12, 1917

Moscow Nov. 15, 1917 March 1918 Government moved from Petrograd

Nizhniy Novgorod (Gorky) Nov. 10, 1917

Kazan Nov. 8, 1917

R U S S I A

Ufa Nov. 8, 1917

Warsaw

Brest-Litovsk

Gomel Nov. 12, 1917

Kaluga Dec. 11, 1917

Tula Dec. 20, 1917

Trans-Siberian Railway

Czechs

Poles

Orël Nov. 14, 1917

Tambov Feb. 13, 1918

Penza Jan. 4, 1918

Samara (Kuybyshev) Nov. 9, 1917

Orenburg Jan. 31, 1918

Zhitomir Jan. 22, 1918

Kiev Feb. 8, 1918

1919 Denikin

Voronezh Nov. 12, 1917

Saratov Nov. 9, 1917

1918–20 Ural Cossack Army

AUSTRO-HUNGARIAN EMPIRE

Poltava Jan. 19, 1918

Kharkov Dec. 24, 1917

1917–19 Don Cossacks

Yekaterinoslav (Dnepropetrovsk) Jan. 11, 1918

Tsaritsyn (Stalingrad Volgograd) Nov. 27, 1917

Volga R.

Kishinev Dec. 10, 1917

Nikolayev Jan. 27, 1918

Novocherkassk Feb. 25, 1918

Romanians

Rostov-on-Don Nov. 10, 1917

Astrakhan Feb. 7, 1918

Odessa Jan. 31, 1918

1920 Wrangel

ROMANIA

Danube R.

Sevastopol Dec. 29, 1917

Simferopol Jan. 26, 1918

Novorossiysk Dec. 14, 1917

French

BULGARIA

Black Sea

British

French

British

Entente fleet

British

1919–20 Georgians

Caspian Sea

1919–20 Mensheviks

Batumi

Kars

Tbilisi (Tbilisi)

Baku Nov. 15, 1917

Krasnovodsk

OTTOMAN EMPIRE

0   200 km
0   200 miles

PERSIA

1918–19

British

Tabriz

THE NEW RUSSIA

By the end of the 1930s, the Soviet Union had been through a tremendous upheaval. Between seventeen and eighteen million people had been lost in the First World War and the Civil War, and a large number through famine and disease. A repressive totalitarian system had been put in place to maintain in power a monolithic party that had no legitimate democratic authority.

After the death of Lenin, Stalin, once in power, secured his position through ruthless policies of industrialization, collectivization, and a system of terror and repression that grew with the spread of the Gulag system of "corrective labor"—linked with the Great Purges, or Yezhovschine, of 1936–1941, named after the eponymous Commisar for Internal Affairs from September 1936 to July 1938, Nicholas Yezhov, during which it has been estimated that ten million were arrested and three million executed.

Despite this the vision of a new Russia that was a thriving and happy society was carefully fostered by the Soviet government and its organs. They harnessed the forces of Socialist Realist art and cinema, to provide images of happy agricultural workers and tractor drivers, gathering the harvests, alongside loyal Stakhanovites (named after Alexis Stakhanov, a coal miner who persistently exceeded his alloted quota), toiling cheerfully in the mines and factories, doubling or tripling production levels and yields.

In industry priority was given to producers' goods over consumer goods, and all available resources were channeled into heavy industry. Before the Great Patriotic War, the Stalinist organization of the Soviet economy was realized through a series of three Five-Year Plans involving the expansion of industry. Although production rates were generally increased, this was often at the expense of quality. Despite the hardships in which workers accused of industrial sabotage were sent to the Gulag, on the outbreak of war, the foundations of an industrial base had been well laid.

Collectivization was forced upon the countryside and would change the lives of over 75 percent of the Soviet population. By 1937, almost all cultivated land was in collective farms (*kolkhozi*) or the state farms (*sovkhozi*) which were more directly controlled on factory lines by the state. In the Soviet Union many collective farms were inefficient.

With the increase in international tensions in the 1930s, an even more ferocious event was about to be unleashed on the Soviet people. On the eve of the German invasion in 1941, agricultural production still had not returned to its 1928 levels.

A poster designed by Victor Deni, Enemies of the Five-Year Plan, *1928–33.*

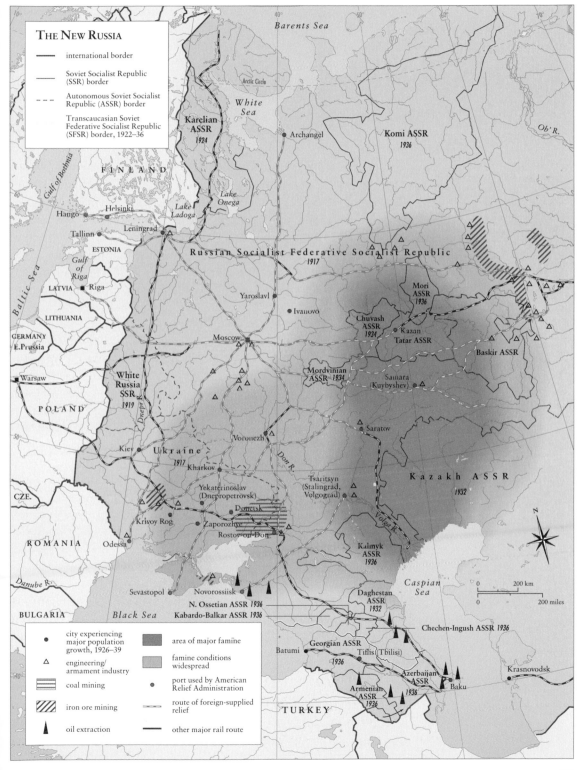

THE NEW RUSSIA

— international border

— Soviet Socialist Republic (SSR) border

- - - Autonomous Soviet Socialist Republic (ASSR) border

Transcaucasian Soviet Federative Socialist Republic (SFSR) border, 1922–36

- • city experiencing major population growth, 1926–39
- △ engineering/ armament industry
- coal mining
- iron ore mining
- ▲ oil extraction
- area of major famine
- famine conditions widespread
- • port used by American Relief Administration
- route of foreign-supplied relief
- other major rail route

Barents Sea

Arctic Circle

White Sea

Karelian ASSR *1924*

• Archangel

Komi ASSR *1936*

Ob' R.

F I N L A N D

Lake Onega

Gulf of Bothnia

Hango •
Helsinki •
Tallinn •
Lake Ladoga
Leningrad

ESTONIA

Gulf of Riga

LATVIA • Riga

LITHUANIA

GERMANY E.Prussia

Baltic Sea

Russian Socialist Federative Socialist Republic *1917*

Yaroslavl •

• Ivanovo

Mori ASSR *1936*

Chuvash ASSR *1934*
• Kazan
Tatar ASSR

Baskir ASSR

Moscow •

Mordvinian ASSR *1934*

Samara (Kuybyshev) •

• Warsaw

White Russia SSR *1919*

Dnepr R.

P O L A N D

• Saratov

CZE.

Kiev •

U k r a i n e *1917*

Kharkov •

Voronezh •

Don R.

K a z a k h   A S S R *1932*

Tsaritsyn (Stalingrad), Volgograd) •

Yekaterinoslav (Dnepropetrovsk) •

Krivoy Rog •

Donetsk •

Zaporozhye •
Rostov-on-Don •

Volga R.

R O M A N I A

Odessa •

Kalmyk ASSR *1936*

Danube R.

Sevastopol •

Novorossiisk •

N. Ossetian ASSR *1936*
Kabardo-Balkar ASSR *1936*

BULGARIA   *Black Sea*

Caspian Sea

Daghestan ASSR *1932*

Chechen-Ingush ASSR *1936*

Georgian ASSR *1936*

Batumi •

Tiflis (Tbilisi) •

Azerbaijan ASSR *1936*

Krasnovodsk •

Baku •

Armenian ASSR *1936*

T U R K E Y

N

0   200 km
0   200 miles

PART VII: IMPERIAL ECHOES

The First World War ended a century of scientific, industrial, and cultural progress. Events conspired against Europe: war, nationalism, imperialism, the alliance systems, armed peace, and a total failure to establish a system of international arbitration that ensured carnage on the battlefield and the spread of a European into a global war. This conflict gave a new impetus to nationalisms that were developing in Asia and Africa even before 1914. Anti-imperial feeling and failure to repress it demonstrated structural weaknesses in Europe, and the nationalisms of colonial peoples continued until they achieved independence after the Second World War.

The breakdown of the balance of power in 1914, the impact of war, chaos, poverty, and hunger in east and central Europe, and badly designed peace treaties left a legacy of hatred and revenge that raged after 1945. The war also brought into focus the economic decline of Europe compared with the United States, and the U.S.-exported 1929 stock market crash and the following Depression exacerbated problems caused by debts and war reparation payments. The next war threw into sharp relief Europe's exhaustion and imperial overstretch, a humiliating counterpoint to apparent strength and pride at the end of the New Imperialist surge in the late nineteenth century.

The decades before World War I saw a relative decline in religious idealism and an increase in secular attacks on religion as demonstrated by Bismarck's Kulturkampf, the French Third Republic's onslaught on the Roman Catholic Church after the Boulanger Crisis, and the hostility between the new Italian state and the pope. British urbanization and the failure of the Anglican Church to build enough places of worship in towns allowed congregations to drift away, with many working-class men and women switching to dissenting movements such as Methodism. The spread of education and literacy allowed the general population to be more aware of foreign affairs. The breakdown in rural extended kinship patterns and community in the face of industrialization produced a new hierarchy of values whereby nationalism exalted the motherland and fatherland on whose altars the good patriot should sacrifice himself. This new sense of identity was subject to manipulation by governments and newspapers raising the specter of chauvinism, fanaticism, and hysteria in times of national crisis. The breakdown in the old Concert of Europe meant the lack of an arbitration system to orchestrate diplomatic peace processes. The result was mistrust leading to even more secret diplomacy and foreign policies. Even when governments desired moderation, the newly literate populace sometimes imagined insults to national pride, thereby exerting undue pressures on government. New ideologies and movements were spawned: Russian state-sponsored Pan-Slavism; the Pan-German Alldeutscher Verband; French revanchists uniting behind General Boulanger, advocating war to regain Alsace-Lorraine; the Action Française with Charles Maurras's ideal of total nationalism; extremist Italian irredentism; and British imperialism, jingoism, and the Primrose League. Exaggerated national egos fueled an aggressive realpolitik, first introduced in a moderate form by Bismarck. Reasons of state became the ideal and could legitimize any policy.

Europe rapidly deteriorated into an armed peace with two opposing camps competing in military and naval arms races: the Triple Alliance and the Triple Entente. Both systems were permanently renewing themselves as long as the other existed. Now any crisis, however minor, could escalate out of all proportion and blow up as one did in 1914. Serious crises were endemic: the first Moroccan Crisis between France and Germany (1905); the Bosnia-Herzegovina Crisis between Russia and Austria-Hungary (1908); the second Moroccan Crisis between the same protagonists (1911); the crises surrounding the Balkan Wars involving Russia and Austria-Hungary (1913); and, finally, the Black Hand's murder of Archduke Franz Ferdinand in Sarajevo in 1914, which tipped Europe into disaster.

European statesmen considered that the scramble for empire would be a safety valve. The emergence of new states in Europe—Italy and Germany—reduced opportunities for expansion in Europe. The virtual end of free trade and the establishment of protectionism by industrializing countries generated a search for new overseas markets and their seizure by all force necessary. The development of new technologies aided imperialism: steamships needed regular coaling stations like Aden and Mauritius, stepping-stones to British India and French Indochina respectively; and the innovation of ships with refrigeration compartments meant food could be transported longer distances to feed the industrial, urbanized masses. The rifle and the machine gun made violent policies easier but not without the occasional mishap, such as Zulus slaughtering a British force at Isandhlwana, and the Ethiopians overwhelming an Italian force at Adowa. The French became very careful when Dahomey's fighting women leaped from jungle cover wielding spears. Nevertheless, the colonization of the world rolled on, and Europeans transported the balance of power to Africa and Asia. Jules Ferry, French premier in 1881 and supporter of imperialist mercantilism, saw the conquest of Tunisia as being restitution for the loss of Alsace-Lorraine. All imperial powers sought to partition areas, seek compensation, and create buffer states. Siam, Iran, and Afghanistan retained independence to separate France and Britain, or Britain and Russia.

Equality of commercial access was also important, as evidenced in 1900, when Europeans endorsed the United States suggestion of an Open Door policy in China and in 1906 when a conference at Algeciras announced such equality regarding Morocco. By 1914, all continents were held in thrall, except where the Monroe Doctrine held sway, and the great powers seemed to have settled their colonial differences bilaterally.

Even while pursuing the New Imperialism, the European states faced almost constant rebellion. Both Africa and Asia provide examples of determined stands by peoples seeking independence, resisting encroachment, and establishing nationalist parties and associations. In Indochina, De Tham fought the French until 1913, the year that saw the foundation of Vietnam Quang Phuc Ho (Association for the Restoration of Vietnam), a revolutionary organization started by Phan Boi Chau. In Africa, Britain met fierce resistance from the

Ashanti, Zulu, and Matabele, while tyrannical German rule provoked a Herero revolt in South-West Africa (1904) after many had been subject to genocide; the anti-German Maji-Maji Rebellion (1905) in Tanganyika is another example. Some anticolonialist movements were traditionalist and religious, notably the Mahdi's seizure of the Sudan in 1881. A holy war against the Dutch in northern Sumatra (1881–1908), the Chinese Boxer uprising (1900), and the attack on foreign legations in Peking brought fearful European retaliation. More peaceful means were explored by the Indian National Congress founded in 1885, the Egyptian National Party (1899), and Egyptian People's Party (1907). The year 1912 saw the birth of the Indonesian National Party (Sarekat Islam) and the South African National Congress. The First World War gave new encouragement to Asian and African nationalisms. In China, Sun Yat-sen saw the Japanese victory over Russia in 1904–1905 as the "defeat of the West by the East," showing the art of the possible. In 1916, major anti-Russian uprisings took place in Muslim central Asia; the Saharan Senussi helped an anti-French rebellion in Tunisia (1915–1916), while France also had to cope with rebellion in Annam (1916); and the British had to suppress an antisettler movement in Nyasaland. Although these and other nationalist activities stimulated resistance of those resentful and in despair, little was achieved except that European rule was exposed as insecure, and myths grew that in later years led to the collapse of European imperialism and freedom for dominated peoples. The colonial powers faced further difficulties after 1918, especially with the inheritance of League of Nations' mandates in the Middle East. In Syria, the French suppressed a nationwide revolt (1925–1927). Between 1935 and 1939, Britain faced a large Arab revolt in opposition to Jewish immigration into Palestine, having granted independence to Egypt (1922) while retaining control of the Suez Canal and military matters. Elsewhere in North Africa, the 1930s saw early nationalist movements applying pressure on the French in Morocco, Algeria, and Tunisia. In Asia, Gandhi linked nationalism to Hinduism and engaged in civil disobedience campaigns against British India, thereby raising the profile of the Indian National Congress. Eventually, the British were persuaded to introduce the Government of India Act (1935), which allowed political participation in central and provincial governments. By 1937, the Congress controlled a majority of the provincial ones.

The depression and subsequent unemployment were a major factor in causing unrest. The West Indies saw strikes and riots, as did the Gold Coast, which again pressured the British into rethinking colonial policy. Ceylon was given a new constitution in 1931, and Burma was split from India and given a degree of autonomy in 1935. Other colonial powers adopted a recalcitrant attitude of no concession. French Indochina experienced outbreaks of violence, leading to the creation of the Vietminh by Ho Chi Minh in 1941. The Dutch East Indies saw unsuccessful Communist outbreaks demanding self-determination. Eventually, the Second World War changed the nature of European colonialism in Asia. The failure of the imperial powers in the face of Japanese aggression gave an impetus to popular nationalisms, and after 1945, the Europeans either granted independence or were kicked out.

The colonial experience demonstrated the inherent fragility of European power. The Great War of 1914–1918 ruined Europe financially and wiped out so much youth that some European towns and villages were denuded of an entire generation of young men. The advent of the United States into the war (April 1917) turned the tide for the Entente powers but introduced President Wilson into European politics. His peace aims were idealistic and predicated upon ignorance of Europe, and his plans for the postwar world ushered in a new diplomacy based upon a League of Nations that the U.S. Senate so disliked that the United States was prevented from joining. However, his failure and that of all statesmen at Versailles to address the nationality issue in its entirety left a legacy of hatred, especially after the victors penalized the defeated with territorial losses and reparations, and saddled the Germans with a war-guilt clause. According to A. J. P. Taylor, a controversial British historian, the Second World War was fought to rewrite Versailles. For Europe, the interwar years were characterized by moral regression and political insanity in an apparent lemminglike drive to shrug off the last vestiges of culture and civilization. The new Europe of Versailles and its associated treaties destroyed Austria-Hungary and constructed a jigsaw of small successor states, none being economically viable and all containing ethnic minorities. The dissolution of the Habsburg empire removed the last foreign policy restraint from Germany, a factor that Hitler rapidly noted and appreciated.

The fragmentation of Europe was extensive and posed infinite dilemmas for the future. The new states were generally aggrieved at not receiving enough territory or resentful that kinfolk were minorities in other countries. The new states included Czechoslovakia, a reestablished Poland, Finland, Estonia, Latvia, and Lithuania, while others were enlarged, such as Romania and the hotchpotch state of Yugoslavia. This was based upon an expanded Serbia, ushering in a political nightmare whose inhabitants are still trying to eradicate each other, giving humanity an exercise in ethnic cleansing. The nadir of interwar Europe appeared in its mix of ethnic grievances, compounded by the economic poverty and decline during the Great Depression.

The farrago of small, strategically vulnerable states faced two new economic, social, and ideological systems challenging and criticizing capitalism and democracy. In Italy, Mussolini coined the term "totalitarianism" when building the Fascist Party, while the Soviet Union offered the world a Communist blueprint. More significant was the German appointment of Adolf Hitler as chancellor, then führer. Europe was drawing the lines for renewed conflict. Fascist and military dictatorships spread rapidly, while the League of Nations collapsed in the face of the Spanish Civil War, Italy's attack on Abyssinia, and the Japanese invasion of Manchuria. European democracies were outnumbered and, still recovering from the Depression, now faced darkness in six years of organized savagery.

GLOBAL EMPIRES

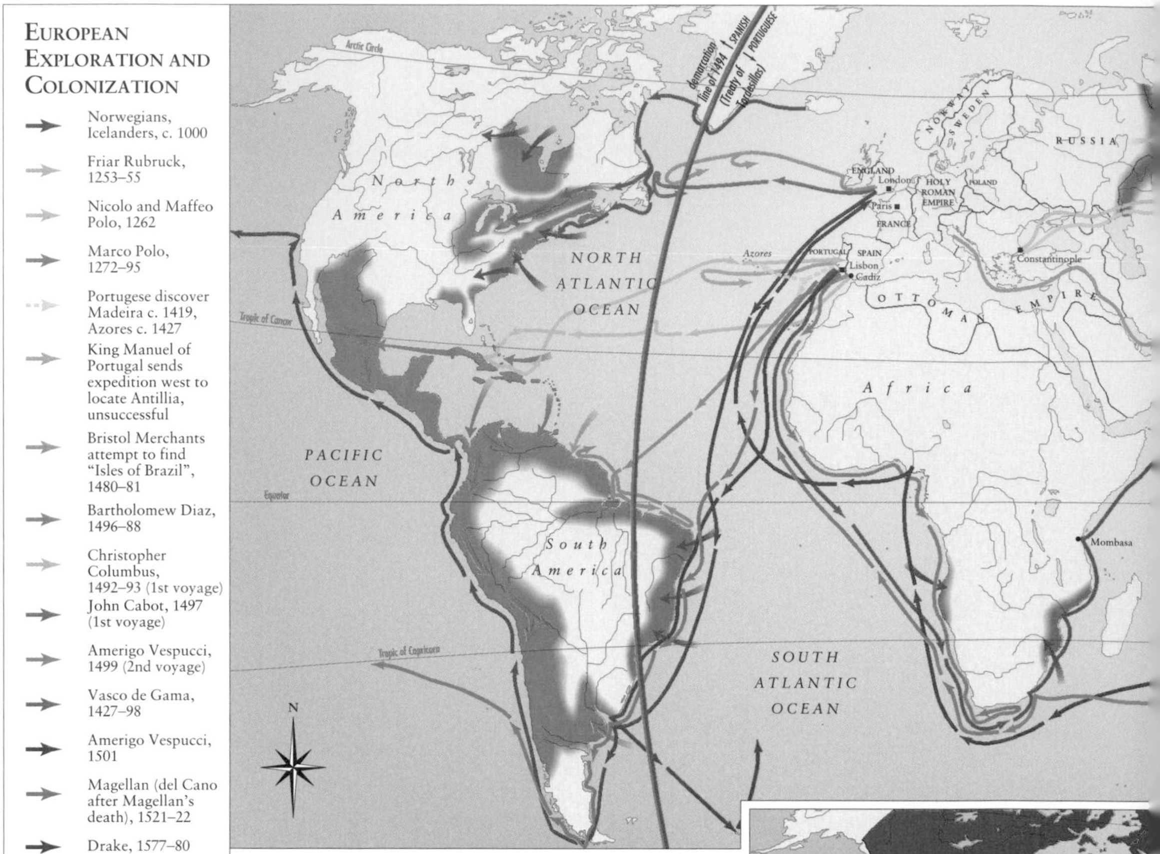
EUROPEAN EXPLORATION AND COLONIZATION
Norwegians, Icelanders, c. 1000
Friar Rubruck, 1253–55
Nicolo and Maffeo Polo, 1262
Marco Polo, 1272–95
Portugese discover Madeira c. 1419, Azores c. 1427
King Manuel of Portugal sends expedition west to locate Antillia, unsuccessful
Bristol Merchants attempt to find "Isles of Brazil", 1480–81
Bartholomew Diaz, 1496–88
Christopher Columbus, 1492–93 (1st voyage)
John Cabot, 1497 (1st voyage)
Amerigo Vespucci, 1499 (2nd voyage)
Vasco de Gama, 1427–98
Amerigo Vespucci, 1501
Magellan (del Cano after Magellan's death), 1521–22
Drake, 1577–80
Abel Tasman, 1642–43
main directions of European colonization or control, 1450–1600
Spanish
Portuguese
English
French
Dutch
Russian
under European colonization or control mid. 17th C.
Arctic Circle
demarcation line of 1494 (Treaty of Tordesillas)
SPANISH
PORTUGUESE
North America
NORTH ATLANTIC OCEAN
Azores
ENGLAND
London
Paris
FRANCE
HOLY ROMAN EMPIRE
POLAND
NORWAY
SWEDEN
RUSSIA
PORTUGAL
SPAIN
Lisbon
Cadiz
Constantinople
OTTOMAN EMPIRE
Tropic of Cancer
Africa
PACIFIC OCEAN
Equator
South America
Mombasa
Tropic of Capricorn
SOUTH ATLANTIC OCEAN
N

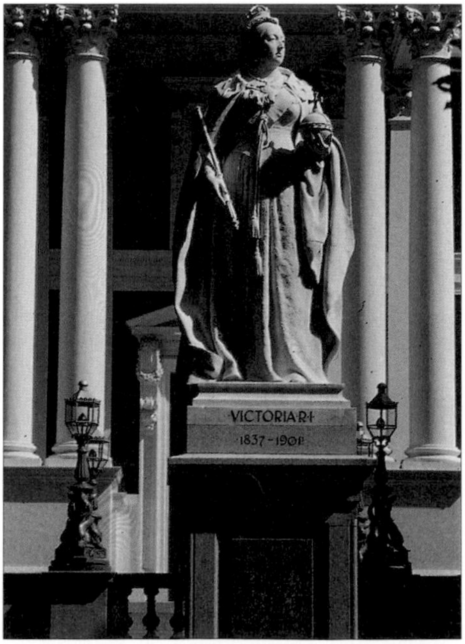
VICTORIA R.I.
1837-1901

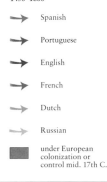

As a symbol of domination, Queen Victoria looks across yet another possession, this time Cape Town, South Africa.

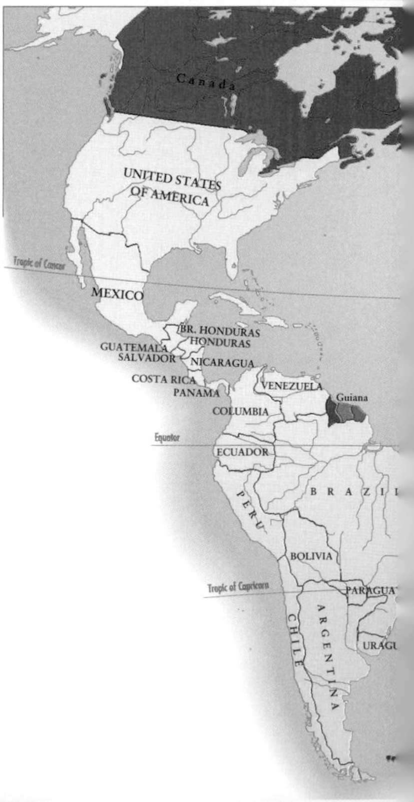
Canada
UNITED STATES OF AMERICA
Tropic of Cancer
MEXICO
BR. HONDURAS
HONDURAS
GUATEMALA
SALVADOR
NICARAGUA
COSTA RICA
PANAMA
VENEZUELA
Guiana
COLUMBIA
Equator
ECUADOR
PERU
BRAZIL
BOLIVIA
Tropic of Capricorn
PARAGUAY
CHILE
ARGENTINA
URAGU

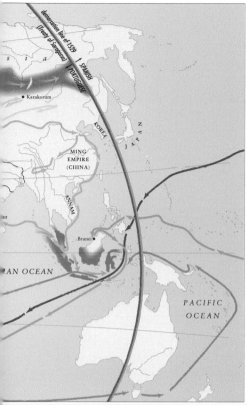

From the late 1400s Europeans began to sail the oceans, trading, conquering, and colonizing the world. In this painting by Diego Velasquez, Christopher Columbus (Cristobal Colon), navigator and explorer who made four voyages across the Atlantic, offers the New World to the Catholic king of Spain.

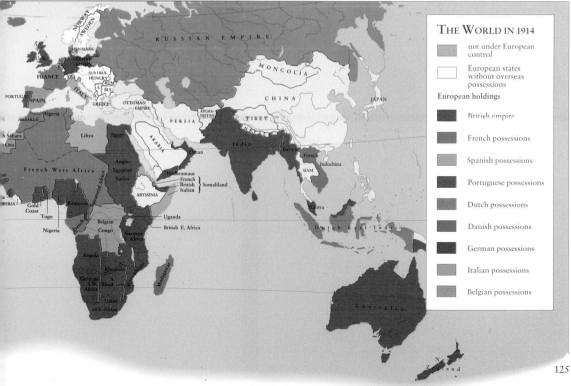

THE WORLD IN 1914

	not under European control
	European states without overseas possessions

European holdings

	British empire
	French possessions
	Spanish possessions
	Portuguese possessions
	Dutch possessions
	Danish possessions
	German possessions
	Italian possessions
	Belgian possessions

"The colonies
are millstones
round our
neck."
Disraeli, 1852

The late nineteenth century introduced the "New Imperialism," a period when the great powers partitioned the world into economic and political empires. Historical explanations for this phenomenon are legion, such as the Marxist surplus capital theory, export of excess population, strategic defense of existing empire, and the belief that empire aided the balance of power and a nation's international prestige.

Prior to 1871, European overseas possessions were confined to British India and South Africa, the Dutch East Indies, French Algeria and Cochin-China, Spanish Cuba and Philippines, and Russian Siberia and central Asia. Otherwise, European influence was limited to trading stations (Lagos, Hong Kong), Chinese treaty ports such as Shanghai, and strategic posts (Aden). The new expansionism is best exemplified by the "scramble of Africa." The French empire spread throughout north and west Africa and Madagascar; the Germans moved into German East Africa, South-West Africa, the Cameroons, and Togoland; Britain acquired Egypt, the Sudan, Kenya, Uganda, the Rhodesias, Nyasaland, Nigeria, and the Gold Coast; Leopold II of Belgium gained the Congo as a personal possession; the Portuguese expanded their trading stations into Angola and Mozambique; and the Italians seized Eritrea, parts of Somaliland, and Libya but failed to capture Abyssinia, the Italian army being overwhelmed at Adowa (1896). China provided the other main area of competition in the "battle for concessions" when interested powers jockeyed for commercial advantages, development projects, and territory. Although various ports were lost to European powers and areas penetrated economically (most noticeably Britain controlling the Yangtse-Kiang river basin trade), China managed to retain independence. Even the Sino-Japanese War (1895) and the loss of Formosa failed to destroy the remnants of Chinese sovereignty. Events adjacent to China illustrate the peculiar British approach to empire. Despite Disraeli's declaration that colonies were a drain on economic resources, Britain continued to acquire lands to safeguard influence and to act as a bulwark for existing empire. Hence, when France added Tonking (1885) and Laos (1893) to Cambodia and Cochin-China, Britain acquired Burma (1886), and the two powers divided Siam into spheres of influence. Elsewhere, in the Pacific, Britain took Fiji, parts of Borneo, and New Guinea; other islands were the subject of British, French, and German competition. By 1914, Britain had accumulated 20 percent of the world's land surface, one-quarter of the world's population, and all the trade routes in the Indian Ocean. Simultaneously, non-European empires threatened European dominance; the Spanish-American War (1898) allowed the United States to obtain Cuba, Puerto Rico, Guam, and the Philippines; Hawaii was annexed the same year, but Cuba was granted independence in 1902, although remaining under U.S. influence. Nationalism and imperialism propelled Japan into wars against China (1895) and Russia (1905), gaining Formosa (1895), the lease of the Liaotung Peninsula, south Sakhalin, and considerable rights in south Manchuria, and recognition of Japanese supremacy in Korea, formally annexed in 1910.

The First World War provided nationalists with an opportunity to voice their resentment against imperial control. When Britain made Egypt a protectorate (1914), latent anti-British feelings sprang forth. French possessions were also susceptible to uprisings in Tunisia (1915–1916), while Italy had never crushed the Sanusi tribesmen in Libya. The peace treaties ending World War I altered the imperial map: in the Middle East, Britain was given Palestine, Transjordan, and Iraq, and France gained Lebanon and Syria, all as League of Nations mandates. Germany's former African possessions were mandated to Britain (Tanganyika) and South Africa (South-West Africa), while Britain and France shared Togoland and the Cameroons. In the Far East, Japan and Australia divided Germany's Pacific islands. The interwar years exposed the weaknesses of the imperial powers: rule was gradually understood to be temporary as expressed in the new concept of British "dominion" and in the mandate system itself. Nationalist movements grew as a result of armed conflict such as that led by Abdel-Krim against France and Spain (1921–1926). Educated elites commenced mobilization of wider support as in Gandhi's Indian civil disobedience campaign. Elsewhere, in Asia, Communist revolts (1926) burst out in the Dutch East Indies, and such militancy exemplified a group of emerging radical leaders such as Ho Chi Minh in Vietnam, Nehru in India, and Sukarno in Indonesia. The Second World War further explored the frailty of empire with the loss of colonies to Japan and the sheer exhaustion of the imperialists shown in financial, military, and demographic terms.

Reaction against imperialism articulated itself in a number of ways: indigenous nationalism, especially in Algeria and Southeast Asia; pressure exerted by the United States desiring emancipation and new markets, and the USSR's offering ideological blueprints based on class struggle and revolution; and worldwide anticolonialism being given a forum in the United Nations, allowing the nonaligned a stage, resulting in the uncompromising 1960 Declaration on the Granting of Independence to Colonial Countries and Peoples.

The speed of decolonization was probably occasioned by military weakness, and new plans for European cooperation and economic integration made Europe less expansionist with a realization that it had shrunk in terms of power and influence. France was pushed out of southeast Asia by Ho Chi Minh (1954) and Algeria became independent in 1962. Most French colonies were freed in 1960, many joining a French community. Spain liberated most of its African colonies peacefully, but Nehru seized Portugal's Indian colonies while guerrilla liberation movements brought independence to Angola and Mozambique (1974). The Dutch faced similar problems, unable to reassert authority in the East Indies. The UN arranged a transfer of sovereignty in 1949; next it helped the Belgian Congo after 1960. Britain, pressured into emancipating the Indian empire (1947), conferred independence in Africa from 1957 onwards. After the 1950s, some remnants of colonialism remained, such as Rhodesia.

THE ROAD TO SELF-DESTRUCTION

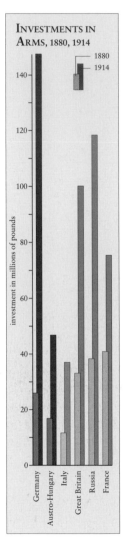

INVESTMENTS IN ARMS, 1880, 1914

— 1880
— 1914

investment in millions of pounds

140 —
120 —
100 —
80 —
60 —
40 —
20 —
0 —

Germany
Austro-Hungary
Italy
Great Britain
Russia
France

"Fritz," the giant steam hammer at a Krupps armament works, c. 1914.

The creation of the German Reich (1871) ushered in a new balance of power. All states accepted the change except France, which lost Alsace-Lorraine and felt increasingly isolated over colonial differences with Britain and Italy. When Bismarck fell from power (1890), his foreign policy of alleviating international tension ended. Imperial antagonism, the nonrenewal of the Reinsurance Treaty with Russia, and the character of Kaiser Wilhelm all combined to aggravate the international system. All major states sought security but were prepared to seek varied combinations of alliance partners to achieve their aims. Russia attempted to prevent any unfriendly power from controlling the Straits at Constantinople and feared Austro-Hungarian influence spreading into the Balkans, and to this end signed military conventions with Bulgaria (1902) and Serbia (1903). Britain wanted to protect her empire and sought ways of preventing perceived Russian expansion in Persia and Afghanistan as a thrust toward India. A 1907 Anglo-Russian agreement allayed fears and prepared the way for the Triple Entente. France drew closer to Russia when the failure of the Reinsurance Treaty forced Russia to find a new partner. The need to industrialize required financial loans, and the closure of the Berlin stock exchange to such transactions prevented Russia's borrowing to rearm and build. Stategic railways had opened the way to a Franco-Russian alliance in 1894. The Anglo-French Entente (1902) enabled the two countries to settle their differences over Morocco and Egypt. The entente faced its first test in the 1905–1906 Morocco Crisis; the Anglo-French-Russian Triple Entente followed in 1907. A naval arms race between Germany and Britain in battleship construction increased tensions brought to a head in the second Moroccan Crisis, when France occupied Fez. The dispatch of a German warship and the resultant crisis were only resolved by an agreement over a French protectorate in Morocco, with German compensation in the Cameroons. The fluid situation allowed Italy to seize Tripoli and the Dodencanese. The Balkans provided the other flash point. In 1908, Austria-Hungary annexed Bosnia-Herzegovina from the Turks, angering Serbia by destroying one element of its plans for a Greater Serbia. German support for the seizure intensified international problems, and Russia saw a Germanic march on the Straits (Dardanelles). In 1909, Russia and Italy signed a secret Treaty of Racconigi to keep a Balkan status quo. The crisis also sealed the 1879 Austro-German alliance, tying the latter to Austrian aims in the Balkans. Further concern was caused by the Austro-Serb "Pig Wars" (1906–1911), unrest in Albania, and the two Balkan Wars of 1912 and 1913, which saw Turkey virtually thrown out of Europe, and large territories added to Greece, Bulgaria, and Serbia, the last being disappointed over the nonacquisition of an Adriatic outlet due to Austrian interference. By 1914, German Weltpolitik challenged the old imperial powers, and Germany and Austria felt encircled by the entente. When Archduke Franz Ferdinand was killed in Sarajevo, Serbia appeared to reopen its ambitions, and the subsequent Austrian ultimatum backed by Germany was the final step to war and self-destruction.

ALLIANCES ON THE EVE OF
WAR, JULY 1914

- Austro-German Alliance,
  1879–1918
- Triple Alliance, 1882–1915
- Franco-Russian Alliance,
  1894–1917
- Triple Entente, 1907–1917
- varying independence and
  nationalist movements sponsored
  by Russia, 1879–1914
- sympathetic to 'Central Powers'
- sympathetic to 'Entente Powers'
- neutrality guaranteed by United
  Kingdom
- neutral

WORLD WAR I

WORLD WAR I

- Central Powers
- Allied Powers
- joining Allied Powers at a later date
- declaration of war surrender
- Central Powers attack, 1914
- Allied attack, 1914
- front line, late 1914
- Central Powers attack, 1915–17
- Allied attack, 1915–17
- front line, mid 1917
- Central Powers occupation of Russia, Feb.–May 1918 and occupation of Georgia by Ottoman empire, May 1918
- Allied attack, 1918
- front line, Nov. 1918
- naval battle

The First World War inaugurated new modes of warfare, resulting in hitherto unknown destruction of human life, material, and landscape. When war began in August 1914, all countries based their plans on a short war, but best-laid plans went astray; the conflict developed into long lines of entrenched armies in almost immovable seigelike conditions in a war of attrition. The German Schlieffen Plan intended to encircle and destroy the French Army by a sweeping hook through neutral Belgium, but nervousness in execution and events on Germany's eastern front drew troops from the west, allowing the Allies to consolidate their front into a 400-mile complex

of trenches and barbed wire extending from the English Channel to the Swiss frontier. The stalemate in the west occasioned total war, with intense mobilization of both people and industry. Various innovations attempted to end the deadlock; the Germans used poisoned gas at Ypres (April 1915) and the British the newly developed tank on the Somme (July 1916) and at Cambrai (November 1917). The land battle spread to the skies and seas in a hopeless search for victory. Primitive aircraft grew into sophisticated forms such as the Sopwith Camel and Fokker Triplane, and Germany developed the Zeppelin airship and Gotha long-range bomber capable of bombing enemy cities. Meanwhile, the Allies' naval blockade tried to starve the Central Powers, stimulating a submarine counter-offensive. Continued stalemate led the Allies into opening new war fronts in Europe: landing in the Dardanelles (April 1915–January 1916) this staggered to a halt with over 200,000 casualties; likewise, an attempt to help Serbia through Salonika, bogged down. The Italian entrance into the war on the Allied side in an attack on Austria on the Isonzo also failed.

On the eastern front, the Germans defeated a Russian invasion at Tannenberg (August 1914), while the Russians defeated Austria at Lemberg (September 1914). Despite a German offensive at Gorlice-Tarnow in 1915 and the Russian Brusilov advance in 1916, no decision resulted. Only when Russia dissolved into revolution did the Germans finally manage to advance through the Ukraine and force the Bolsheviks to sign the Treaty of Brest-Litovsk (December 1917). The entry of the United States into the conflict (April 6, 1917) after Germany declared unrestricted submarine warfare turned the tide for the Allies. The extra Allied manpower limited German territorial acquisitions in new offensives, the counterattacks under Marshall Foch pushed back the Germans, and the tank onslaught at Amiens (August 1918) was partially responsible for the German retreat to the Hindenburg Line. Austria's last offensive at the Piave against Italy (June 1918) failed, and the Allies finally broke through enemy lines in Macedonia (September 1918); in the face of this advance the Bulgarian army collapsed. As a result of this deteriorating situation, General Ludendorff called for an armistice, thereby acknowledging the defeat of the Central Powers. The mutiny of the German fleet (1918), revolutionary eruptions throughout Germany, and the kaiser's abdication with the proclamation of a republic led to an armistice (November 11, 1918), ending a European conflagration that had spread to the Middle East, Africa, and Asia. The victors now had to make the peace based upon U.S. President Wilson's Fourteen Points.

> "And by his smile, I knew that sullen hall. By his dead smile I knew we stood in Hell."
> *Wilfred Owen*

This detail of a painting by the British artist Paul Nash shows the Menin Road, giving an idea of the destruction and squalid horror of life on the western front between 1914 and 1918.

131

VERSAILLES, 1919

At the end of World War I, the Allies imposed a series of peace treaties upon the defeated Central Powers. From a European perspective the most important were Versailles on Germany, Trianon on Hungary, and St. Germain on Austria.

Opening in January 1919, the Versailles conference sought to follow the Congress of Vienna (1814) in the redrawing the map of Europe. Taking certain principles into consideration, nationalist demands for independence in eastern and central Europe would receive attention using principles of democracy, freedom, and self-determination and U.S. President Wilson's Fourteen Points.

The participants at Versailles sought to rationalize the incoherent mess that was the aftermath of war. Eventually, the three main political figures, Wilson, Lloyd George, and Clemenceau, fought it out for their separate interests. Wilson wanted open diplomacy and a League of Nations; Lloyd George saw Britain as a naval and imperial power, viewing Germany as a bastion against France and Bolshevik Russia, and he also desired Germany's African colonies. Clemenceau sought revenge, a weakened Germany, and four Allied military-controlled Rhine bridgeheads, eventually established by treaty.

Conflicting interests meant that Wilson's idealism remained unfulfilled. Ultimately, Germany lost territory to Poland, France, Belgium, and Denmark; and was virtually disarmed. Germany also had its colonies seized as League of Nations mandates, had the Saarland occupied by French troops, and was saddled with a war guilt clause and huge reparations.

Austria-Hungary was sundered, leaving the rump states of Austria and Hungary.

The end product of these treaties were excessive German reparations, while a variety of peoples were still intermingled in new multinational states throughout central Europe and the Balkans. Throughout the region, railway communications and banking systems were fragmented, and economically viable areas were destroyed.

EUROPE IN 1914

EUROPE IN 1919

0   200 km
0   200 miles

N

Iceland
to Denmark

Arctic Circle

Norwegian
Sea

Faeroe Islands
to Denmark

N O R W A Y

S W E D E N

F I N L A N D

Oslo

Helsinki
Leningrad
Tallinn
Stockholm
ESTONIA

North
Sea

Riga
LATVIA

LITHUANIA
Kaunas

DENMARK
Copenhagen
Königsberg

Glasgow
Edinburgh

UNITED KINGDOM

Liverpool

Danzig
free city under
League of Nations
East
Prussia

U.S.S.R.

Bristol

Hamburg
Berlin

Warsaw

Brest Litovsk

Amsterdam

Birmingham
London
Calais
Brussels
NETHERLANDS

G E R M A N Y

P O L A N D

Cracow
Lvov

BELGIUM
Rhine R.
Frankfurt
Prague

SAAR
autonomous under
League of Nations

Paris

CZECHOSLOVAKIA

Orléans

Vienna
Budapest

ATLANTIC
OCEAN

F R A N C E

Bern
SWITZ.

AUSTRIA
HUNGARY
R O M A N I A

Lyon
Milan
Trieste

Bucharest
Danube R.

Bordeaux
Genoa
Venice

Belgrade

Black Sea

Marseille

I T A L Y

YUGOSLAVIA

BULGARIA

Sofia

ANDORRA

Adriatic Sea

PORTUGAL

Barcelona

Rome

ALBANIA

TURKEY

Lisbon
Madrid

S P A I N

Naples

GREECE

Aegean
Sea

Smyrna

Balearic Is.

Alicante

Athens

Cádiz
Gibraltar
to Great Britain
international
zone
Almería

Italian
occupied

Tangier

M e d i t e r r a n e a n

A l g e r i a
to France

Tunisia
to France

S e a

Morocco
to France

Libya
to Italy

THE GREAT DEPRESSION

All over Europe workers were laid off in huge numbers. In towns like Jarrow in the northeast of England, the only people working were the few organizing the soup kitchens for the relief of the unemployed.

The Great Depression began in 1929, its impact, rippling out from the United States, affecting nearly every country in the world, whether industrial producers or agricultural countries. The increased economic interdependence in the world heightened the problems and showed how the world economy was flawed. Industrial production increased in Europe during the 1920s, especially in traditional industries such as coal, steel, and shipbuilding, at the expense of newer consumer industries. The United States developed the latter, particularly the motorcar industry, and the American economic growth rate outstripped Europe's, leaving Britain, France, and Germany with a relative decline in their share of world trade. Agricultural prices were falling under the impact of mechanization, so producers of raw materials had to reduce the quantity of imported manufactured goods to compensate. U.S. tariff barriers against European products had a harsh effect. Investments left Europe in search of higher interest rates elsewhere, and the cycle of indebtedness established around German reparations payments merely confused matters further. American loans were made to Germany to help reparations payments to France and Britain, who could then repay interest to the U.S. for wartime loans. In this situation the Wall Street crash caused severe hardship, especially with the recall of U.S. European loans, damaging Germany in particular. Many industrial countries incurred 25 percent unemployment rates (Germany 30.1 percent, France 24.3 percent, Austria 26.1 percent, Denmark 31.7 percent); industrial production fell to 53 percent in Germany, and social distress was immense. In Germany, malnutrition was rife, meat consumption fell, and the death rate increased, while in England this despair is best exemplified by the hunger marches from the Jarrow shipyards to London. Government reactions to the Depression sometimes exacerbated the distress. Import tariffs were strictly applied all over Europe, and even Britain ended its eighty-six years of free trade by the 1932 Import Duties Act and the Ottowa Imperial Conference, which granted preferential treatment to Dominion agricultural products, while British manufactured goods received reciprocal treatment in Dominion markets. France adopted similar tactics regarding her own colonies. Additionally, European states adopted deflationary policies, especially in Germany and France; budgetary control in Britain; and government intervention in Nazi Germany, concentrating on promoting heavy industry and a public works program. In Britain, the revival of domestic consumer demand provided with cheap money helped private enterprise and gradually turned around the economy. The Depression had a significant impact on domestic and international politics. Democracies experienced unusual political tendancies. Ministerial crises in France and the development of Fascist leagues, the Croix de Feu, led in 1936 to Leon Blum's Popular Front government, a sister system to that in Spain. Britain ended the normal single-party government and switched to a multiparty national government in the face of international events and Mosley's British Union of Fascists. Support for right-wing extremist parties grew, from the Lapua movement in Finland to the Hungarian Arrow Cross. Ruined farming interests backed the right (Romania's League of the Archangel Michael), and many middle-class voters in Germany brought Hitler to power.

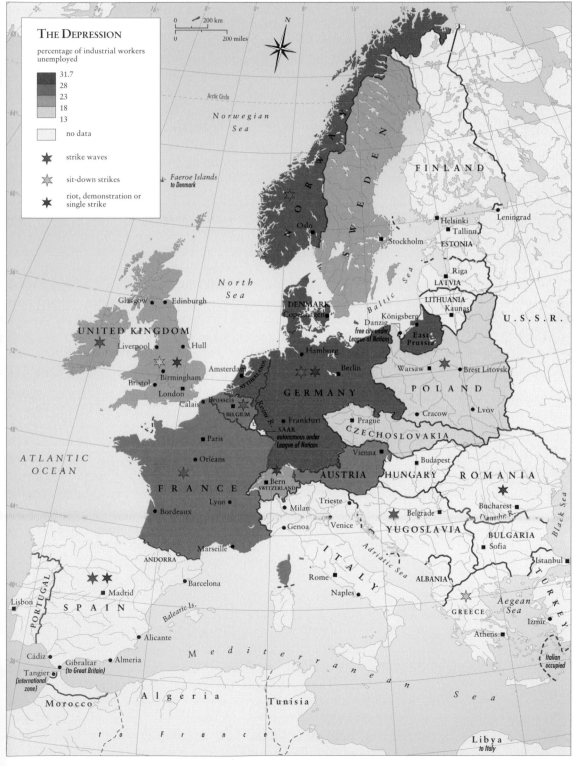

THE DEPRESSION

percentage of industrial workers unemployed

- 31.7
- 28
- 23
- 18
- 13
- no data

★ strike waves

☆ sit-down strikes

✦ riot, demonstration or single strike

PART VIII: MODERN TIMES

A poster supporting the Hitler Youth, a march and rally to be held in Nuremberg, 1938.

All the states of continental Europe, with the exceptions of Sweden, Switzerland, and Portugal, had been occupied, defeated, bombed, pillaged, fought over, and liberated between 1939 and 1945; Spain was suffering from the effects of its civil war between 1936 and 1939. Europe had suffered; Europe had been broken, national institutions and infrastructures had been suppressed and wrecked, and millions of European citizens had been thrown into prison, murdered, or carried off into slavery. All, whether conquerors or conquered, underwent a terrible experience during these war years, and with hindsight it might not seem unnatural that many intelligent citizens of European nation-states should have begun to nurse apparently heretical doubts about the continuing validity and sacrosanctness of the nation-state. It was such a mood that not only gave rise to the project of European integration, but also to the intellectual movements of existentialism and, in more recent times, postmodernism.

The first need was to rebuild Europe, first through the Marshall Plan, officially termed as the European Recovery Program, then, after 1950, through European-led initiatives. It was these initiatives that led to the establishment, in 1950, of the European Coal and Steel Community, which paved the way for the 1957 Treaty of Rome, and the hopes, of some, for a federated Europe.

Without doubt the overriding issue confronting Europeans in the aftermath of the Second World War was the impact of the Cold War. The origins of the Cold War may be found in the Yalta Conference of February 1945, when the "Big Three" Allied powers, the United States, the Soviet Union, and Great Britain, began to plan the peace that would follow the Second World War. Some commentators, including this writer, believe that with hindsight the Cold War can actually be predated to the period of the Russian Civil War (1918–1921), during which Allied military intervention in Russian affairs led to deep-seated Soviet suspicions of the Western powers. Whatever the case, growing suspicions of Soviet intentions by the United States and Great Britain were fueled by their inability to resolve satisfactorily disagreements between the Allied powers. As former allies ceased to be friends, the European continent fell subject to a bitter bipolar cleavage, based upon the ideological difference of two entirely different political, social, and economic systems held between "East" and "West."

The Soviet Union and its satellites–Albania (until 1961), Bulgaria, Czechoslovakia, Eastern Germany, Hungary, Poland, and Romania–were supported through the Zhdanov policy of 1948, which was the ideological and economic alternative to the rejected Marshall Aid and the Truman Doctrine. To a lesser extent this was bolstered by the ideological campaigns of Communist parties and their fellow travelers in Western Europe, where Communists in the first decade after the war were winning 25 percent of the electorate in countries such as France and Italy. It cannot be denied that Communism had a strong appeal in some European states in the immediate postwar period, and this was built upon the link between Communist parties with resistance movements after the German invasion of the Soviet Union in 1941. For example, in France the Communist Party was seen by many as being the *Parti des fusillés*, since 75,000 Communist "patriots" had been executed by the German occupiers between 1940 and 1945.

The Cold War was dominated by the interests of the two superpowers, whereby the United States aimed to contain the Soviet Union and the spread of Communism, while postwar Soviet leaders aimed to provide for the total security of their country; hardened as they were by the expenditure of tremendous efforts and vast population losses suffered during the First World War, the Civil War, and the Second World War, or Great Patriotic War as the Soviets termed it. Europe was divided into two hostile blocs ranging along the "iron curtain," which cleaved Europe into two. Europe, especially the north German plain, became one of the "front lines" of the East-West divide, where NATO forces confronted Warsaw Pact forces, without a shot being fired in anger. Western leaders were concerned with the threat of a Warsaw Pact Blitzkrieg-type attack, which might sweep rapidly through Germany to the North Sea coast. To counter this situation, nuclear weapons held the stalemate, since throughout the Cold War, in order to maintain peace, both sides believed in the strategies of deterrence and relied upon the existence of nuclear weapons in the face of protests against European governmental policies by peace movements in the early 1960s and 1980s.

Despite this the wishes and aspirations of the peoples of eastern Europe were not taken into account. During the slight thaw that followed the death of Stalin in March 1953, there was discontent in Poland and East Germany; then, in 1956, revolution broke out in Hungary, where nationalist opinion was influenced by the recent granting of independence to Austria as a neutral state in 1955. Soviet forces invaded Hungary, and the streets of Budapest were shelled by the Red Army. Some 190,000 Hungarians fled into exile, while their leader, Imre Nagy, was executed. Hungary was soon forced back into the Soviet fold.

The period 1963–1978 witnessed a gradual détente, or relaxation, of East-West tensions, despite the Soviet invasion of Czechoslovakia in 1968, when Czechoslovaks had rallied to General Secretary Alexander Dubcek's (1927–1993) appeal to "socialism with a human face," expressing themselves in lively debate and criticism and demonstrating in the streets of their capital, in what was known as the short-lived Prague Spring, only to be crushed by Soviet tanks.

The Conference on Security and Cooperation in Europe, held at Helsinki in August 1975, accepted the need for developing economic relations and recognized the postwar frontiers of Europe. The mood of the conference was one of conciliation and détente. As part of Willy Brandt's Ostpolitik, the Federal Republic of Germany accepted the postwar frontier with Poland, and West Berlin was no longer interpreted as part of the Federal Republic.

By the 1960s, the Soviet Union had achieved parity with the United States in the military sector. This parity, however, led to a huge drain on Soviet resources. The Soviet Union's GNP was only half the size of that of the United States, yet it had to devote a far greater proportion of its resources to defense in order to compete. A two-track economy developed in the Soviet Union between military and consumer needs. In addition, ten years of warfare in Afghanistan proved a costly failure to the Soviet Union and ended in ignominious defeat in 1988–1989.

"Die breite Masse eines Volkes...einer grossen Lüge lieber zum Opfer fällt als einer kleinen."

"The broad mass of the nation...will more easily fall victim to a big lie than to a small one."
Adolf Hitler

The problems of a devided Europe are commented on in this German magazine of 1949; two peoples, two countries, two leaders.

Maintaining Soviet control over the economically weak Eastern European buffer zone was costing too much and producing little of any benefit. President Reagan's Strategic Defense Initiative (Star Wars) eventually constituted an even greater strain on the Soviet economy.

The Cold War had entered a second phase of deteriorating relations with Soviet intervention in Afghanistan; this was reinforced by the election of Ronald Reagan as U.S. president in 1980, with his invective against the "evil empire." Similarly, the imposition of martial law in Poland in December 1981 led to a further deterioration of East-West relations, which, with the shooting down of the Korean airliner, flight KAL 007, by Soviet fighter aircraft, resulted in what some commentators have termed as the "Second Cold War."

Because of the great importance attached to military security during the Cold War, other issues and events in international relations were considered to be of lesser importance, such as the project of European integration that stemmed from the Treaty of Rome in 1957, or the degree of communication between the two halves of Europe. These either played a subordinate role or were treated as security issues in themselves. From a United States point of view this often meant two conflicting attitudes toward European integration, either as a vital necessity to the cohesion of the West, particularly in support of the NATO alliance, or as a potential threat to both the economic and political leadership of the United States.

In the 1980s, the cost of the Afghan War and "Star Wars" rivalry were placing great strain upon the Soviet economy. The USSR was spending between 11 and 15 percent GNP on defense in comparison with between 6 and 7 percent in the United States. The gap between military and civilian economies demonstrated a need for greater dialogue with the West, and a series of reforms, known as *perestroika* and *glasnost,* advocated economic reform and greater transparency.

By the end of 1989, the once monolithic Soviet Communist Party was losing its political preeminence, against a background of popular dissatisfaction with the Soviet government and the rising problem of nationalism and interethnic disputes. By the time of a failed coup of August 1991, it was clear that the Soviet Communist Party had lost its authority and that the Soviet Union was rapidly disintegrating. In December 1991, the Soviet Union ceased to exist, giving place to a loose alliance called the Commonwealth of Independent States. The political and social upheaval in the fifteen successor states to the former USSR constitutes one of the most momentous events affecting Europe in the latter part of the twentieth century.

After the end of the Cold War, the whole issue of European security and defense underwent tremendous transformation. Before the end of the Cold War, the threat of interstate conflict in western Europe had been almost unimaginable. But the experiences of former Yugoslavia and Chechnya have shown different, and the issues of nationalism and minority rights in eastern and central Europe have caused considerable concern. Since 1991, concerns have been expressed not so much over the possibility of interstate conflict, as that of intrastate conflict—a non-European as well as a European issue. In moments of pessimism, some influential European politicians even talked of "former" Yugoslavia as being a laboratory for the rest of Europe, although at the time of writing, the Yugoslav experience has been shown to be an exception rather than a norm. Likewise minorities' issues have soured relationships between the Hungarian, Romanian, and Slovak governments over the 9 percent Hungarian minorities living in both Slovakia and Hungary, or in the Baltic States of Latvia and Estonia and Lithuania, which have 30 percent or more Russian minority populations. In the West, regional movements have asserted themselves in Spain since the transition period following the death of Franco in 1975 (Basques, Cataláns, and Galicians), in Italy (Umberto Bossi's Northern League, which even tried to establish an independent Padania in September 1995), and in Belgium, where tensions between Walloon French speakers and the Flemish have consistently influenced Belgian politics since the 1950s. Oft-perceived regional and national differences are becoming more and more blurred. Whereas in the period 1989–1992 academics and political commentators argued that European integration was becoming a greater reality in contradistinction to the breakup of eastern and central European states, throughout the 1990s the idea of a Europe of the regions, with greater decentralization, has become the reality. In the mid-1990s, a sense of failure concerning European-led security projects led to reliance again upon the military and political weight of the United States in what had been described euphemistically as "Europe's backyard."

The conflicts in Bosnia-Herzegovina have also demonstrated a change in attitude to peacekeeping; since the Dayton agreements of November 1995, peacekeeping based upon impartiality has been transformed into the more interventionist and proactive policy of peace enforcement, with the introduction into Bosnia of IFOR, then SFOR troops, who work to keep the different factions apart.

Current developments on the European political scene gravitate around different issues, such as: the deepening and widening of the European Union; the impact of defense organizations, such as NATO in East Central Europe, upon the CIS, with the policy of "Partnership for Peace," which has caused great concern in Russia; minority and human rights issues and internal security issues with the policies of ending borders within the EU, the Schengen policy set against concerns expressed over the influx of economic and political migrants from East Central Europe; European initiatives in developing security and defense organizations, such as "Eurocorps," the European Community for Security and Cooperation (ECSC); and the Western European Union and the changing nature of Europe, whereby North-South divisions and tensions have replaced East-West tensions, resulting in growing tensions between richer and poorer states and societies. If Hungary, Poland, the Czech Republic, and Slovenia are in the next round of negotiations for entry into Europe, one wonders what will happen in turn to some of the Balkan states, such as Albania, Bulgaria, Macedonia, Romania, and Yugoslavia (Serbia and Montenegro). Will these states and peoples, which have played their role in the European mainstream across the centuries, now be excluded from the new European *imperium*, as their ancestors were one and a half millennia previously? Perhaps the biggest problem in Europe at the dawn of the new millennium is that of exclusion and identity.

THE FASCIST STATES

A poster from 1938 celebrating the Hitler-Mussolini Pact.

"Fascism accepts the individual only insofar as his interests coincide with the state's."
Benito Mussolini

The aftermath of the First World War with its peace treaties of Versailles, St. Germain, Neuilly, and Trianon reconstructed much of Europe into a patchwork of new and economically unviable states. The resentment felt by the defeated powers and the failure to put President Wilson's principle of the self-determination of peoples into practice left ethnic minorities in virtually every country, creating irredenta all over Europe. The subsequent growth or resurgence of intense nationalism was further fueled by inflation, the economic adjustment to peace.

The response to social, economic, and political change and dislocation spawned protest movements throughout Europe; the weaker the democratic traditions and institutions, the more likely that a country would flirt with some form of right-wing political movements or parties. A further event coloring European political views was the apparent success of the Bolshevik Revolution in Russia, the consequent fear of the spread of Communism after the failure of socialist revolutions in Finland, some Baltic states, Germany, Hungary, and Romania, and the founding of the Soviet Comintern, probably reinforced the development of right-wing parties, especially those of the fascist variant.

The difficulties of the interwar years were a fertile ground for fascism and its specific programs to end national problems. Fascism sought to construct a society wherein the individual was subordinated to an organic state, where economic conflicts were reconciled in the corporate state, and where duty and service to the state was accompanied by unquestioning loyalty to the leader, the *Führerprinzip*. Fascist regimes flourished between the wars, establishing themselves through the ballot box as in Germany and Italy, or by these countries' sponsoring or protecting such regimes in conquered or Allied states like Croatia, Slovakia, and Albania.

Although fascist ideas developed before 1914, the concept of "action" derived from Sorel found a particular home in Benito Mussolini's Italy. The Italian dictatorship began in 1922, and despite his claims to be totalitarian, fascism never managed to permeate all aspects of society. Based on a leadership cult, Mussolini's Italy sought: domination over the Adriatic by backing the Fascist Croatian Ustashe and penetrating Albania economically; hegemony in the Mediterranean, with dreams of acquiring French Tunisia and Corsica; and extending her East African possessions into Abyssinia. The desire to rebuild a new Roman empire led to Italy's ruin in the Second World War.

The German variant of fascism, National Socialism, redolent of biopolitics, racialism, anti-Semitism, and hostility toward democracy, was more brutal than its Italian forerunner. Successfully revising aspects of the Versailles Treaty, Hitler's foreign policy ambitions were grandiose–fantasies of a Central European empire in the search for *Lebensraum* and a central African imperium were part of a quest for world domination.

Both Hitler and Mussolini supported fascism elsewhere, but other movements never achieved power except through Nazi or Italian support in the war. Even Germano-Italian support for Franco in the Spanish Civil War (1936–1939) failed to sway El Caudillo into a fascist stance: Franco remained a traditional, authoritarian, conservative, military leader, supported by the old Spanish elites.

THE FASCIST STATES

- democratic countries
- repressive or conservative countries
- fascist countries
- communist dictatorship
- right-wing activity

0   200 km
0   200 miles

N

Norwegian
Sea

Arctic Circle

Faeroe Islands
to Denmark

NORWAY

SWEDEN

FINLAND

• Leningrad

■ Helsinki

Oslo •

Stockholm •

■ Tallinn

ESTONIA

North
Sea

• Riga

LATVIA

Baltic Sea

LITHUANIA

Glasgow •   • Edinburgh

UNITED KINGDOM

DENMARK

Copenhagen ■

Königsberg

Kaunas •

U.S.S.R.

• Dublin

Liverpool •

IRELAND

Danzig
(free city under
League of Nations)

East
Prussia

• Warsaw

• Brest Litovsk

Birmingham •

Amsterdam ■

• Hamburg

• Berlin

POLAND

London •

Calais ■

Brussels ■

BELGIUM

NETHERLANDS

GERMANY

Rhine R.

• Frankfurt

SAAR
(autonomous under
League of Nations)

• Prague

CZECHOSLOVAKIA

• Cracow

• Lvov

ATLANTIC
OCEAN

■ Paris

• Orléans

FRANCE

Lyon •

• Bordeaux

Bern ■

SWITZERLAND

Vienna •

AUSTRIA

Budapest •

HUNGARY

ROMANIA

Trieste •

• Milan

• Genoa

Venice

Belgrade ■

YUGOSLAVIA

Bucharest •

Danube R.

Black Sea

BULGARIA

Sofia •

Marseille •

ANDORRA

• Barcelona

Rome •

ITALY

ALBANIA

Istanbul ■

TURKEY

Izmir •

Lisbon ■

PORTUGAL

■ Madrid

SPAIN

Balearic Is.

Naples •

GREECE

Aegean
Sea

Athens •

• Alicante

Cádiz •

Gibraltar
to Great Britain

Almería •

Tangier
international
zone

Mediterranean

Sea

Italian
occupied

Morocco

Algeria

Tunisia

(to France)

Libya
to Italy

WORLD WAR II, 1939–1942

THE AXIS EXPANSION, 1938–42

- Germany, 1939
- German invasion of Poland, 1938–39
- Soviet attack on Baltic states and Poland
- added to the Reich, 1936–40
- Axis satellites, 1939–44
- invasion of Denmark and Norway, April 1940
- Allied landing in Norway and withdrawal
- invasion of Netherlands, Belgium and France, May 10, 1940
- British attack on Libya from Egypt, 1940
- Western states conquered, 1940
- invasion of Yugoslavia and Greece, April 1941
- allied landing in Greece, withdrawal to Crete then Egypt, 1941
- Italian advance, 1941
- Eastern territories and Balkans conquered, 1941
- German support of Italy, campaigns to Egypt, Feb. 1941– Sept. 1942
- invasion of Russia, June 1941
- Soviet industrial plants move east, 1941–42
- conquered, 1942
- controlled by Vichy, 1942
- Allied controlled, late 1942
- neutral states

Nordcape

Norwegian Sea

Narvik

Arctic Circle

NORWAY

SWEDEN

FINLAND

Lulea

Helsinki

Leningrad

Oslo

Stockholm

Baltic Sea

SOVIET

Mosco

DENMARK

Copenhagen

Königsberg

East Prussia

North Sea

Dublin

IRELAND

UNITED KINGDOM

Hamburg

Berlin

Warsaw

POLAND

Kiev

Amsterdam

NETH.

London

Brus.

BELGIUM

GERMANY

Frankfurt

Prague

CZECHO SLOVAKIA

Paris

Munich

Vienna

Aug. 1940, to Hungary

ATLANTIC OCEAN

FRANCE

Bern

SWITZ.

Geneva

AUSTRIA

Budapest

HUNGARY

ROMANIA

Vichy

Nov. 11, 1942 occupied

Milan

Genoa

Venice

YUGOSLAVIA

Belgrade

Bucharest

Danube R.

B

Marseille

Adriatic Sea

Sofia

BULGARIA

Istanbul

PORTUGAL

SPAIN

Corsica

Rome

ITALY

ALBANIA

GREECE

Aegean Sea

T

Lisbon

Madrid

Sardinia

Taranto

Athens

Balearic Is.

Mediterranean

Sicily

Malta to Britain

Crete

Sea

Algiers

Bone

Tunis

N

French North Africa

Tripoli

Benghazi

Lybia to Italy

Lybia to Italy

E

0 200 km

0 200 miles

The Second World War largely originated in the disputes and bitterness that had remained unresolved since the end of the First World War. The Germans were particularly bitter over the severe terms imposed upon them by the Treaty of Versailles.

By 1933, Adolf Hitler, leader of the extremely nationalist, anti-Semitic National Socialist Workers Party (NSDAP), was established in power and immediately began the rearmament of Germany. Benefiting from the reluctance of other European powers, especially Britain and France, to oppose him, he contravened the Versailles Treaty by sending German troops into the demilitarized Rhineland in March 1936. Later that year, Benito Mussolini, the fascist dictator of Italy, signed the Rome-Berlin "axis" agreement and the following year joined the Anti-Comintern Pact signed between Germany and Japan.

In March 1938, German forces occupied Austria, Hitler's birthplace, which was incorporated into the Third Reich (Anschluss). The following year the Germans, having incorporated the so-called Sudetenland by agreement in 1938, then in turn annexed and neutralized what was left of Czechoslovakia.

On September 1, 1939, Hitler having signed a nonaggression pact with the Soviet Union, German forces invaded Poland. Great Britain and France declared war on Germany two days later, and on September 16, Soviet forces invaded Poland from the east, dividing that country between the Third Reich and the Soviet Union. In the winter of 1939–1940, Estonia, Latvia, and Lithuania, independent since 1918, were reoccupied by the Soviet Union, whose forces also invaded Finland and eventually occupied Karelia.

In April 1940, Germany occupied the whole of Denmark and several Norwegian ports and on May 10, launched a Blitzkrieg (Lightning War) offensive in the west, sweeping through the Netherlands and Belgium into France. The bulk of the British Expeditionary Force, together with a large number of French troops, were evacuated at Dunkirk. An armistice was signed between Germany and France in June, with the Germans occupying Paris and the strategic northern and western seaboards of France, leaving central and southern parts to the control of Marshal Pétain's Vichy régime.

In August and September a bombing offensive, the Battle of Britain, was launched by Goering's Luftwaffe against the British, in an attempt to prepare the way for German troops to cross the English Channel and occupy Britain. However, the Royal Air Force won the day, forcing Hitler to break off his invasion plans.

In April 1941, Germany overran Yugoslavia and Greece; this diversion into the Balkans was in support of Hitler's Italian allies.

On June 22, Hitler broke the Nonaggression Pact, caught the Red Army completely by surprise, and drove deep into Soviet territory, overrunning Estonia, Latvia, Lithuania, Belorussia, and Ukraine. However, he was eventually halted before Moscow and Leningrad by Soviet counterattacks and resistance, aided by the long Russian winter.

In the summer of 1942, the Germans drove on toward the Black Sea and toward the Caucasus oilfields, only to be halted at Stalingrad and Ordzhonikidze, a Soviet victory that coincided with that of General Montgomery in El Alamain in Egypt. This was the high-water mark of the Axis advance.

WORLD WAR II, 1942–1945

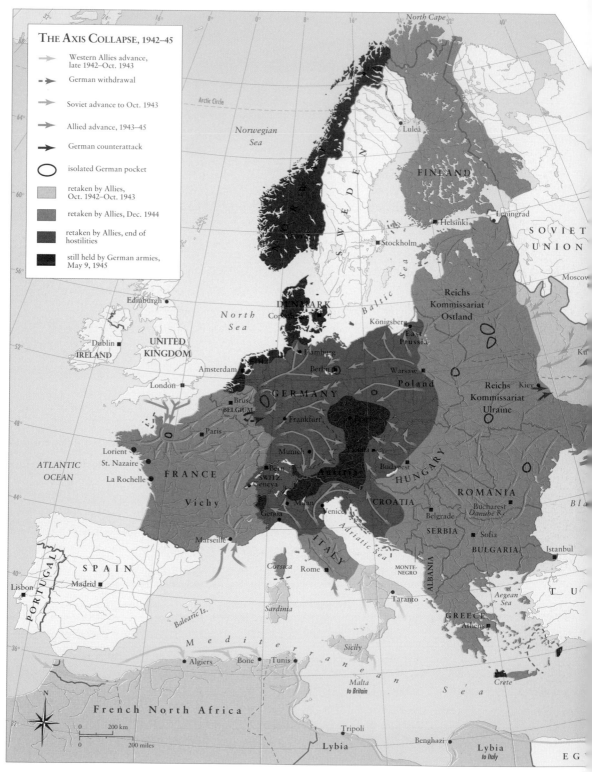

THE AXIS COLLAPSE, 1942–45

→ Western Allies advance, late 1942–Oct. 1943

⇢ German withdrawal

→ Soviet advance to Oct. 1943

→ Allied advance, 1943–45

→ German counterattack

◯ isolated German pocket

▦ retaken by Allies, Oct. 1942–Oct. 1943

▦ retaken by Allies, Dec. 1944

▦ retaken by Allies, end of hostilities

▦ still held by German armies, May 9, 1945

When Japan attacked U.S. installations at Pearl Harbor, Hawaii, and the Philippines in December 1941, the United States declared war against all the Axis powers. Japan lost its initial advantage and momentum with the sea battles of the Coral Sea and Midway in the early summer of 1942.

Meanwhile, in North Africa British and Commonwealth forces who had been victorious against Italian opposition at the beginning of 1941 were now engaged in bitter fighting with Rommel's Afrika Korps with a campaign that swung back and forth across the western desert. Victory at El Alamain in November 1942 turned the tide of the desert war. That same month, U.S., British, and Free French troops landed in North Africa, and the Axis armies were forced out of North Africa into Sicily. By July, Allied troops landed in Sicily, invading Italy in September. The Italian fascist government signed an armistice with the Allies, and in October the Italians declared war on Germany. Harsh fighting ensued with German forces that had moved into Italy. By the end of that summer, the Germans consolidated on the Gothic line, along the River Po, fighting throughout the autumn and winter of 1944.

In the meantime, the Red Army's victory over Von Paulus's Sixth Army at Stalingrad in February 1943 was followed in July by the greatest tank battle of the war at Kursk. The Red Army began to push the Germans back, so that throughout the winter of 1943–44, the Red Army recovered much of occupied Soviet territory and in April 1944, advanced on Central Europe.

In June 1944, the Allies, under the supreme command of U.S. General Dwight Eisenhower, landed in Normandy, establishing a bridgehead in Europe and the much awaited Second Front. By June 18, U.S. General Bradley had gained control of the Cotentin Peninsula, while British and Commonwealth forces took the city of Caen by July 9, and advanced on Falais, helping to surround the German Fifth and Seventh Armies; murderous aerial bombardments resulted in the deaths of some 60,000 German soldiers, thus momentarily breaking the spirit of German resistance. General Patton swept through France as Montgomery moved up the French coast. Paris was liberated by French General Leclerc on August 26, and Brussels was liberated by British forces on September 3.

Despite setbacks at Arnheim in the early autumn and the German counterattack in the Ardennes during the bitter winter weather of December, the Rhine was crossed in February 1945, and the occupation of Germany began, as Soviet forces moved in from the east, occupying Berlin by the end of April. Hitler committed suicide on April 30, and on May 8, all German forces signed an unconditional surrender.

A German V-2 rocket is prepared for launching at a British target, beginning the ballistic missile age.

"Let us therefore brace ourselves to our duties, and so bear ourselves that, if the British empire and its Commonwealth last for a thousand years, men will still say; 'This was our finest hour.'"
Winston Churchill

RUIN, BANKRUPTCY, AND RECOVERY

By 1945 many towns in Europe lay in ruins, such as Nuremberg, above. Only a massive injection of aid from the United States would hasten recovery.

It was a devastated Europe that emerged from the embers of the Second World War, with its prestige in tatters throughout the world, but especially in the European colonies. Europe was economically and spiritually bankrupt, with transport, fuel, food, and housing in short supply, to say nothing of the severe bomb and war damage, highlighted by the destruction of cities such as Berlin, Caen, Coventry, Dresden, and London and many more. The ravages of war were compounded by a massive refugee problem of peoples returning to their homes in both the Soviet and Allied-controlled sectors.

Nevertheless, with the infrastructures of most European states destroyed, Europe had to rebuild itself. Before 1950, this project, at least in the West, was highly dependent upon American aid, especially Marshall Aid, officially known as the European Recovery Program (ERP), established in June 1947. The Soviet Union would refuse to accept Marshall Aid out of fear of American political, cultural, and military hegemony. Consequently Eastern Europe, under Soviet influence, fell under the Zhdanov policy of 1948 with the concomitant internationalist and progressive Peace Movement and Comecon (Council for Mutual Economic Assistance)—a supranational economic agency, established in January 1949.

The ERP provided $6.8 billion in the first fifteen months of operation. Marshall Aid also created Inter Governmental Organizations (IGOs), which acted as agencies for European recovery and cooperation: The Organization for European Economic Cooperation (OEEC), which was made up of eighteen European countries, including the United States and Canada, provided $17,000 million between 1948 and 1952; the Technical Cooperation Administration (TCA) supplied technical and material support rather than financial aid.

The negative side of Marshall Aid was that it was seen by its detractors as being part of the apparatus of the Cold War. At the same time there were fears of Soviet influence, highlighted by large communist support at 25 percent of the electorates of Italy and France. By the end of the 1940s, Europe would be split into two ideological blocs, "East" and "West"; two antithetical political, social, and economic systems that lay at the heart of the Cold War scenario.

Concerns over external influence were felt within several European states, especially France, where a third force, neutralism, was advocated, proposing non-alignment with either Moscow or Washington; nevertheless, this was poorly supported in the national elections of 1951.

The year 1950 proved to be a watershed in the process of European recovery, with the governments of several European states beginning to take greater control of their own affairs and destinies by demonstrating a serious intent toward economic and political collaboration. Recovery and reconstruction would provide the catalyst of the European project, based upon mutual cooperation, that would materialize with the Treaty of Rome in 1957.

The Marshall Plan greatly contributed to the recovery of Europe, restoring industrial and agricultural production and bolstering international trade. Marshall Aid allowed European states to modernize their economies and repair the dislocation of social patterns that had arisen from the Second World War.

"From Stettin in the Baltic to Trieste in the Adriatic, an iron curtain has descended across the Continent."
Winston Chuchill

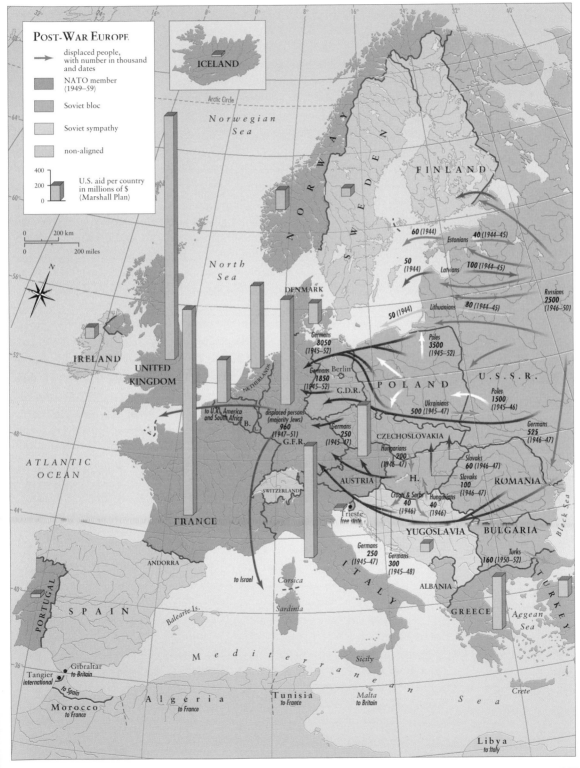

POST-WAR EUROPE

→ displaced people, with number in thousand and dates

■ NATO member (1949–59)

■ Soviet bloc

■ Soviet sympathy

■ non-aligned

U.S. aid per country in millions of $ (Marshall Plan)

ICELAND

Arctic Circle

Norwegian Sea

NORWAY

SWEDEN

FINLAND

North Sea

DENMARK

IRELAND

UNITED KINGDOM

NETHERLANDS

ATLANTIC OCEAN

FRANCE

SWITZERLAND

ANDORRA

PORTUGAL

SPAIN

Balearic Is.

Corsica

Sardinia

Gibraltar to Britain

Tangier international

to Spain

Morocco to France

Algeria to France

Tunisia to France

Malta to Britain

Sicily

Mediterranean Sea

Crete

Libya to Italy

60 (1944)

50 (1944)

50 (1944)

Estonians 40 (1944–45)

Latvians 100 (1944–45)

Lithuanians 80 (1944–45)

Russians 2500 (1946–50)

Poles 3500 (1945–52)

Germans 8050 (1945–52)

Germans Berlin 1850 (1945–52)

G.D.R.

POLAND

U.S.S.R.

Poles 1500 (1945–46)

Ukrainians 500 (1945–47)

Germans 525 (1946–47)

to U.K., America and South Africa

displaced persons (majority Jews) 960 (1947–51)

G.F.R.

B.

Germans 250 (1945–47)

CZECHOSLOVAKIA

Hungarians 200 (1946–47)

Slovaks 60 (1946–47)

Slovaks 100 (1946–47)

ROMANIA

AUSTRIA

H.

Croats & Serbs 40 (1946)

Hungarians 40 (1946)

to Israel

Germans 250 (1945–47)

Germans 300 (1945–48)

SWITZERLAND

Trieste free state

YUGOSLAVIA

BULGARIA

Turks 160 (1950–52)

Black Sea

ITALY

ALBANIA

GREECE

Aegean Sea

TURKEY

147

EUROPEAN UNION

Not everyone was in favor of a new united Europe; a British political poster from the 1970s advocates withdrawal from the European Economic Union.

"The contribution which an organized and living Europe can bring to civilization is indispensible to the maintenance of peaceful relations."
Robert Schuman,
May 9, 1950

In the aftermath of the Second World War, the founding fathers of the project for European integration, among them Robert Schuman, Jean Monnet, Konrad Adenauer, Alcide de Gaspierri, and Paul-Henri Spaak, sought to work together in a spirit of reconciliation to build Europe anew and to strengthen European economic competition in the world marketplace.

Although the European Economic Community was founded by the Treaties of Rome in March 1957, its origins lie in the Schuman Declaration of May 9, 1950, which advocated the pooling together of coal and steel production, by establishing a single higher authority that would merge the coal, iron, and steel industries of France, West Germany, Italy, and the Benelux countries. The European Coal and Steel Community (ECSC) was also designed to be "a first step in the federation of Europe," in a bid to establish peace forever on the European continent by ending the traditional enmity between France and Germany. The ECSC began to function in July 1952 and would be merged with the EEC and Euratom in 1967, within the European Community.

A second significant development was the unsuccessful attempt to establish a European Defence Community among the six ECSC states. This project was launched by French Foreign Minister René Pleven and ratified by five of the member states in 1954, but rejected by the French Assemblée Nationale, due to a growing public opinion that was concerned with the rearmament of Germany.

In accordance with the Treaty of Rome, the European Community established common policies among the six member states for: agriculture, transport, the movement of capital and labor, and the erection of common external tariffs. A European Parliament was set up, meeting alternately in Strassbourg and Luxembourg, alongside the European Commission in Brussels and the European Court. Later the Lomé Conventions of 1975, 1979, 1984, and 1989 would establish development and technical cooperation aid programs, and would ease customs duties for over sixty countries.

The United Kingdom, Ireland, and Denmark joined the EEC in January 1973. The "nine" became ten when Greece followed in 1981, and then twelve in 1986, with the entry of Spain and Portugal. Sweden, Finland, and Austria became members of the European Union in January 1995.

A major development took place in 1992 with the signing of the Maastricht Treaty, which established the Single European Act. At its simplest level, this can be described as "an amendment of the Treaty of Rome plus citizenship," establishing a single European Act and a peoples' Europe based upon the three pillars of European security, the European Community, and internal affairs.

As Europe enters the twenty-first century, two key issues, "deepening" and "widening," confront the European communities. To what extent does the Union progress further down the road toward becoming a federal, supranational state with, for example, its own army and a common European currency; and how does the European Union respond to the enormous changes that have taken place in Eastern Europe since the fall of the Berlin Wall in 1989 and the end of the Cold War?

EUROPEAN UNION

development of the European Community

- signature of the Treaty of Rome, 1957
- EEC member added 1973
- EEC member added 1981
- EEC member added 1986
- became part of the EEC after union of Germany, 1990
- EEC member added 1995
- membership pending, 1996

military alliances

- original member of North Atlantic Treaty Organization, 1949
- later NATO member
- Warsaw Pact, 1955–90
- neutral state

0   200 km
0   200 miles

Norwegian Sea

ICELAND

FINLAND

Helsinki
Leningrad
Oslo
Tallinn
Stockholm   ESTONIA
Baltic Sea   LATVIA
Riga
LITHUANIA
Konigsberg   Vilnius
DENMARK   Gdánsk   RUSSIA   (U.S.S.R.)
Copenhagen   (until 1991)

North Sea

Glasgow   Edinburgh
UNITED KINGDOM
Dublin
IRELAND   Liverpool   Hamburg   Berlin   Warsaw
Amsterdam   POLAND
Birmingham   The Hague   GERMANY
Bristol   NETHERLANDS   (GERMAN FEDERAL REPUBLIC)   (GERMAN DEMOCRATIC REPUBLIC)   Cracow
London   Brussels   *Rhine R.*   Frankfurt   Prague   Lvov
Calais   BELGIUM   Prague   CZECH
Paris   *1965*   Vienna   SLOVAKIA
FRANCE   Bratislava
1966 withdrawal   Bern   AUSTRIA   HUNGARY   ROMANIA
SWITZERLAND   Budapest
ATLANTIC OCEAN   Lyon   Milan   SLOVENIA   Zagreb   Bucharest
Bordeaux   Genoa   Trieste   Ljubljana   *Danube R.*   *Black Sea*
Venice   CROATIA   BOSNIA HERZEG.   Belgrade   BULGARIA
Marseille   Monaco   *Adriatic Sea*   Sarajevo   SERBIA   Sofia   Istanbul
ANDORRA   ITALY   MONTE-NEGRO
Corsica   Rome   ALBANIA   Skopje   TURKEY
Barcelona   Tiranë   *Aegean Sea*   Izmir   *1952*
SPAIN   Madrid   *Sardinia*   Naples   *1968 withdrawal*   GREECE   *1952*
1982   Athens
Lisbon   Balearic Is.
PORTUGAL   Alicante
Cádiz   Gibraltar   Almeria
Tangier   *to United Kingdom*
Mediterranean Sea   Sicily   Crete
MOROCCO   ALGERIA   TUNISIA   CYPRUS
LIBYA

NEW HOPE, OLD DIVISIONS

The fall of the Berlin Wall in November 1989 and the subsequent wave of change that swept through eastern Europe arose from a popular desire for liberalism and democracy nurtured by new hopes for a better standard of living and quality of life after forty-five years under the control of rigid, totalitarian Communist governments and their systems.

The early 1990s witnessed a difficult social and economic transition, which led to unemployment, where previously there had been overmanning or where technologies and industrial processes were considered to be behind those of the West; this coincided with cuts in welfare and social support and led to a new underprivileged class, whose sense of bitterness and feelings of exclusion and frustration was sometimes vented in sporadic outbursts of violence, tainted by nationalistic yearnings that hearkened back, in some cases, to deep-rooted dissatisfactions with settlements that had been established by the Paris Peace Conference of 1919–1920. Some historians saw in this a "rebirth of history" whereby the traditional bipolar and economic cleavage between East and West that had existed since the end of the Second World War had gone, replaced by older divisions and tensions such as ethnic nationalism, national and regional identity, and religious difference.

With these developments there has been a rise in organized crime, black marketeering, and mafia-related activities, particularly in some of the less economically advantaged east-central European states. Many commentators have also remarked upon the lack of a fully developed civil society, due to the former presence of a monolithic Communist party and earlier political and cultural differences from the West, which as this survey has shown, have existed since the end of the middle ages, if not since the fourth century. Since the time of the French Revolution these differences have often been expressed in terms of economic, social, and political "backwardness" in the region.

In the 1990s outbursts of nationalism were experienced in both eastern and western Europe; with the rise of the NPD (National Democratic Party) in Germany and the MSI (Movimento Sociale Italiano) in Italy, and regular returns

NEW AND OLD STATES EMERGE, 1991–93

reunited, 1990

new state, 1991

new state, 1992

new state, 1993

area not under control of new government

■ capital of new state

1 Serbian backed 'Independent Krajina'.

2 Serbian and Croatian populations seize control of their own ethnic areas.

3 Russian majority form Transnistrian Republic.

4 Gagauzian separatist movement.

5 Abkhazian separatist movement.

6 South Ossetian separatist movement.

7 Chechenian separatist movement.

8 Armenian population struggle to control Nagorno-Karabakh and adjacent territory to the south.

of between 12 and 15 percent for the Front Nationale in the first rounds of successive French elections, or for the Vlaams Blok in the Flemish part of Belgium; nevertheless, nationalism has, by and large, remained a marginalized protest vote in the West.

In the East, by contrast, experience has been somewhat different. Extremes of ethnic nationalist violence were experienced in parts of the region after the breakup of the Soviet Union, particularly in Chechnya, and also during the bitter wars of "former" Yugoslavia, most notably in Bosnia-Herzegovina and Croatia, with the attendant horrors of ethnic cleansing carried out by all factions. But Yugoslavia did not become the benchmark of nationalist difference for the rest of eastern and central Europe; indeed, even among the Yugoslav successor states, Macedonia, Slovenia, and Yugoslavia (Serbia and Montenegro) were spared the horrors of war and bitter interethnic conflict. Nevertheless the ordinary citizens of Serbia and Montenegro suffered considerably the economic effects of sanctions and hyperinflation prior to the signing of the Dayton Accords in November 1995.

Against this background concerns over the security of Europe in the aftermath of the Cold War have been placed high on the European agenda, and one wonders if the announced withdrawal of SFOR troops from Bosnia-Herzegovina in June 1998 will lead to further outbreaks of conflict in southeast Europe, or whether the recent tensions in Albania and their potential implications upon Albania's neighbors: Montenegro, Serbia, Greece, Macedonia, Bulgaria, and Turkey will transform the Balkans once again into a European "powder keg"?

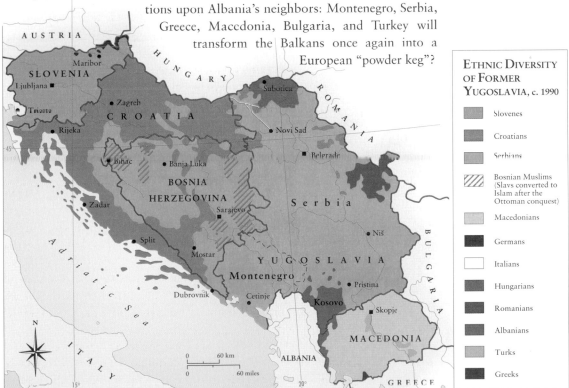

ETHNIC DIVERSITY OF FORMER YUGOSLAVIA, c. 1990

Slovenes

Croatians

Serbians

Bosnian Muslims (Slavs converted to Islam after the Ottoman conquest)

Macedonians

Germans

Italians

Hungarians

Romanians

Albanians

Turks

Greeks

CHRONOLOGY

7,000 BC Agriculture appears in the Aegean, begins spreading northwards.

4,000 BC Metal smelting begins in the Balkans.

3,000-2,000 BC First Cycladic civilization (Aegean). The use of bronze (copper and tin).

2,000 BC Minoan civilization (Crete). Trading begins throughout region.

1,800 BC Stonehenge completed (Britain).

1,600 BC Rise of Mycenaean civilization (Greece).

1,300 BC Fortification of Athens' acropolis.

1,000 BC Rise of the Etruscans (northern Italy). Iron-working in Germany and Austria spreads westwards.

750 BC Formation of Greek city-states, throughout the Mediterranean. Rise of Athens and Sparta. Scythian horseman, from the Russian steppes, begin to spread into eastern Europe.

510 BC Foundation of the Republic of Rome.

505 BC Establishment of democracy in Athens.

500 BC Germanic peoples expand through northern Europe.

490 BC Greeks in Asia Minor rebel against Persian rule. Persians defeated by Athenians at Battle of Marathon.

480 BC Greeks defeat Persian invasion forces under Xerxes at the Battles of Salamis, Plataea and Mycale. Greeks form the Delian League alliance.

450 BC Celtic 'La Tène' culture emerges in central Europe, spreads through northern Europe.

443 BC Pericles elected to power in Athens.

432 BC War begins between Athens and Sparta.

404 BC Sparta victorious over Athens, but then goes to war with Persia.

395 BC Athenian coalition defeats Sparta.

390 BC Gauls invade early Rome.

338 BC Philip II of Macedon defeats the Greeks at the Battle of Chaeronea.

331 BC Philip's son Alexander defeats the Persians under Darius III and enters Egypt, founding Alexandria and his empire.

290 BC Rome controls central Italy.

280 BC Alexander's empire splits into "Hellenistic" kingdoms.

264-241 BC First of three 'Punic' (Phoenician) Wars between Rome and Carthage for control of the Mediterranean.

218-201 BC Second Punic War. Carthaginian General Hannibal crosses the Alps and invades Italy from the north.

206 BC The Romans conquer Spain.

149-146 BC Third Punic War ends with the Romans razing Carthage and founding North African colonies. Macedonia and Greece fall under Roman control.

60 BC Germanic and Celtic tribes attack central Gaul, prompting the campaigns of conquest by Julius Caesar.

49 BC Julius Caesar becomes Emperor after civil war in Rome.

31 BC Octavian victorious at the Battle of Actium, annexes Egypt, and becomes Emperor Augustus.

AD 43 The Romans invade Britain.

AD 70 Jewish revolt in Palestine; the Romans take Jerusalem. Christianity begins to spread through the eastern provinces.

AD 114 Roman Empire at its height under Trajan.

AD 193 A year of six Roman Emperors, assassinations and upheaval, resulting in civil war.

AD 195-217 Wars between the Romans and the Parthians, from Asia Minor.

AD 240-270 Encroachments on the Empire by Goths, a Teutonic people from the River Vistula region. Eventually the Goths are driven back, but the Empire is fragmenting.

AD 294 The Empire reorganized and strengthened by Emperor Diocletian .

324 Constantine defeats his rival Licinius and reunites the Empire, making Constantinople (formerly Byzantium) his new capital. Constantine declares Christianity the Empire's official religion. Henceforth, the Roman Emperors are all nominally Christian.

375 The Visigoths (western Goths) are driven by marauding Huns from central Asia across the River Danube and into the Roman Empire.

378 Romans defeated by the Visigoths at the Battle of Adrianople.

395 The Roman Empire is once again divided, between the two sons of Theodosius I. Visigoths invade Greece. Incursions from the north into Gaul and Spain by other Germanic tribes, the Vandals and the Suebi.

410 Rome sacked by the Visigoths under Alaric.

439 The Vandals capture Carthage; western Roman Empire in collapse.

451 Germanic Angles, Saxons and Jutes invade Britain.

476 The German Odoacer proclaimed king of the western Empire, usurping Romulus Augustulus.

486 Clovis founds Merovingian kingdom of the Franks in northern Gaul.

493 Ostrogoths (eastern Goths) seize power in Italy.

533 The Romans under Justinian regain control of Italy and North Africa.

600-1,000 The eastern Byzantine Empire, based on Constantinople, grows steadily more powerful in Asia Minor and southeastern Europe, spreading Greek Orthodox Christianity and resisting Persian and Arab invasions. Slavs spread westwards and southwards.

650 Muslim Arabs begin attacking Byzantium.

680 Bulgars invade the Balkans, establishing a rival empire north of the Byzantine.

687 The foundation of the Carolingian dynasty.

711 Muslims invade Spain from Morocco.

718 The Byzantines resist Arab siege of Constantinople.

732 Muslims defeated by Franks at the Battle of Poitiers.

774 Carolingian Emperor Charlemagne invades northern Italy.

790 From Scandinavia, Viking and Danish raids begin on northern Europe, Britain and Ireland.

800 Charlemagne becomes Emperor in Rome. Foundation of the Holy Roman (western) Empire.

830 The Vikings reach Constantinople.

843 The Carolingian Empire is divided by the Treaty of Verdun into areas roughly corresponding with modern France and Germany.

860-880 The Vikings seize Novogorod and Kiev, capital of Russia, and attack Constantinople.

890 Incursions begin into central and southern Europe by non-Christian Magyar horsemen from around the Danube (Hungary).

911 Vikings gain Normandy (northwestern France).

929 A Muslim caliphate is established at Cordoba (Spain).

955 The Magyars are defeated by German King Otto I at the Battle of Lechfield (Augsburg).

959 England is unified under King Edgar.

960 Poland is unified by Miesko I.

962 Otto is declared Emperor in Rome.

983 The Slavs rebel against Germanic expansion eastwards.

1014 In Ireland, the Vikings are defeated by Munster King Brian Boru at the Battle of Clontarf.

1018 The Byzantines gain control of Bulgaria.

1031 The Caliphate at Cordoba is overthrown.

1066 The Norman invasion of Britain.

1071 The Normans invade Italy. The Seljuks decisively beat the Byzantines at the Battle of Manzikert (Turkey).

1085 In Spain, Toledo is recaptured from the Muslims by King Alfonso I of Leon.

1096 The First Crusade is launched to liberate Palestine.

1125 The Germans expand eastwards.

1147 The Second Crusade to Spain; Lisbon is recaptured.

1154 Angevin Henry II becomes King of England and France.

1170 Anglo-Normans seize Dublin (Ireland).

1204 The Franks conquer Byzantium in the Fourth Crusade.

1215 In England, King John's Magna Carta makes concessions to the barons.

1230 Mongol incursions into Russia begin.

1241 The Mongols invade Russia, Ukraine, Poland, Hungary and Bohemia.

1250 With the death of Frederick II, the Holy Roman Empire collapses in Italy and Germany.

1261 Greek control of Constantinople is restored with coronation of Michael VIII.

1309 The Papacy is moved from Rome to Avignon (France).

1337 Start of the Hundred Years War between France and England.

1378-1417 The Great Schism between rival papacies at Avignon and Rome.

1389 The Ottoman Turks gain control of the Balkans at the Battle of Kosovo.

1418 Henry the Navigator launches Portuguese explorations of Africa.

1447 Gutenberg invents the printing press.

1453 The French recapture England's continental possessions. The Ottomans take Constantinople, bringing an end to the Byzantine Empire.

1455-1485 The Wars of the Roses (Lancaster and York) in England.

1480 Ivan III, the first Russian Tsar, overthrows the Mongols.

1492 The Granada emirate falls, ending Muslim rule in Spain. Columbus' landfall in the West Indies.

1494 Franco-Habsburg wars begin for control of central Europe.

1519 Charles V of Spain and Holland is elected Holy Roman Emperor. Magellan circumnavigates globe.

1521 The Protestant Reformation

1534 English King Henry VIII breaks away from Rome; establishment of the Church of England.

1545 Counter-Reformation discipline instituted by the Roman Catholic Church at the Council of Trent.

1556 Ivan IV of Russia invades Volga basin.

1560-1598 Religious wars in France.

1572 The Dutch, aided by the English, rebel against Philip II of Spain.

1588 The Spanish Armada invasion force is defeated by the English.

1609 Dutch Republic gains independence.

1618-1648 The Thirty Years War between the Catholic and Protestant powers ends with the Treaty of Westphalia.

1642-1646 English civil wars result in the execution of the King.

1654 Ukraine ceded by Poland to Russia.

1660 The Restoration of the English monarchy under Charles II.

1661 Louis XIV accedes to French throne, initiating French expansion.

1683 The Ottomans besiege Vienna.

1699 Hungary ceded by the Ottomans to the Habsburgs.

1700 The Great Northern War begins between Sweden and Russia.

1702 The War of Spanish succession begins. England allies with Holland and Austria to stifle Louis XIV's ambitions.

1707 England and Scotland unite.

1709 The Swedes are defeated by the Russians under Peter the Great at the Battle of Poltava.

1713 The War of Spanish succession ends with the Treaty of Utrecht .

1740-1748 The War of Austrian succession. England supports Maria Theresa against France, Spain and Prussia. Prussia annexes Silesia.

1756-1763 The Seven Years' War. England and Prussia fight France, Spain and Austria.

1776-1783 The American War of Independence from Britain ends with Treaty of Versailles.

1783 Russia annexes the Crimea.

1789-1802 The French Revoluton.

1791 Russia captures Black Sea steppes from Turks.

1795 Partition of Poland.

1804 Napoleon becomes Emperor of France .

1805 French and Spanish navy defeated by British at Trafalgar.

1805-1812 Napoleonic defeats of Austrians and conquest of Prussia, Italy, and Spain. Napoleon invaded Russia.

1815 Napoleon finally defeated by the British at Waterloo (Belgium). Congress of Vienna.

1821 Greek war of independence.

1845 Great Famine in Ireland starts heavy emigration to U.S.A.

1848 'The Year of Revolutions'; violent suppression widespread.

1852 The French Republic falls; Napoleon III declared Emperor.

1854-1856 The Crimean War.

1859 War between France and Austria over Lombardy.

1861, 1862 Italy and Romania proclaimed kingdoms.

1864 Russia stifles rebellion in Poland.

1866 Prussia annexes Schleswig-Holstein from Denmark, threatens Austria.

1867 Austro-Hungarian alliance forms with dual monarchy.

1870 Italian troops expel French from Rome.

1871 Prussia annexes Alsace and Lorraine from French, forms unified German Empire. Establishment of the third French Republic.

1878 The Treaty of Berlin, Bulgaria, Romania, Serbia and Montenegro become independent states.

1879 German alliance with Austro-Hungarians. Expansion of German navy.

1894 French alliance with Russians.

1904 French Entente Cordiale with Britain.

1905 The first phase of the Russian Revolution. The Tsar suppresses the revolt but grants civil liberties. Norway gains independence from Sweden.

1907 British entente with Russia.

1908 Austria annexes Bosnia and Herzegovina.

1912-1913 War in the Balkans.

1914-1918 The First World War.

1917 The Tsar abdicates, Bolshevik takeover in Russia. America enters War.

1918 Tide turns against the Germans, who sue for peace.

1919 Treaty of Versailles dismantles Austro-Hungarian Empire, leaves Germany reduced, indebted and stripped of colonies. The League of Nations founded.

1922 Union of Soviet Socialist Republics (USSR) established by Lenin. Fascists under Mussolini gain power in Italy. In Ireland, 26 southern counties win independence (Eire), 6 northern counties (Ulster) remain British.

1923 French occupation of the German Ruhr.

1931 Spain declared a Republic.

1933 Hitler becomes German Chancellor; Nazis seize power, start rearming.

1936 German occupation of the Rhineland. In Spain, General Franco seizes power, overthrowing the Republic; civil war begins. In Russia, Stalin embarks on 'Great Purges'.

1938 Germany annexes Austria. Munich conference. Germany occupies the Sudetenland (Czechoslovakia). The Nazis initiate violent persecution of Jews.

1939 German-Russian non-aggression pact. Franco victorious in Spain. Second World War.

1945 United Nations established. The 'Cold War' begins.

1947 Americans' Marshall Plan for economic reconstruction of Europe.

1947-1949 Greek civil war.

1948 Communist regimes installed in Czechoslovakia and Hungary. The Berlin airlift.

1949 North Atlantic Treaty Organization (NATO) founded.

1955 Warsaw Pact (Eastern Bloc treaty) instituted.

1956 Russians crush revolts in Poland and Hungary.

1957 European Economic Community (EEC) founded by the Treaty of Rome.

1959 Britain and non-EEC states form the European Free Trade Area (EFTA).

1961 East Germans erect the Berlin Wall. Russian Gargarin the first man in Space.

1962 Crisis over Russian attempt to station nuclear missiles in Cuba.

1968 'Prague Spring' in Czechoslovakia crushed by Russian troops.

1969 British troops sent into Northern Ireland; start of 'the troubles'.

1972 USSR signs SALT I arms limitation treaty with USA.

1974 Turks invade and occupy half Cyprus

1975 Democracy restored in Spain.

1979 USSR invades Afghanistan. SALT II arms limitation treaty between USSR and USA, but not formally ratified.

1983 Beginning of Strategic Arms Reduction Talks (START) between USSR and USA.

1985 Gorbachev becomes reformist leader of USSR, introduces 'Glasnost' and 'Perestroika'.

1989 Fall of Berlin Wall. Uprising in Romania.

1990 Reunification of Germany.

1991 Formal dissolution of USSR and Warsaw Pact, establishment of CIS (Russian Federation).

1992 EU recognizes former Yugoslav republics of Croatia, Slovenia and Bosnia-Herzegovina. Civil war in Bosnia. Denmark votes against membership in EU.

1995 Czechoslovakia splits into the Czech Republic and Slovakia. Dayton Accord brings NATO-enforced peace in Bosnia.

1997 Negotiations underway for admission to EU of Norway, Austria, Slovenia, Poland, Hungary and Czech Republic.

SELECT BIBLIOGRAPHY

The authors readily acknowledge the work of many scholars and works in publication, which have been consulted in the preparation of this atlas.

Many remain in publication and can be recommended for further reading on the topics covered in this atlas. Among this selected bibliography are the following:

Anderson, M. S., *The Eastern Question*, Macmillan, 1966

Angold, Michael, *The Byzantine Empire, 1025-1204*, Addison Wesley Longman, 1997

Asch, Ronald G. *The Thirty Years' War, The Holy Roman Empire and Europe 1616-1648*, Macmillan, 1996

Ball, Simon, *The Cold War, An International History 1947-1991*, Arnold, 1997

Bell, P. M. H., *The Origins of the Second World War in Europe*, Longman, 1986

Bennett, Martyn, *The English Civil War*, Addison Wesley Longman, 1995

Boxer, C. R., *The Dutch Seaborne Empire 1600-1800*, Penguin, 1965

Bradford, Alfred S. (ed), *Philip II of Macedon*, Praeger, 1992

Bradley, Richard, *Rock Art and the Prehistory of Atlantic Europe*, Routledge, 1997

Bremner, Ian and Taras, Ray, *New States, New Politics: Building the Post-Soviet Nations*, Cambridge University Press, 1996

Brown, P., *The World of Late Antiquity*, Thames and Hudson, 1971

Browne, H., *Spain's Civil War*, Addison Wesley Longman, 1996

Bury, J. B., *A History of Greece*, Macmillan, 1977

Cain, P. J., and Hopkins, A. G., *British Imperialism, Crisis and Deconstruction 1914-1990*, Longman, 1993

Cain, P. J., and Hopkins, A. G., *British Imperialism, Innovation and Expansion 1688-1914*, Longman 1993

Calvocoressi, Peter, *Resilient Europe, 1870-2000*, Longman, 1991

Cameron, A., *The Later Roman Empire*, Fontana, 1993

Cameron, Euan, *The European Reformation*, Clarendon Press, 1991

Cawkwell, George, *Thucydides and the Peloponnesian War*, Routledge, 1997,

Coppa, F. J., *The Origins of the Italian Wars of Independence*, Addison Wesley Longman, 1992

Cottrell, Leonard, *Hanibal: Enemy of Rome*, Da Capa Press, 1992

Cunliffe, Barry, *The Ancient Celts*, Oxford University Press, 1997

David, Jean-Michel, *The Roman Conquest of Italy* Blackwell, 1996

Davies, J. K., *Democracy and Classical Greece*, Harper Collins, 1993

Davis, R. H. C., *A History of Medieval Europe from Constantine to Saint Louis*, Longman, 1988

De Blois, *An Introduction to the Ancient World*, Routledge, 1997

Dolukhanov, Pavel M., *The Early Slavs, Eastern Europe from the Initial Settlement to the Kievan Rus*, Addison Wesley Longman, 1996

Elton, G. R., *Reformation Europe*, Fontana, 1963

Esdaile, Charles J., *The Wars of Napoleon*, Addison Wesley Longman, 1995

Fisher, D. J. V., *The Anglo-Saxon Age, c. 400-1042*, Addison Wesley Longman, 1976

Freeman, Charles, *Egypt, Greece and Rome: Civilisations of the Ancient Mediterranean*, Oxford University Press, 1996

Furet, Francois, *The French Revolution, 1770-1814*, Blackwell, 1996

Gates, David, *Napoleonic Wars*, Arnold, 1997

Green, Miranda J., *The Celtic World*, Routledge, 1996

Grey, Ian, *Ivan III and the Unification of Russia*, Penguin, 1972

Hale, J. R., *Renaissance Europe, 1480-1520*, Fontana, 1971

Higgins, R. A., *Minoan and Mycenaean Art*, Thames and Hudson, 1967

Hosking, G., *A History of the Soviet Union*, Fontana, 1985

Huizinga, J., *The Waning of the Middle Ages*, London, 1924

Joll, James, *Europe since 1870, An International History*, Penguin, 1990

Jones, Martin, *The Counter Reformation*, Cambridge University Press, 1995

Judt, T., *A Grand Illusion, an Essay on Europe*, Penguin, 1997

Kennedy, Hugh, *Muslim Spain and Portugal*, Longman, 1997

Kershaw, Ian, *The Nazi Dictatorship, Problems and Perspectives of Interpretation*, Arnold, 1993

Kindleberger, Charles P., *The World in Depression, 1929-1939*, Allen Lane, 1973

Kirby, D., *Northern Europe in the Early Modern Period. The Baltic World 1492-1772*, Addison Wesley Longman, 1990

Klinchevskii, V. O., *A History of Russia*, Russell and Russell, 1960, 5 vols

Koenigsberger, H. and Mosse, G., *Europe in the Sixteenth Century*, Longman, 1968

Kunte, Martin (ed), *Suleyman the Magnificent and his Age*, Addison Wesley Longman, 1995

Lewis, G., *The French Revolution, Rethinking the Debate*, Routledge, 1993

Lewis, Paul G., *Central Europe since 1945*, Addison Wesley Longman, 1994

Macfie, A. L., *The Eastern Question, 1774-1923*, Longman, 1989

McAuley, M., *Societ Politics, 1917-1991*, Oxford University Press, 1992

McCauley, M., *The Soviet Union since 1917*, Longman, 1981

McGregor, Malcolm F., *The Athenians and their Empire*, UCL Press, 1991

Martel, G., *The Origins of the First World War*, Addison Wesley Longman, 1996

Martin, Janet, *Medieval Russia, 980-1584*, Cambridge University Press, 1995

Mason, John, *The Dissolution of the Austro-Hungarian Empire 1867-1918*, Longman, 1997

Megarry, Tim, *Society in Prehistory, The Origins of Human Culture*, Macmillan, 1995

Mellars, P., *The Neanderthal Legacy. An Archaeological Perspective from Western Europe*, Princeton University Press, 1996

Mitchell, Lynette G. and Rhodes, P. J., *The Development of the Polis in Ancient Greece*, Routledge, 1997

Moorhead, John, *Justinian*, Addison Wesley Longman, 1994

Niewyk, D. L., *The Holocaust: Problems and Perspectives*, Houghton Mifflin, 1997

Oakley, Stewart P., *War and Peace in the Baltic, 1560-1790*, Routledge, 1992

Okey, R., *Eastern Europe, 1740-1985, Feudalism to Communism*, Routledge, 1992

Ostrogorsky, G., *History of the Byzantine State*, Blackwell, 1968

Outram, Dorinda, *The Enlightenment*, Cambridge University Press, 1995

Parker, Geoffrey, *Europe in Crisis, 1598-1648*, Fontana, 1979

Parker, Geoffrey, *Spain and the Netherlands, 1559-1659*, Fontana, 1979

Payne, Stanley, *A History of Fascism*, University of Wisconsin Press, 1996

Polisensky, J. V., *The Thirty Years' War*, NEL, 1974

Porter, A. H., *European Imperialism*, Macmillan, 1994

Rankin, David, *Celts in the Classical World*, Routledge, 1996

Riasanovsky, N. V., *A History of Russia*, Oxford, 1984

Roberts, Michael, *Gustavus Adolphus*, Addison Wesley Longman, 1997

Runciman, Steven, *A History of the Crusades*, Cambridge University Press, 1951-54, 3 vols

Runciman, Steven, *The Fall of Constantinople, 1453*, Cambridge University Press, 1965

Sawyer, Peter (ed), *The Oxford Illustrated History of the Vikings*, Oxford University Press, 1997

Scharma, S., *Citizens, A Chronicle of the French Revolution*, Penguin, 1898

Schlieder, Theodor, *Frederick the Great*, Addison Wesley Longman, 1997

Service, R., *The Russian Revolution, 1900-1927*, Macmillan, 1986

Smith, Christopher, *Late Stone Age Hunters of the British Isles*, Routledge, 1992

Sonnino, Paul, *Louis XIV and the Origins of the Dutch War*, Cambridge University Press, 1989

Steinberg, S. H., *The Thirty Years' War and the Conflict for European Hegemony*, Edward Arnold, 1966

Stone, Norman, *Europe Transformed, 1878-1919*, Fontana, 1983

Stoneman, Richard, *Alexander the Great*, Routledge, 1997

Sutherland, D. M. G., *France, 1789-1815, Revolution and Counter-revolution*, Fontana, 1985

Taylor, A. J. P., *The Habsburg Monarchy*, Penguin, 1948

Thorpe, I. J., *The Origins of Agriculture in Europe*, Routledge, 1996

Urwin, D. W., *The Community of Europe, A History of European Integration since 1945*, Longman, 1994

Vernadsky, G., *A History of Russia*, Yale University Press, 1961

Vernadsky, G. A., *The Mongols and Russia*, Yale University Press, 1953

Waley, D., *Later Medieval Europe, From Saint Louis to Luther*, Longman, 1985

Wallace-Hadrill, J. M., *The Barbarian West, 400-1000*, Blackwell, 1996

Wedgewood, C. V., *The King's War 1641-1647*, Collins, 1958

Wedgewood, C. V., *The Thirty Years' War*, Penguin, 1957

Wegs, R., *Europe since 1945, A Concise History*, Macmillan, 1996

Wehler, Hans-Ulrich, *The German Empire 1871-1918*, Berg, 1985

Wells, Colin, *The Roman Empire*, Fontana, 1992

White, Steven, *After Gorbachev*, Cambridge University Press, 1993

Whittow, Mark, *The Making of Orthodox Byzantium, 600-1025*, Macmillan, 1996

Yapp, M. E., *The Near East since the First World War*, Longman, 1991

INDEX

A

Achean League, 31
Actium, battle of, 31, 45, 49
Adelard, of Bath, scholar, 65
Adenauer, Konrad, 148
Adria, 11
Aeolian, 22
Aegates Islands, battle of, 42
Aegean,
  agriculture, 16,
  culture, 10,
  trade, 16, 60, 80
Aequi, tribe, 40
Aeschylus, 30
Afghanistan, 10, 36, 137
Africa, 121, 31, 126
Agamemnon, 20
  death mask, 11
Aghlabids, 68
Alalia, battle of, 24
Albert, of Habsburg, 90
Alcium, of York, 66
Alemanni, 58
Alesia, battle of, 44
Alexandria, 37
Alexander I, 112
Alexander, the Great, 31, 36
Alfonso V, 78
Alfonso VI, 65
Alhambra, 78
Alsace-Lorraine, 115, 120-1, 128
Altimira, 9
Amber Road, 32
Ampuria, 24
Amphictyonic League, 36
Amphipolis, battle of, 35
Anabaptist, 88, 106
Anatolia, 18, 20, 22, 31, 33, 38
Angles, 57
Anglo-French Entente, 128
Anti-Comintern Pact, 143
Antioch, 36, 72
Antonine, 51
Antony and Cleopatra, 31, 45
Apollo, temple of, 38
Arab, 31, 78, 80
Aragon, 78
Architecture
  Athens, 34
  Cretan, 18
  Dutch, 106
  Etruscan, 24
  Italian, 46
  Minoan, 11
  Muslim, 78
  Mycenean, 11, 20
  Roman, 46
Argos, 20
Aricia, 40
Aristophanes, 30, 33
Aristotle, 30, 33
Armenia, 51
Art
  Académies, 96
  Aegean, 10
  Agamemnon, death mask, 11
  Athens, 34
  Cretan frescoes, 18
  Cro-Magnon, 14
  Dutch school, 106
  Etruscan, 13, 24
  Flemish School, 106
  Greek, 20

Holbein, 80
La Tène, 38
Minoan, 10
Muslim, 78
Mycenaen, 11, 20
Paleolithic, 9
Socialist Realist, 118
Starcevo-Körös, 14
Therack, 11
Theran Frescoes, 10
Asia, 31, 122, 126
Asia Minor, 34, 53, 60
Astrakhan Khanate, 95
Astronomy, 85
Athens, 22, 28, 30, 36
  Golden Age, 34
  plague, 34
Attica, 22
Attila, 58
Augustus, Caesar, 24
Aurelius, Marcus, Roman
  emperor, 46, 51
Australopithecus africanus, 14
Austria, 63, 66, 86, 108, 110
  independence, 137
  unemployment, 134
  World War I, 131
  World War II, 143
Austria-Hungary, 103, 132
Avar, 61, 66
Axis Powers, 143, 145

B

Babylon, 31, 32
Balearic, 32, 78
Balkans, 61, 64, 76, 103, 128, 132
  Ottoman expansion, 86
  World War II, 143
Baltic, 93, 98, 106
Barcelona (Catalonia), 78
Basil II, 64
Basque, 100, 139
Bastile, 108
Baudoin, founder of Jerusalem, 72
Bavaria, 110
Belgium, 108, 110, 112
  Vlaams Blok, 151
  World War I, 130, 132
  World War II, 143
Belgrade, 38
Belisarius, General, 60
Belorussia, 143
Berber, 78
Berlin Wall, 148, 150
Bismarck, Otto von, 103, 114,
  120, 128
Black Death, 80
Black Sea, 33, 35-6, 80
Blitzkrieg, 143
Blizingsleben, 8
Blum, Leon, 134
Bogomils, 65
Bohemia,
  Habsburg rule, 90
  Thirty Years' War, 93
Bohemond, 72
Boin settlements, 16
Bolshevik, 103, 116, 131, 140
Bonaparte, see Napoleon
Book of Kells, 39
Bosnia-Herzegovina, 139, 151
Bossi, Umberto, 139
Boudicca, Queen of the Iceni, 26, 51
Boulanger, General, 120

Bradley, General, 145
Brandenburg-Prussia, 98
Brandt, Willy, 137
Brennus, 38
Breton, 100
Brienne, Jean de, 72
Britain, 108, 112, 116, 132, 134
  battle of, 143
  Celts, 26, 38
  Civil War, 104
  Colonial policy, 122
  Constantius I, reconquers, 54
  Crusades, 72
  empire, 127
  India, 122
  invasion, 44, 51, 56, 102
  political, 100-2
  religion, 88, 104-5, 120
  Second Civil War, 105, 136
  trade, 10, 65, 80, 100, 104,
  110, 134
  World War I, 130, 131
  World War II, 143
  Viking, 68
British Expeditionary Force, 143
Bronze Age, 9, 22
  culture, 16, 18, 20, 26
  religion, 10
Brünn, 14
Bulgar, 61, 74
Bulgaria, 76, 128
Burgundy, Duke of, 73
Byzantine empire, 47, 53, 58, 60,
  63, 72, 86
  decline, 62, 64, 68
  religion, 62
  trade, 126

C

Cabot, 85
Cairo, 73
Caligua, Roman emperor, 51
Calvin, John, 88, 101, 106
Campania, 13, 33
Canada, 146
Capua, 11
Carausius, Emperor of Britain, 54
Carinus, 53
Carnac, 16
  Carthage, 32, 40, 42,
  seige of, 43
  Vandal capital, 58
Carolingian empire, 62-3, 66, 70
  religion, 68,
Carthusian Order, 63
Castile, 78
Castlereagh, 112
Catalonia, 110, 139
Catholic Church, 83, 104
Cato, Roman Senator, 43
Cavour, 114
Celtic Fringe, 38
Celts, 26, 28, 38
  agriculture, 26
  art, 2
  political, 38
  religion, 38
  trade, 26
Central Powers, 131
Ceos, 11
Charlemagne, 62-3
  empire, 66
Charles I, of England, 101, 104-5
Charles I, of Spain, 90

Charles II, of England, 101, 105
Charles V, Roman emperor, 88, 90
Charles XII, of Sweden, 98
Charthage, 40, 42-3
Chechnya, 151
China, 122, 126
  trade, 31
Chosroes I, Sassanid king, 61
Christian Roman empire, 47
Church of Rome, 64
Cistercian Order, 63
Civil War,
  England, 10, 104-5
  Roman, 49
Claudius, Roman emperor, 51
Cleisthones, 23
Clemenceau, George, 132
Clement III, 70
Clermont,
  council of, 72
  synod, 65
Clovis I, Krank King, 58
Cochin-China, 126
Codex Justianus, 60
Cold War, 136-8, 146, 148, 151
College of Cardinals, 70
Columbus, Christopher, 85
Commonwealth of Independent
  States (CIS), 138-9
Communist Party, 136-8, 140, 146,
  150
Concert of Europe, 103, 120
Concordat of Worms, 70
Congress of Berlin, 103
Congress of Paris, 103
Congress of Vienna, 112, 132
Conrad III, emperor, 72
Constance, council of, 83
Constantine, the Great, 46, 60
Constantinople, 72, 86
  fall, 76,
  Patriarchate, 64
  siege, 64
  trade, 60, 63, 65
Constituent Assembly, 116
Continental System, 110
Constantius, Ceasar, 54
Copernicus, 85
Córdoba,
  Caliphate of, 78
  emirate of, 68
Corfu, 80
Corinth, 34
  conflict, 28
  trade, 20
Corneille, writer, 96
Corsica, 24, 42, 58, 60
Cortéz, Hernán, 90
Counter-Reformation, 83, 93
Crete, 9, 10, 20, 22, 66
  architecture, 18
  art, 11
  religion, 18
  trade, 18, 20
Crimean War
Croatia, 54, 64, 66, 86, 151
  Habsburg rule, 90
Croix de Feu, 134
Cro-Magnon, 14
Cromwell, Oliver, 101, 105
Crusades, 72, 80, 86
  Albigensian, 65
  Eighth, 73

Fifth, 72
First, 64, 72
Fourth, 72, 76, 80
Second, 72
Seventh, 73
Sixth, 73
Third, 72
Cumae, sea battle, 24
Cyclades, 10, 18, 20, 22
Cyprus, 20, 32, 66, 80
    trade, 10
Cyrene, 32
Czechoslovakia, 123
    German invasion, 143
    Soviet invasion, 137

D
Dacia, 51
Dalmatia 61, 66, 80, 110
    trade, 24
Dandaldo, Enrico, Doge, 80
Danelaw, 68
Danish War, 93
Danube, 14
Dardanelle, 86
Darian League, 34
Darius, 31
Dark Ages, 22
Dayton Agreements, 139, 151
Decabulus, 51
Demosthenes, 36
Denmark, conflict, 95, 98
    reform, 98
    unemployment, 134
    World War I, 132
    World War II, 143
Descartes, René, 85
Devolution, war of, 96
Diniz, farmer king, 78
Diocletian, Roman emperor, 47, 53-4, 60
Disraeli, Benjamin, 126
Dodecanese, 21-2
Dorians, 20, 23, 28
Dionysus I of Syracuse, 33
Divine Right of Kings, 104
Dubcek, Alexander, 137
Dubrovnik, trade, 87
Dunkirk, 143
Dutch, 20
    Golden Age, 106
    Independence, 90
    republic, 96
    revolt, 106
    rule, 112
    trade, 106
Dutch East India Company, 106
Dutch East Indies, 122, 126

E
East Germany, 137
Eighty Years' War, 93
Einhard, writer, 66
Eisenhower, General Dwight, 145
Egypt, 60, 72, 122, 127-8, 143
    art, 18
    conquest of, 31, 33, 54
    trade, 10, 18, 22
Egyptian National Party, 122
Egyptian Peoples Party, 122
El Alamain, 143
El Caudillo, 140
El Cid, 65
Elton, G. R., 85

England
    civil war, 101, 104
    invasion, 102, 105
    naval war, 106
Enlightenment, 85
Ephesus, 22
Erasmus, Djesiderius, 84, 88
Estonia, 95, 123, 139, 143
Etruria, (Tuscany), 13, 31, 40
Etruscan, 9, 10-11, 38
    architecture, 24
    art, 13, 24
    religion, 13
    trade, 10, 24
Etruscan League, 24
Euoboea, 22
Euphrates, 18
Euric, King, 58
Euripides, 30, 33
Eurocorps, 139
European Coal and Steel Community, 136, 148
European Commission, 14
European Defence Community, 148
European Economic Union, 148
European Parliament, 148
European Recovery Program, 146
European Union, 139
Evans, Sir Arthur, 18, 20
Ezhov, Nicholas, 118

F
Fascist Party, 123, 134, 140
February Revolution, 116
Ferdinand I, 78
Ferdinand II, 78
Ferdinand, Archduke Franz, 121, 128
Ferry, Jules, 121
Finland, 98, 123, 140, 143
First World War, *see* World War I
Flanders (Bruge), 80
France, 61, 68, 93, 110, 112, 116, 128, 134
    Abolition of Feudalism, 108
    Algeria, 126
    ambitions, 98
    Americas, 126
    Committee of Public Safety, 108
    Declaration of the Rights of Man, 108
    empire, 126
    Front Nationale, 150
    National Guard, 108
    trade, 106, 134, 148
    uprisings, 127
    World War I, 130-2
    World War II, 143
Franche Comté, 96
Franco-Dutch War, 96
Franco, General Francisco, 139-40
Franco-Habsburg War, 93
Franco-Russian Alliance, 128
Franks, 57-8, 64, 66, 68
Frederick II, 63, 70, 73
French empire, 63
French Revolution, 100, 102, 107, 150
Fyodor I, 95

G
Gaiseric, Vandal leader, 58
Galatia, 38
Galerius, Caesar, 54
Galileo, 85

Gandhi, 122
Garibaldi, Giuseppe, 114
Gaugamel, battle of, 31
Gaul, 13, 24, 47, 61
    conquest of, 38, 44
Genoa, 65, 80
George, Lloyd, 132
Germany, 68, 70, 112, 116, 121-2, 132, 134
    anticlericalism, 88
    early settlements, 16
    empire, 103, 126
    Federal Republic, 137
    federation, 112
    National Democratic Party, 150
    nazi, 103, 134
    political, 114
    rearmament, 143
    Reich, 115, 128
    renaissance, 84
    Social Democratic Party, 103, 140
    trade, 65, 80, 103, 134
    universities, 83,
    Weltpolitik, 128
    World War I, 130-1
    World War II, 143, 145
Getae, 36
Geza, Magyar leader, 68
Glasnost, 138
Godonuv, Boris, Tsar of Muscovy, 95
Golden Age, 30
Golden Horde (Great Mongol empire), 74
Goths, 57
Government of India Act, 122
Granicus, battle of, 31
Great Depression, 123, 134
Great Northern War, 98
Great Schism, 83
Greece, 34, 58
    architecture, 20
    art, 20
    culture, 20, 23, 28, 36
    mythology, 28
    occupation of, 86
    political, 22-3, 31, 33, 36
    religion, 13, 23, 28, 46
    trade, 22, 28, 37
Gregory VII, 70
Grenada, 78
Grimaldi, 14
Grotius, Hugo, 106
Guiscard, Robert, Norman duke, 70
Gustav, Adolf, of Sweden, 93

H
Habsburg, empire, 90
    conflict, 98,
    dissolution of, 123
    spread of power, 87, 96
Hadrian, Roman emperor, 51
Hagia Sophia, 76
Hallstatt Culture, *see* Celts
Hannibal, 31, 42
Hanseatic League, 80
    ports, 93
Hawaii, 145
Hellenic Culture, 30
Henry I, Saxon emperor, 68
Henry II, Saxon King, 63, 70
Henry IV, 70
Henry VIII, 88
Heodotus, 30, 33

Heraclitus, 23
Hercules, 54
Hesiod, 28
Hindenburg Line, 131
Hitler, Adolf, 123, 134, 140, 143, 145
Hittite empire, 10
    trade, 10
Hohenstaufen, dynasty, 70
Holbein, 82
Holland, 112
Holstein-Gottorp, duchy, 98
Holy Land, 70
Holy Roman empire, 87-8
Holy Sepulchre, 72
Holy War, 72
Homer, 10, 20, 28
Hominids, 8, 14
Homo erectus, 8, 14
Homo habilis, 14
Homo sapiens, 8
Hoplites, 28,
    battles, 30
Hugh of Vermandois, 72
Huguenots, 96
Humanism, 84, 99
Hungarian Arrow Cross, 134
Hungary, 68, 74, 86, 139
    revolution, 137, 140
Huns, 57, 58
Hutton, Ulrich von, 84

I
Iberia, 26, 58, 60, 79
    religious conflict, 65
    trade, 106
Ice Age, 14
Ignatius Loyala, 83
Illyrian provinces, 110
Import Duties Act, 134
India,
    British, 126
    trade, 31
Indian National Congress, 121
Indonesian National Party, 122
Indus, 32
Innocent III, 65
Inquisition, 78, 83
Inter Governmental Organizations, 146
Investiture Controversy, 62, 70
Investiture Struggles, 63
Ionian, 22
Ireland,
    Celts, 38
    civil war, 101, 105
    religion, 39, 68
    Vikings, 68
Irminsul wood, 66
Iron Age, 26
Iron Curtain, 137
Isabella of Castile, 78
Islam, 70, 74, 86
Isle of Man, 39
Istria, trade, 24
Italy, 58, 68, 70, 112, 121, 126
    culture, 46,
    MSI, 150
    trade 20, 148
    World War II, 145
Ivan III, "The Great," 94
Ivan IV, "The Terrible," 94

J
Jacobin Committee of Public Safety, 102

James II, of England, 101
Japan, 122, 143
  attacks U.S., 145
Javan Sultans, 106
Jerusalem, 65
  crusaders, 70
Jesuit Order, 83
Jews, 106, 122
  exploitation, 78
Jove, 54
Juana of Castile, 90
Julius Caesar, 38, 44
Justinian, Roman emperor, 47, 60
Jutes, 57
Jutland, 98
K
Karanovo, 16
Karos, 10
Kazan Khanate, 95
Keivan Rus, 63, 64, 68
Kerensky, Alexander, 116
Khan, Batu, 74
Khan, Ghengis, 74
Khan, Ogedei, 74
Kimon, General, 34
Kingdom of Antigonus, 36
Kjöge Bay, 98
Knossos, 10, 16, 18, 20-1
Kornilov affair, 116
Kosovo, battle of, 76, 87
Kraljevic, Marko, of Serbia, 87
L
La Cotte de St. Brelade, 8
La Tène,
  trade, 24
  culture, 38
Lake Neuchâtel, 38
Lapua Movement, 134
Latin Empire, 70, 76
Latium, 40
Latvia, 95, 123, 139, 143
Laudism, 104
Laugierie Basse, 14
Lawrence, D. H., 13
Lazar, Ottoman prince, 76, 86
League Council, Corinth, 36
League of Nations, 123, 132
League of Twelve Cities, 24
Lechfeld, battle of, 62, 68
Leclerc, General, 145
Lenin, V. I., 103, 116, 118
Leon, 78
Leonodis, King of Sparta, 30
Leopold II, of Belgium, 126
Lesbos, 22, 34
Levellers, 101
Linear A, 21
Linear B, 21
Literature
  Homer, 10
  Lawrence, D. H., 13
Lithuania, 80, 123, 143
  conflict, 95
Livonia, 98, 138
Livonian War, 95
Livy, 38, 40
Lombardy, 66
Lomé Convention, 148
Los Navas de Tolosa, 78
Louis VII, of France, 72
Louis XIV, 96, 98
Louis XVI, of France, 108
Louis, the Pious, 66

Low Countries, 110, 112
  early settlements, 16
  political, 100
  trade, 100
Luftwaffe, 143
Lutherans, 106
Luther, Martin, 85, 88
Lvov, prince, 116
Lydia, 33
M
Macedonia, 20, 32, 38, 43, 63, 151
  occupation of, 86
  rise of, 31, 36
  trade, 36
Magellan, 85
Magyar, 62, 68
Mallia, 18
Malta,
  trade, 10
Manzikiertt, battle of, 64
Marathon, battle of, 30
Marcus Furius Camillus, 38
Marie-Antoinette, Queen of
  France, 108
Marie-Louise, Princess, 110
Marshall Aid, 146
Marshall Plan, 136
Marston Moor, battle of, 105
Mary II, Stuart, 106
Malmesbury, William of, scholar,
  65
Margaret of Austria, 90
Marseille, 26, 28
Mary of Hungary, 90
Mas d'Azil, 14
Mathematics, 85
Maximian, 54
Maximilian I, Roman emperor,
  88, 90
Mazarin, Jules, 93
Mediterranean, 80
  tade, 86
Mehmet II, Sultan, 76, 86
Melanchton, Philipp, 84
Memphis, 32
Mercatir's chart, 85
Mesopotamia, 51, 61
Michael I, Byzantine emperor, 66
Middle Ages, 62
Middle East, 126
Minoan,
  architecture, 11
  art, 10
Mohacs, battle of, 86
Mongols, (Tatars), 62, 74
Monmouth, Geoffrey of, scholar, 65
Monnet, Jean, 148
Monroe Doctrine, 121
Montgomery, General, 143, 145
Moors, 65, 78
More, Sir Thomas, 84
Moroccan Crisis, 128
Mosley, Sir Oswald, 134
Mount Olympus, 28
Mount Pangaeus, 36
Murad, Sultan, 76
Muscovy, 80, 94
Muslim, 65, 66, 68, 72, 78
Mussolini, Benito, 123, 140, 143
Mycenae, 9, 20-2
  architecture, 11, 20
  art, 11, 20
  culture, 18, 20

religion, 11
  trade, 10, 20
N
Nagy, Imre, 137
Naples, 11, 28, 78
Napoleon, Bonaparte, 63, 102,
  110, 112
Napoleon III, 114
  Code, 110
Napoleonic Wars, 102, 112
Narses, King of Persia, 54, 60
Nasrid, dynasty, 78
National Assembly, 108
National Socialism, 140
National Socialist Worker's Party,
  143
NATO, 137-9
Navarre, 78
  King of, 73
Navigation Act, 106
Naxos, rebellion, 34
Nazi Party, 103, 140
Neanderthal, 8, 14
Nebuchadnezzar II, 32
Neolithic,
  agriculture, 16
  Nero, Roman emperor, 51
Netherlands,
  revolt of, 93
  Spanish, 96
  trade, 84
  World War II, 143
New Imperialism, 121, 126
New Model Army, 104, 105
New World,
  explorers, 90
  Jesuit mission, 83
Ninevah, 32
Norman, occupation, 64
Normandy, 68
North Africa, 122, 126
  World War II, 145
North America, 126
North German Federation, 115
Norway, 80, 143
Nuclear weapons, 137
Numerian, emperor, 53
O
Obolensky, 64
Odoacer, Italian ruler, 58
Octavian, Augustus, 31, 46, 49
Octavian, emperor, 44-5, 49
Olympic Games, 776 BC, 28
Open Door Policy, 121
Oracle, Delphie, 30
Organization for European
  Econmic Cooperation, 146
Osmanli, dynasty, 86
Ostrogoths, 47, 57-8, 60
Otto I, of Saxony, 62, 68, 70
Otto II, 63, 70
Otto IV, 70
Ottoman empire, 7, 86-7, 98, 112
Ottowa Imperial Conference, 134
Out of Africa Theory, 8
P
Paine, Tom, 102
Palarinate War, 93
Pamphylia, 34
Pannonian Plain, 86
Paris, Congress of, 103
Parthians, 46, 51

Pascal, Blaise, 85
Patarenes, 65
Patton, General, 145
Pax Roma, 46, 51
Peace Conference, 150
Peace of Nikias, 35
Peace of Philocrates, 36
Peace of Schönbrunn, 110
Pechenegs, 64
Peloponnesian War, 30, 34
Peloponnesus, 22
Peninsula War, 110
Pericles, 34
Peristroika, 138
Persia, 30, 32, 34, 36, 46, 51, 60
Peter the Great, 98
Phaestos, 18
Phoenicia, trade, 32
Philip II, 36, 90
Philip V, of Macedon, 31
Philip of Hesse, 88
Pian de Carpine, John of, 74
Piedmont-Sardinia, 114
"Pig Wars," 128
Pilgrims, 70
Pius, Antonius, Roman emperor,
  46, 51
Pizzaro, Francisco, 90
Plataea, 34
Plato, 30, 33
Pleven, Réné, 148
Poland, 74, 80, 87, 98, 123
  conflict, 95
  discontent, 137
  martial law, 138
  trade, 98
  World War I, 132
  World War II, 143
Pompeii, 11
Pompey, Roman dictator, 46
Pope Gregory VII, 70
Pope Honorius III, 73
Pope Innocent III, 70
Pope John XII, 70
Pope Leo III, 66
Pope Nicholas II, 70
Pope Paul III, 83
Pope Urban II, 65, 72
Portugal, 78, 126
Posena Lars, 40
Poussin, writer, 96
Po Valley, 11-2, 24
Prague Spring, 137
Presbeterianism, 105
Printing, 85
Protestantism, *see* Reformation
Provence, 58
Prussia, 98, 103, 108, 110, 114
Ptolemaic Egypt, 36
Punic Wars, 42
Punjab, 36
Puritanism, 104
Pylos, 20, 22
Pyrrhus, King of Epirus, 40
Pythagoras, 23
R
Racine, writer, 96
Reagan, Ronald, President, 138
Red Army, 137, 143, 145
Reformation, 83, 85, 88, 90, 100,
  101,104
  Habsburg, 90

ideals, 85
rise of, 82
Reichstaat, 103
Reichstag, 103
Renaissance, 82, 104
birth of, 84
humanism, 85
German, 84
Republicansim, 101
Rhineland, 16, 143
Rhodes, 18, 22
Rhodesia Man, 8
Richard, the Lionheart, 72
Richelieu, Cardinal, 93
Robert of Flanders, 72
Robespierre, 108
Roman Catholic Church, 101,
    106, 120
Roman empire, 10, 13, 31, 38, 42,
    51, 57-8, 60, 63
culture, 40, 46,
golden age, 46, 51
legacy of, 46
literature, 46
political, 38, 43-4, 46, 49, 52
religion, 46, 53-4, 57, 60
superpower, 43-4
trade, 44, 46
Rome, 114, 126
Rome-Berlin Axis Agreement, 143
Rommel, Erwin, 145
Romulus and Remus, 40
Roumania, 123, 140
Roundheads, 101
Royalists, 104-5
Rump Parliament, 101
Russia, 74, 110, 120
abdication of Tsar, 116
bolshevik, 103, 132
civil war, 136
expansion, 95, 98
First World War, 131
foreign policy, 98
political, 103
Reinsurance Treaty, 128
Revolution, 100, 116
"Russian Question," 74
Second World War, 103
trade, 64, 80, 116
S
Sabine, tribe, 40
Saladin, 72
Salian, dynasty, 70
Samnite Wars, 40
Sardinia, 32, 42, 58, 78, 80
trade, 10, 20
Sassanian empire, 60
Saxon, 57
religion, 66, 68, 70
wars, 66
Scandinavia, 80
Schengen policy, 139
Schism, 1054, 62
Schleswig-Holstein Question, 115
Schlieffen Plan, 130
Schliemann, Heinrich, 20
Schmalkaldic League, 88
Schuman, Robert, 148
declaration, 148
Scipio, Roman commander, 42
Scotland, 101, 105
Scottish Covenantors, 105
Scythians, 26

Sea of Atov, 38
Second Civil War, 105
Second Cold War, 138
Second Front, 145
Second World War, see World War II
Seleucid empire, 36
Serbia, 76, 86, 128
nobility, 86
Sexi, 32
Shakespeare, William, 84
Siberia, 126
Sicily, 32-3, 38, 42, 58, 114
occupation of, 64, 78
trade, 10, 18
World War II, 145
Sieyes, Abbé, 108
Silesia, early settlements, 16
Sino-Japanese War, 126
Slavs, 64
Slovenia, 151
Society of Jesus, (Jesuits), 83
Socrates, 30, 33
Solon, 23
Sophocles, 30, 33
South Africa, 126
Soviet Comintern, 140
Soviet Union, 143
Spaak, Paul-Henri, 148
Spain, 42, 47, 106, 110, 136
Americas, 126
civil war, 123, 140
Cuba, 126
culture, 16
Inquisition, 83
Muslim, 78
Reconquista, 65, 80
Spanish-American War, 127
trade, 10, 24
Tudor wars, 101
Sparta, 28, 30, 34
Spina, 11,
trade, 24
Spinoza, 106
Spinoza, Benedict, 85
St. Bruno, 63
St. Cyril, 64
St. Lois, 73
St. Methodius, 64
St. Patrick, 39
Stalin, J. V., 103, 116, 118, 137
Star Wars, 138
Stephen I, Magyar king, 68
Stone Age, 9
Stonehenge, 16
Sublime Porte, 87
Suez Canal, 122
Suleiman II, Sultan, 86
Sulla, Roman dictator, 44
Sweden,
conflict, 95
trade, 98
Swedish War, 93
Switzerland, 112
Sybaris, culture, 22
Syracuse, trade, 28
Syria, 31, 36, 54, 60
trade, 18
T
Tarquin kings, 13, 24, 40
Tartessos, 24
Tatars (Mongols), 65, 74
culture, 74
Tawney, R. H., 100

Taylor, A. J. P., 123
Tepes, Vlad, of Transylvania, 87
Terralba-Ambrona, 8
Tetrarchy, 54
Tetzel, Cardinal, 88
Teutonic knights, 80
Thasos, rebellion, 34
Thebes, 20, 28, 34, 36
Theodoric I, King, 58
Therack (art), 11
Third Reich, 143
Thirty Years' War, 93
Reformation, 90
Treaty of, 83
Thrace, 36, 38, 86
Thucydides, 30, 33
Tilly, Johann, General, 93
Tiryns, 20, 22
Tortessus, 32
Totalitarianism, 123
Trajan, Roman emperor, 51
Treaty of Aix-La-Chapelle, 66, 96
Treaty of Augsburg, 88
Treaty of Brest-Litovsk, 131
Treaty of Maastricht, 148
Treaty of Nymwegen, 96, 106
Treaty of Paris, First, 112
Treaty of Paris, Second, 112
Treaty of Pressburg, 110
Treaty of Racconigi, 128
Treaty of Rome, 136, 138, 146, 148
Treaty of Ryswick, 96, 106
Treaty of Tilsit, 110
Treaty of Utrecht, 96, 106
Treaty of Verdun, 66
Treaty of Versailles, 140, 143
Treaty of Westphalia, 83, 93, 101
Treaty of Windsor, 78
Trent, council of, 83
Triple Alliance, 120
Triple Entente, 120, 128
Tripolye, 16
Trotsky, 116
Troy, 40
Truman Doctrine, 136
Tudor wars, 101
Tuilleries Palace, 108
Turkey, 128
Turks, Seljuk, 64, 72
Tyre, 32
U
Ukraine, 143
early settlements, 16
Unetice, culture, 16
Union of Kalmar, 80
Union of Soviet Socialist Republics,
    (USSR), 116, 127, 136
Afghanistan, 138
art, 118
cold war, 137-8
communism, 123
Five Year Plans, 118
German invasion, 118
Great Patriotic War, 137
Gulag system, 118
trade, 118
United Nations, 127
United States of America, 116, 136
beginnings, 130
cold war, 137
economic, 120
First World War, 123, 131
Great Depression, 134

Second World War, 143, 145
territories, 127
Universal Church, 88
Urnfield, culture, 16, 26
Utica, 32
Uzbekistan, 36
V
Valmy, battle of, 108
Vandals, 47, 57-8, 60
Vardar River, 14
Vatican City, 115
Veii, seige of, 24
Venice, 66, 72, 76, 115
trade, 65, 80, 87
Vercingetorix, Gallic leader, 44
Versailles, 96, 108, 123, 140
conference, 132
Vértessoölös, 14
Vespucci, 85
Vichy Régime, 143
Victor, Emmanuel, King of
    Piedmont, 114
Vienna, siege of, 87, 90
Congress of, 103
Vikings, 62, 66, 126
settlements, 68
trade, 68
Visigoths, 47, 57-8, 61
Vladimir, 64
Volsci, tribe, 40
W
Wales, 104
Wall Street Crash, 134
War of Spanish Succession, 96
Warsaw Pact, 137
Waterloo, battle of, 102
Water Road, 74
Weber, Max 101
Wellington, Duke of, 110, 112
West Berlin, 137
West Germany, 148
West India Company, 106
Western European Union, 139
Western Pomerania, 98
Westphalia, 110
White Mountain, battle of, 93
Wilhelm, Kaiser, 106
William II, King of England, 106
William III, of Orange, 101-2, 106
Wilson, President, 123, 140
Fourteen Points, 131-2
World War I, 116, 120, 122, 130, 132
aftermath, 142
aircraft, 131
peace treaties, 127, 140
origins, 121
World War II, 120, 122, 136, 140,
aftermath, 146, 148
origins, 144
Y
Yalta Conference, 136
Yernack, cossack, 95
Yugoslavia, 123, 138-9, 151
Z
Zakros, 18
Zama, battle of, 42
Zeno, emperor, 58
Zhdanov policy, 136, 146
Zwingli, Huldrich, Swiss
    reformer, 88

ACKNOWLEDGMENTS

Pictures are reproduced by permission of, or have been provided by the following:

Bibliothèque Historique de la Ville de Paris: p. 47.
e.t. archive: pp. 12, 13, 20, 22, 24, 29, 31, 32, 36, 38, 40, 42, 48, 50, 57, 58, 60, 62, 66, 72, 77, 87, 88, 90, 96, 98, 100, 102, 104, 108, 118, 125, 128, 131, 136, 138, 140, 146, 148.
Gibert, Elsa: p. 51.
Hulton Deutsch Picture Library: pp. 115, 134.
Image Bank: p. 124.
Imperial War Museum: p. 145.
Lauros-Girandon: p. 110.
Metropolitan Museum of Art: p. 55.
Novosty, London: p. 95, 116.
Peter Newark's Historic Pictures: p. 83.
Private Collections: pp. 10, 18, 44, 114.

Illustrations: Peter A. B. Smith

Design: Malcolm Swanston

Typesetting: Shirley Ellis, Marion M. Storz

Cartography: Peter Gamble, Elsa Gibert, Peter A. B. Smith, Malcolm Swanston, Isabelle Verpaux, Jonathan Young

Production: Marion M. Storz